I QUIT MY JOB AND HIKED THE APPALACHIAN TRAIL

BY MICHAEL 'MOUNTAIN GOAT' FALDUTO

Independently published

Printed in the United States of America
First Printing, 2019

ISBN 9781798658437

This book is dedicated to my parents for always supporting me through all of my endeavors that drive them absolutely crazy.

FOREWARD

This book gives you insight into what it's like living on the beautiful, yet demanding Appalachian Trail. The following are the daily journal entries that I kept while preparing for and hiking the AT for 5 months in 2016. While I made minor post trail edits to each post, they serve to capture the events and emotions as they occurred. I held nothing back. I hope you enjoy my stories. Here goes...

PREPARATION

The Decision

When I graduated college, I obtained an excellent job - I was an engineer for an international automation company. I was paid well, I liked the people I worked with and I had the unique opportunity to travel around the world. The company was small so I also had the benefit of gaining work experience outside the field of engineering. However, the fact remained that 90% of my job consisted of sitting in the same chair at the same desk in the same cubicle with no window for at least 40 hours a week. When I hit the inevitable wall in the middle of the afternoon each day, I would search the internet looking for an adventure I could fantasize about. I quickly discovered the Appalachian Trail and developed an obsession with the concept of this long distance hike. As soon as I walked into the office every morning, I found myself checking the Appalachian Trials website before my Outlook inbox.

Then, I read "AWOL on the Appalachian Trail" by David 'AWOL' Miller (which I highly recommend by the way). I remember reading the first two pages of Chapter 8 and immediately knowing that I needed to hike the Appalachian Trail:

> "Doc and Llama are on their second thru-hike of the AT. They did the PCT the same year as Ken and Marcia. They are in a small sect of thru-hikers that could be dubbed "career hikers." During the off-season, Doc does landscape work and Llama waits tables. These aren't jobs with "a future"; they're jobs that will fund their next adventure.

People living normal lives are ruffled by folks like Doc and Llama. Nonconformity is an affront to those in the mainstream. Our impulse is to dismiss this lifestyle, create reasons why it can't work, why it doesn't even warrant consideration. Why not? Living outdoors is cheap and can be afforded by a half year of marginal employment. They can't buy things that most of us have, but what they lose in possessions, they gain in freedom.

In Somerset Maugham's The Razor's Edge, lead character Larry returns from the First World War and declares that he would like to "loaf." The term "loafing" inadequately describes the life he would spend traveling, studying, searching for meaning, and even laboring. Larry meets with the disapproval of peers and would be mentors: "Common sense assured...that if you wanted to get on in this world, you must accept its conventions, and not to do what everybody else did clearly pointed to instability."

Larry had an inheritance that enabled him to live modestly and pursue his dreams. Larry's acquaintances didn't fear the consequences of his failure; they feared his failure to conform.

I'm no maverick. Upon leaving college I dove into the workforce, eager to have my own stuff and a job to pay for it. Parents approved, bosses gave raises, and my friends could relate. The approval, the comforts, the commitments wound themselves around me like invisible threads. When my life stayed the course, I wouldn't even feel them binding. Then I would waiver enough to sense the growing entrapment, the taming of my life in which I had been complicit.

Working a nine-to-five job took more energy than I had expected, leaving less time to pursue diverse interests. I grew to detest the statement "I am a..." with the sentence completed by an occupational title. Self-help books emphasize "defining priorities" and staying focused", euphemisms for specialization and stifling spontaneity. Our vision becomes so narrow that risk is trying a new brand of cereal, and adventure is watching a new sitcom. Over time I have elevated my opinion of nonconformity nearly to the level of an obligation. We should have a bias toward doing activities that we don't normally do to keep loose the moorings of society.

Hiking the AT is "pointless". What life is not "pointless"? Is it not pointless to work paycheck to paycheck just to conform? Hiking the AT before joining the workforce was an opportunity not taken. Doing it in retirement would be sensible; doing it at this time in my life is abnormal, and therein lay the appeal. I want to make my life less ordinary."

This passage echoed the battles I was having in my own mind so accurately that it was almost creepy. However, when I thought about it, I realized literally every human being in their 20s that is stuck in a cubicle like I was must research the same fantasies on the internet when they get hit by that inevitable wall in the middle of the afternoon. More often than not, turning that fantasy into a reality is too large of a step for most people to take. Well, I didn't want to rationalize my current reality any longer so I pulled the trigger (really, I just turned the safety off - the trigger pulling would come a bit later). The impact AWOL's words alone had on me was so strong that I literally scheduled an AT thru-hike in my Microsoft Outlook calendar for March of 2016. If you bear with me and my story, you'll be ready to pull the trigger soon, too.

Fast forward to the summer of 2015 - I walked into work just like I did every morning, but when I pulled up my Outlook, I had a reminder to 'Thru-Hike AT' in 9 months. While I had not been idle the past year or so (I had been scouring gear websites like Backcountry and Steep and Cheap for deals so I could acquire the necessary equipment for the hike), I did have some pretty big decisions to make regarding the renewal of my apartment lease and my job, of course. I broke the news to my parents (Dad was relatively indifferent as he calmly asked me to come home normal and Mom, of course, broke down sobbing at the bar in Houlihan's) and then my roommates as I informed them I would be moving home when our apartment's lease was up in October to save money prior to the trip. The trigger had finally been pulled.

I won't bore you with a detailed overview of the Appalachian Trail – Google or Bill Bryson can do a far better job of summarizing the history of the AT than I can. Suffice it to say that it's an approximately 2,189 mile trail through the woods and small Appalachian towns from Springer Mountain in Georgia to Katahdin in Maine. The trail passes through 14 states and has the combined elevation gain of sixteen summits of Mt. Everest.

"Take Half the Clothes and Twice the Money"

Unfortunately, even spending 5 months in the woods isn't enough to avoid spending money. It costs money to thru-hike and quite a bit of it. So, I put together a rough, preliminary budget based on my research.

As an engineer, I naturally tend to look at the worst case scenarios so my budget is admittedly very, very conservative. Here are my assumptions:

- I am estimating that it will take me 160 days (just over 5 months) to hike the trail.
- I am estimating I will make 30 trail town stops (including zero days) during the hike.
- I am allocating 3 months to decompression, or integration back into society (basically until I can get another job). I do not believe it will take even half that time, but again, I'm trying to prepare for the worst case scenario.
- 5 months of hiking and 3 months of decompression amounts to 8 months total.

I am very grateful to my parents who paid for the transportation expenses to Georgia and back home from Maine since they would like to join me at both terminuses.

My trail expenses will include food, supplies, lodging, restaurant food, miscellaneous items like laundry, and bounce box / mail drops. These estimates total $3670. I have allocated $500 to replacement gear, though I'm not really sure how much of this I will actually need to use. That brings the trail total to $4170, which isn't that bad.

Off Trail expenses are easily the largest portion of the cost based on my estimates. A personal investment, health insurance and car insurance are a whopping $5989. Decompression costs can also be considered Off Trail expenses and I have estimated $700 a month for three months based on my spending patterns the past 6 months (without the cost of rent). I am leaving myself with $1000 for an emergency fund just in case anything unexpected happens that will sideline me for a week or more. Obviously, I hope this isn't touched throughout the hike or after, for that matter.

My conservative estimate for the entire 8 months totals to $13259. I do not expect to use anywhere near that much, but it will be in the bank come March 24, 2016.

I have read that a thru-hike costs, on average, between $5000 and $7000. At a conservative estimate of $4170 (trail costs), I am looking pretty good. Then again, that assumes I have any idea what I am talking about. So, this budget will be continually revisited in the time until my hike, but at least I have a baseline. In the end, it's just important to have more than enough money in the bank to ensure I can finish the hike.

Resignation Woes

I am submitting my resignation on February 22 and I am absolutely dreading the confrontation with my managers. I work for a small, relatively close-knit company and I am 95% sure that neither of them will be very happy nor approve of my decision. I am 1,000% sure that my Irish boss overseas will disapprove. He is a very intense man with a personality to match his tolerance at the pub. I feel incredibly guilty even though I know I shouldn't.

I am offering four weeks notice in lieu of the standard two weeks in an effort to help my company adjust, but I am afraid it will be a very uncomfortable month. Then again, there is always the possibility that they will refuse my four weeks. If that's the case, then I'm looking at two horribly boring and empty weeks to kill before my start date. It's a gamble, but one I'm willing to take to assuage my unnecessary feelings of guilt and help my colleagues with the transition.

Don't get me wrong, I don't hate my job. It's actually a great job and I really like the people I work with. The money never mattered as much to me as the learning experience work provided and how work improved me as an overall person. Even though I am still challenged at work, I simply desire a change and I'm not sure how else to put it. Call me crazy, but I'm looking forward to not having a job and facing the challenge of having to figure things out (not to mention the challenge of nearly 2,200 miles of up and down). I think it will make me a better person in the end.

I'm quitting my good job and hiking the Appalachian Trail. It reminds me of the time I went skydiving where a large poster was tacked to the wall that said: "What's the worst that could happen?...Just shut-up and jump".

Mental Prep

Thru-hiking the AT is, without a doubt, a physical challenge, but that's not why only 25% of people that start the trail actually finish it. People quit because they lose the mental battle while on trail. I read "Appalachian Trials" by Zach Davis because it's the only book relating to mental preparation out there. It's an excellent book and it is very apparent that Zach is the man so I definitely recommend it. Zach suggests spending some time defining why I want to thru-hike the AT by addressing the three topics below. I already started to define why I wanted to hike, but Zach's layout forces me to take a more in depth look. I will be writing these reasons down and taking them with me so I can remind myself why I'm hiking when (not if) I want to quit, which seems inevitable from everything I've read. So here goes...

I am thru-hiking the Appalachian Trail because:
- I can and I want to
- I want to wake up and watch the sunrise every morning
- I want to be outdoors and far away from a computer screen
- I want to push myself to the edge, face pain and true adversity and know that I stayed positive and willed myself to overcome it
- I want to understand myself better
- I want to learn to live simply
- I want to further develop my self-confidence and independence
- I want to meet new people and share with them the experience of a lifetime
- I want to get in touch with simplicity and what really matters in life
- I want to overcome conformity and be less ordinary
- I want to really feel alive
- I want to see a moose in person
- I want to attend as many all-you-can-eat pizza places as possible

When I successfully thru-hike the Appalachian Trail, I will:
- Have accomplished the goal of a lifetime

- Have increased my level of self-confidence and independence
- Know that there is no task or obstacle that I cannot achieve or overcome
- Have a true appreciation for the simple things in life
- Have learned to live simply
- Have proved that I am ready for the next challenge
- Have learned to think and have patience (especially when it comes to making decisions)
- Have figured out what I want to do when my thru-hike is over

If I give up on the Appalachian Trail, I will:
- Have constant, haunting feelings of shame and regret
- Have let myself, the charity, and all those people that helped me prepare for my trip down
- Have quit my job for nothing
- Have lost a large measure of my self-confidence
- Want to give it another shot in the future (so why not just complete it now?)

The First Obstacle

I have a tendency to get hurt. Not seriously hurt, but I generally bounce around from injury to injury like a pinball. That's why I regretfully decided to skip two adult hockey seasons in the months leading up to my thru-hike. In spite of my cautious decision, I noticed my right hip cracking pretty loudly while exercising about a month ago. There was no pain, but it definitely didn't feel right. An MRI (I swear those machines remind me of the robot in that horrible Lost in Space movie) revealed that I, in fact, have a labral tear - a whopping TWO MONTHS before starting my hike.

Further research only made the outlook grimmer: labral tears never heal on their own, but require surgery that most surgeons apparently would prefer not to do unless it's absolutely necessary. Physical therapy may help the situation, though. I have a follow-up appointment with a specialist next week to determine a path forward and I can only imagine his reaction when I tell him I still intend to hike almost 2200 miles.

Absolutely none of my plans have changed, but this is undeniably a bummer.

The Deed is Done

I never would have believed it myself, but resigning my job was literally a million times harder than the interview. Holy shit. I mean HOLY SHIT. Like imagine that scene in Animal House where the gun filled with blanks kills the horse and Pluto is freaking out - that kind of holy shit. I can usually mask when I'm nervous pretty well, but all bets were off today - I was sweating, visibly shaking (I think), and my cheeks must have been lit up like a freaking Christmas tree. But it's done!

Contrary to my previous beliefs, both of my managers took the news of an AT thru-hike unbelievably well. Both seemed genuinely happy for me and agreed that now is a great time in my life for such an experience. I believe I was very visibly relieved during the meeting. I'll definitely miss my fellow employees and the relationships I fostered in the last three and a half years. I will most definitely stay in touch with them.

To follow up on a previous post, the labral tear in my hip is of no consequence. The specialist took a look at my MRI as I explained about my upcoming trip and he didn't bat an eye. It was like I was describing a hang nail. Basically, he said don't worry about it as long as you remain asymptomatic. I will be going to physical therapy twice a week until I leave which is definitely helping my lower body prepare for the trip.

In the meantime, my excitement is sky high at the moment - people that know me would say giddy.

The flight is booked, the lodge at Amicalola Falls is booked and everything else is completely ready. 33 days...It just got interesting!

Gear

Two weeks until Amicalola! It's time to finalize my gear. This list is EVERYTHING I own for the next five months, including my home. Everything on this list has been tested multiple times in varying conditions including rain, snow, and cold temperatures as extreme as 4° Fahrenheit. I should be good to go, but I'm sure there will still be some surprises. Here goes:

Cooking and Water
- Aquamira Water Treatment drops - 3 oz
- 2L Platypus Hoser Water Bladder - 3.5 oz

- 2x 1L Platypus Water Bottle – 2.4 oz
- Cook System (Pot, Pan, 4 oz MSR Fuel Canister, Stove, Lighter) – 18.4 oz
- Spork – 0.3 oz

Packing
- Boreas Buttermilks 55 Backpack (w/ Waterproof Pack Cover) – 51.2 oz
- 2x Loksaks with phone, case, charger, credit cards, cash, permits – 9.25 oz
- 4x Sil-nylon Stuff Sacks – 6.75 oz

Shelter and Sleeping System
- Tarptent Notch Tent – 27 oz
- 100% Silk Sleeping Bag Liner – 4.6 oz
- Gossamer Gear Polycryo Ground Sheet – 1.5 oz
- Kelty Cosmic Down 20 DriDown Sleeping Bag – 45 oz
- REI Flash Insulated Air Sleeping Pad – 16 oz

Clothes (Worn + Spare)
- Arc'Teryx Atom LT Hoody Synthetic Insulated Jacket (Sent Home – Cold Only) – 16 oz
- LL Bean 200 Fleece Jacket – 16.75 oz
- SmartWool Merino Wool Gloves (Sent Home – Cold Only) – 1.75 oz
- Marmot Leather Gloves (Sent Home– Cold Only) – 5.25 oz
- 2x Ex Officio Boxers – 6 oz
- 3x SmartWool/Darn Tough Socks – 7.35 oz
- Columbia Evapouration Rain Jacket – 11.3 oz
- Red Ledge Thunderlight Rain Pants – 8.9 oz
- Silk Long Jons – 4.25 oz
- Balaclava (Sent Home– Cold Only) – 1.125 oz
- Smartwool NTS Lightweight Crew (Sent Home– Cold Only) – 8.75 oz
- Icebreaker Sphere Crew T Shirt (Mail Drop – Warm Only) – 5.375 oz
- Prana Zion Stretch Pants – 14 oz
- Kuhl Shorts (Mail Drop – Warm Only) – 9 oz

- Boardshorts (Mail Drop – Warm Only) – 6.75 oz
- Sunglasses – 0.875 oz
- Fleece Hat (Sent Home – Cold Only) – 1.75 oz
- Snapback (Mail Drop – Warm Only) – 3.9 oz
- Synthetic Long Sleeve (Sent Home – Cold Only) – 7.25 oz
- Synthetic T-Shirt (Mail Drop – Warm Only)– 5.125 oz
- Keen Targhee II Trail Shoes – 36.8 oz

Miscellaneous
- Duct Tape – 0.5 oz
- Compass – 0.32 oz / SPOT – 4.5 oz
- Headlamp (w/ Batteries) – 3.4 oz
- 3x AAA Batteries (Spare) – 0.75 oz
- 2x Bandana – 1.5 oz
- Notepad – 1.9 oz
- Pen – 0.25 oz
- Eyeglasses + Sunglasses (w/ Cases) – 3.5 oz
- AT Guide by AWOL – 7.8 oz
- Mini Deck of Cards – 1.375 oz
- Knife + Leatherman – 13.75 oz
- 4x Latex Gloves (Waterproof) – 1.5 oz
- Parachute Cord – 3.875 oz
- Trash Compactor Bag – 1.625 oz
- Spare Ziploc / Trash Bag – 0.875 oz
- Mountainsmith Trekking Poles – 24 oz

Hygiene
- Includes TP, Ear Plugs, Chap Stick, Hand Sanitizer, Pack of wipes, Castile Soap, Contact Case, Contact Solution, 3x Spare Contacts, Toothbrush, Toothbrush, Sunscreen, Bug Spray, Gold Bond Friction, Gold Bond, Medicine – 21.5 oz

First Aid
- Includes Floss, Moleskin, Gauze, Band Aids, Tape, Antiseptic Wipes, Crazy Glue, Scissors, Tweezers, Whistle, Safety Pins, Sewing Needle, Povidone Iodine – 2.75 oz

Fire
- Includes Fire Starter, Lighter, Tinder, Matches - 2.75 oz

TOTAL (Cold Weather – Worn + Pack) - 27.3 lbs
TOTAL (Warm Weather– Worn + Pack) - 24.6 lbs

My pack base weight will hover between 19 and 21 lbs (not counting the clothes I'll be wearing).

I have a mail drop planned for Bland, VA around mile 587 to exchange my colder clothes and gear for my warmer clothes and gear, which will definitely make my pack lighter.

This list could obviously be better, but I don't care. I'm happy with it.

ALL MY GEAR FOR THIS 2,189 MILE ENDEAVOR.

The Calm Before the Storm

On the way to the airport, the anxiety was tangibly building, but in a good way, I think.

I received a complimentary upgrade to a First Class seat on the plane so that was definitely a good start to the trip.

The rents and I stopped in a town called Alpharetta, which is on the way to Amicalola, for a crazy evening of walking around town and grabbing an early dinner. While talking, we realized there's actually nothing to do around Amicalola Falls and, rather than wallow in our collective anxiety all day, we agreed that I'll start the hike tomorrow morning. Plus, this way, my mom can attempt to hike the 8.8 mile approach trail with me like she wanted to.

DAY 1

Starting Location: Amicalola Falls State Park
Destination: Hawk Mountain Campground
Today's Miles: 7.4 (The 8.8 mile approach trail doesn't count)
Trip Miles: 7.4

Mar 25, 2016 - And so it begins...what was my first thought as I started walking into the woods? My own rendition of the Hi Ho song that the dwarves sing in Snow White: "Hi Ho Hi Ho it's into the woods we go!". Don't ask me why though because I don't know.

The sign at the start of the Approach Trail said the 8.8 miles required an average of 6 hours. After taking my first step at 8:30, I didn't think it was too difficult and managed Springer Mountain in about 3 hours. This may have had something to do with the combination of gut wrenching anxiety I was feeling and the adrenaline coursing through my veins. I don't know why I was nervous exactly, but it was like butterflies were having a party in my stomach. I'm glad I did the Approach Trail though as it was very satisfying to summit Springer and see the first white blaze.

My initial plan was to stop at the Stover Creek shelter for the night, but I got there about six hours before sunset so I pushed the remaining 5 miles to the new campsite near Hawk Mountain Shelter. All in all, my first day was 16.2 miles even though only 7.4 miles counted as part of the AT.

I couldn't find my spork so I whittled a small spoon from a thick branch. I honestly probably won't bother buying a new one because the branch is killing it.

So far I've met three other thru-hikers: Todd, Aaron, and Joe. Todd helped quell some of the butterflies still flying around inside me by sharing a few sips of his Jim Beam. No trail names yet though.

DAY 2

Starting Location: Hawk Mountain Campground
Destination: Rockram Mountain
Today's Miles: 11.6
Trip Miles: 19

Mar 26, 2016 - A beautiful first day yesterday gave way to a pretty amazing sunrise this morning. After some breakfast, Todd and I broke camp at Hawk Mountain campsite and headed north.

We crossed Horse Gap, hiked Sassafras Mountain, Cooper Gap, Justice Mountain, Gooch Gap and finally Ramrock Mountain where we made camp making for a modest 11.6 mile day.

We experienced Trail Magic a whopping three times today. At the bottom of Sassafras Mountain, someone had stowed three bottles of beer against a tree - they were still cold! Plus beer at 10:00 am is always extremely satisfying, especially when you're hot and sweaty from trekking over mountains. Next, at Cooper Gap, someone left a large truck full of water for a quick refill. Finally, at Gooch Gap, a family had set up a tent and were giving away apples, cold cut wraps, coffee, hot chocolate and cheese. If it wasn't for this last bit of magic, I would not have made it to Ramrock.

Todd, who I had been hiking with all day, and I met two section hikers on the way to Ramrock Mountain - Pillows and Iron Man. They were hiking the Approach Trail and the first 37.7 miles of the AT and were extremely friendly.

I think I earned a trail name today courtesy of Iron Man. I had planned on 'Dute' (my current nickname and the nickname I carried throughout college – I'm pretty sure some people didn't even know my actual name was Mike until I graduated), but I found I kept introducing myself as Mike. On the hike up Ramrock Mountain, Iron Man stopped, pulled to the side and addressed me as Mountain Goat when he told me to take the lead. I strongly dislike going downhill, but I do enjoy the uphill. I quickly and strongly stride up the hills without stopping and without trekking poles (very few people choose to not carry trekking poles). Apparently, I make hiking up a mountain with a 30 pound pack look very easy. We'll see if Mountain Goat sticks.

The summit of Ramrock was shrouded in fog and it appeared some rain would be moving in tonight. Todd, Iron Man, Pillows, and Doug (a friend of Pillows) got a fire going with some difficulty and made some dinner. After dinner, Jared, a 19 year old that honestly looked like a lost puppy, stumbled into camp. Todd and I recognized him from Hawk Mountain campground and asked him to join us by the fire.

It's about 13 miles to Neel Gap tomorrow where a few of us (Todd, Jared, Pillows, Iron Man, and I) will be renting a cabin so we can grab a shower and sleep indoors. Blood Mountain is the only significant obstacle standing in the way.

As I crawled into my sleeping bag, I noticed a cloud of some exceptionally foul air that collected at the bottom and continually assaulted my face. Just imagine trying to sleep in an ice hockey bag with your wet jock strap still tight against your skin.

DAY 3

Starting Location: Ramrock Mountain
Destination: Neel Gap
Today's Miles: 12.7
Trip Miles: 31.7

Mar 27, 2016 - The rain started around 9 pm last night and did not stop until mid-afternoon today. We woke up to extreme fog, which crushed any hope of a beautiful sunrise from our perch on Ramrock Mountain. In fact, we couldn't even tell the sun had risen until close to lunch time.

Todd, Jared, Iron Man, Pillows and I set out from camp with Neel Gap as our ultimate destination for the day. I had heard of the magical outfitter, Mountain Crossings, located on trail in Neel Gap. It was the first opportunity on trail for hot food and a shower (and for some, to adjust their packs).

Today was Easter Sunday! On our way to Woody Gap, we met a woman dressed as the Easter bunny walking south and passing out candy from a basket. Trail Magic! I was a little bummed that I had to miss my family's Easter dinner at Tatia and Dan's, but I hoped they understood. Part of thru-hiking means accepting that you're going to miss a few important events with friends or family. However, as I rapidly approached Blood Mountain, I had absolutely no problem staying in the present.

Blood Mountain is a slow, drawn out climb up to 4,457 feet. The mountain has its name due to a long, bloody battle between the Cherokee and Creek

Native Americans that caused the mountain to 'turn red with blood'. Though blood wasn't an issue today, we did have to beat a thunderstorm that was scheduled to hit later in the afternoon. As we approached the summit, I actually said aloud to Pillows, "I bet you the storm hits as soon as we hit the summit". Sure enough, lightning and thunder struck when we were only about 200 yards from the summit - talk about bad timing. All five of us literally sprinted the last 200 yards as lightning visibly struck the ground around us. Honestly, despite being soaked to the bone, my first thunderstorm in the wilderness (on top of a summit, unfortunately) was a terrifying and exhilarating experience.

A steep descent of about 2 miles brought us to Neel Gap, home of the famous Mountain Crossings outfitter and hiker hostel. The hiker hostel there was full so the cashier called a local Trail Angel to see if she would house the five of us in one of her cabins for the night.

We waited about 45 minutes for 'Happy' to pick us up from the outfitter and take us to the cabin. It was immediately obvious why people called her Happy - she was the bubbliest person I've ever met. Not only did she drive us to the cabin, she drove us to Wal-Mart to resupply, to Little Cesar's (bonus points in my book - you had to know me in college to understand) for pizza and then insisted on doing our laundry for us. This was all for $25 per person, and honestly made me feel a little guilty because I am not used to such ridiculous kindness. Apparently, this type of southern hospitality is normal down here, but I find that hard to believe because it just doesn't exist where I come from.

The cabin was beautiful and fully equipped with 5 beds, a bathroom and a small kitchen. We crushed pizza, some beers and each took indescribably amazing showers. When you can smell your own brand of stink, you know it's bad.

MOONSHINE, PILLOWS, IRON MAN, SURVIVOR AND MYSELF AFTER NARROWLY ESCAPING A THUNDERSTORM AT THE SUMMIT OF BLOOD MOUNTAIN.

DAY 4

Starting Location: Neel Gap
Destination: Low Gap Shelter
Today's Miles: 11.5
Trip Miles: 43.2

Mar 28, 2016 - Happy needed to get to work by 7:15 am so she dropped us off back at Mountain Crossings at about 5:30 am. Jared needed to mail a package home from Mountain Crossings so we waited for almost 2 hours in the cold morning air for the outfitter to open. The hiking began around 8:45 am.

We covered a total of 11.5 miles today - we summited Levelland Mountain, Cowrock Mountain, Wildcat Mountain, and Poor Mountain. Unfortunately, we had to say goodbye to Pillows and Iron Man as they ended their section hike at Hogpen Gap. Before they left, Pillows insisted on capturing a short video of the "Mountain Goat" powerfully striding up Cowrock Mountain with his trekking poles dangling uselessly from his hands.

All day we heard stories about the hiker hostel at Mountain Crossings the night before and it sounded like a blast. Beer and pot sounded like they were very prevalent as the group apparently stayed up well past midnight (not hiker midnight). I already made reservations at the next one near Hiawassee at Dicks Creek Gap: Top of Georgia Hostel.

We made camp at Low Gap Shelter with around 60 other hikers - from above it looked like a shanty town in the middle of the woods. So, of course we made a large campfire and I had the chance to meet a bunch of other thru-hikers: Tim, Hand Turkey and her dog Lucy, Princess Peach (this is actually a guy that won his New Belgium hat in an N64 Mario Kart Tournament playing as "...Princess Peach, of course"), Rocky, Waterbug, Lauren, Harrison, and a few delightful section hikers.

Todd and Jared both acquired their trail names today. Todd had forgotten a belt for the first 30 miles of the trail so we all saw quite a bit of his ass if we walked behind him on the uphills. Pillows appropriately dubbed him "Moonshine". Jared's story is hilarious - when he came out here to hike, he had no idea the Appalachian Trail was a long distance hiking affair. He thought it was a 6 month survival expedition; consequently, he had all the wrong equipment: a machete, a survival knife, vegetable seeds, emergency food rations, 3 different methods for treating water, and fishing equipment. Honestly, even for a survival expedition, he didn't seem very prepared - his hammock and sleeping system were not rated properly for the cool temperatures typical of late March in the Georgia mountains. Moonshine and I thought the name "Survivor" was extremely fitting.

Because the campsite was so crowded, bedtime tonight was incredibly late: 9:45 pm. Seriously though, it's very rare for thru-hikers to not be in their tents 30 minutes after dark.

DAY 5

Starting Location: Low Gap Shelter
Destination: Sassafras Gap
Today's Miles: 20.1
Trip Miles: 63.3

Mar 29, 2016 – My goal today was Trey Mountain Shelter: 15.4 miles away. That was until Tim mentioned Big Al's Pizza and Buffet in Hiawassee, GA. So instead, Tim, Moonshine and I legged it 20.1 miles to Sassafras Gap – my first 9 hour workday. It's amazing what the words 'pizza' and 'buffet' can make you do.

After summiting the unruly bitch that is Trey Mountain, we stopped at the shelter to eat some much needed lunch. There we met another Tim, 11:30 (he always sets up camp before lunch), Eucalady (she carries a eucalaly and yes I know I spelled that incorrectly), and Anna. Princess Peach was there already, had finished setting up camp, and changed into his nighttime clothes when we arrived. When we told him about the pizza and the plan (see below), he immediately packed back up, changed and left for Sassafras Gap with the three of us. I left a note for Survivor in the shelter letting him know where we went.

Just an aside, but Survivor and I split an entire box of Twinkies today and I forgot how damn good they were.

So with storms forecast for Thursday / Friday, here's the grand plan:
1. Up at sunrise

2. Hike about 6 miles to the hostel (Top of Georgia)
3. Launder and shower our filthy, foul smelling, sweat soaked clothes and bodies
4. Shuttle into Hiawassee, GA
5. Hit up Big Al's and put them out of business by noon
6. Each obtain a 12 pack of beer
7. Shop for food / supplies
8. Wait! At the Dicks Creek Gap, we heard of a 2nd buffet for $8 = dinner
9. Sleep
10. Huge $6 hot breakfast at the hostel
11. Hike around 5 miles to Plumorchard Gap Shelter to beat the storms (11 miles in 2 days is basically a zero day so plenty of time to recover)
12. Drink beer and chill in the shelter until the storms pass
13. Friday – enter NC

Yes, they distribute Yuengling in Georgia.

Finally, some of the lessons I've learned so far:
1. Keep toilet paper in a very quickly and easily accessible part of your pack
2. Downhill is far worse than uphill
3. Shitting in a hole in the ground is way more preferable to privies (unless it's raining)
4. Baby wipes are to hikers as cigarettes are to prisoners
5. If you look into the distance and pick out the tallest mountains you can see, the AT is sure to be in that direction

On the way to Dicks Creek Gap, we passed the "Swag of the Blue Ridge". While this is an epic name, I don't get it because there was absolutely nothing remarkable about that section of the trail. Still, it proved to be a nice picture opportunity.

Tim Adams, the pizza slice count is at 4 (my friend made a bet with me to see how many slices of pizza I could eat while on trail – the more slices I ate, the more he would donate to my charity). I will update you after tomorrow.

DAY 6

Starting Location: Sassafras Gap
Destination: Dicks Creek Gap
Today's Miles: 6.3
Trip Miles: 69.6

Mar 30, 2016 - A hot, sunny day yesterday turned into a windy, beautifully clear morning that made it tough to crawl out of our sleeping bags. With a buffet on our minds, we hiked a short six miles in less than 2 hours. We managed to catch the shuttle at Dicks Creek Gap for the Top of Georgia Hostel.

Upon arriving at this lovely hostel, two hiker terms began to clearly define themselves: hiker hunger and hiker trash. For about two days now, food just isn't enough; I'm always hungry. Now, hiker trash is closely related to hiker hunger. This term was clearly illustrated when I walked into the hostel and sat down next to two complete strangers: Tom and Taylor. Both Tom and Taylor had purchased frozen pizzas and had half eaten leftovers remaining. No food related dialogue took place, but one look at their plates and they were unconsciously pushed in my direction while we made small talk. I crushed those leftovers without a second thought. This behavior is apparently pretty normal around hiker culture. Tim said that on his hike of the PCT, he would take unfinished plates of food off vacated tables at restaurants without even asking. We'll see if the hunger gets to that point.

After a shower, the five of us donned the scrubs the hostel supplied us while laundry was being completed and took the shuttle to Hiawassee, GA.

Big Al's was closed! Thinking about nothing but pizza for almost 48 hours while hiking almost 30 miles and then being denied said pizza is a unique brand of disappointment. We settled for a southern comfort food all-you-can-eat buffet at a steakhouse for $8. Three plates later and we decided it was time for beer so we crossed the street to the Bacchus beer store and bought flights of craft beer.

The owner recommended we take a few growlers down to the lake nearby and sit in the sun while we drank. Good man. He even had cleaned milk jugs especially for hikers due to their lightweight and portable preferences.

Next, I resupplied with food at the local grocery store. Last time I didn't get enough food; this time, I bought far too much. It's a fine line between the two, but I can always unload some extra food in the hiker boxes. It's also not a good idea to resupply after consuming an entire growler of beer. Between the food, water and the 12 pack of beer, my pack weighs over 40 pounds, which will make for a long 5 miles tomorrow morning to Plumorchard Gap Shelter.

I've lost 5 lbs already in 6 days. At least that is what Top of Georgia's scale is telling me.

Tim Adams, the pizza slice count has risen to 7.

DAY 7

Starting Location: Dicks Creek Gap
Destination: Plumorchard Gap Shelter
Today's Miles: 4.5
Trip Miles: 74.1

Mar 31, 2016 - Top of Georgia Hostel was just beautiful. With no alarms, everyone there got up at 6:30 and made their way to the main building for a complimentary, homemade breakfast of pastries, biscuits, and sausage. The staff there (Bob, Jennifer, Jason, Renaissance, Maul and Paul) were ridiculously kind and extremely helpful. During breakfast, Bob's casual conversation with another hiker turned into an impromptu sermon about the 10 keys to thru-hiking that was definitely inspiring and full of useful tips for the next 100 miles.

Tim temporarily said goodbye today - he made a cardboard sign with hopes of hitching a ride to Asheville to see his girlfriend and hopefully convince her to join us on the trail (We actually never saw Tim again - he managed to hitch a ride with a beer distributor. He helped the driver deliver beer the whole way to Asheville).

I set off for Plumorchard Gap shelter around mid-morning carrying 45 pounds including an overly large food bag of 11 pounds, 4 pounds of water and 9 pounds of beer, which I carried in my arms for nearly 5 miles. I may have looked like an asshole carrying it but none of us waiting out the storms at the shelter felt like assholes after a few beers.

On the way to the shelter, I met an older man section hiking southbound. We got to talking and he said he thru-hiked in 2008. This triggered something in my memory and I asked what his trail name was - it was 'Apostle'! He was the same guy that wrote the book Hiking Through that I read before starting my own hike - Paul Stutzman (this also made me feel a lot worse about the beer)! Almost 2,200 miles of trail and I just happen to meet this guy in the backwoods of Georgia! I mean, come on.

The Plumorchard Gap shelter served as a nice gathering spot for those of us waiting out the thunderstorms: Princess Peach, Survivor, Moonshine, Splinter (he picks up a new wooden walking stick everyday), Which Way, Yackie (his wife thinks he talks a lot), Nicole, Sam (she made a dessert called 'Crack' last night so we're hoping that trail name sticks), Green Lady (he took some drug DMT and hallucinated this green lady that followed him for 6 miles...yea...plus all his clothes are green), Sebastian (he rolled in three hours later soaked to the bone), Michael, Crow, and Kane.

Princess Peach made a cribbage board out of a dead branch and we used matchsticks and a deck of cards to play cribbage all afternoon and, of course, eat. Survivor had an emergency 2400 calorie food bar leftover from his misconception of the trail that we all tried because it looked disgusting. It tasted like flavored paper.

All in all, this Nero ("nearly zero day") went by pretty slowly, but it was necessary to allow the legs to recover. Tomorrow, we cross into North Carolina!

PREPARING TO WAIT OUT THE STORM AT PLUMORCHARD GAP SHELTER.

DAY 8

Starting Location: Plumorchard Gap Shelter
Destination: Standing Indian Mountain Summit
Today's Miles: 13.7
Trip Miles: 87.8

Apr 1, 2016 - The storms finally came during the night resulting in about 3 inches of rain. The huge amount of mud actually made the terrain pretty difficult today. The trail was actually a stream in many places. I am definitely hungover from yesterday so that doesn't help matters.

After about 4 miles, we crossed into North Carolina. Other than that, today was fairly uneventful with a tough climb up Courthouse Bald. I did find a field of wild onion (ramps) which kept me busy eating for about 20 minutes...of course, now I reek of onion and am looking at 6 days without a shower.

Moonshine, Survivor, Princess Peach and I finished the day with a relatively easy climb up Standing Indian Mountain - the first summit above 5,000 feet. We met Lou and Louie at the summit where we made camp and shared in their campfire. They were cooking tequila marinated steaks on the fire and generously shared half.

Moonshine realized he left his down jacket at the shelter 13.7 miles back. He quickly left for the previous shelter 1.5 miles away for any hikers behind us. He didn't come back with his jacket, but he did come back with burgers! Trail magic! Two former thru-hikers, Feivel and Littlefoot, were serving burgers, salad, beer and chips. Steak and burgers on the same day in the woods is just nuts.

DAY 9

Starting Location: Standing Indian Mountain Summit
Destination: Rock Gap Shelter
Today's Miles: 18.2
Trip Miles: 106

Apr 2, 2016 – 100 miles! Only 2089.1 to go...

I hiked most of the day alone today, which I think I enjoy the most. It's so easy to get lost in my thoughts, like I'm dreaming while awake. I'll usually have a very random song stuck in my head all day; today, it was Good Charlotte's 'Girls and Boys', which, oddly enough, I haven't heard in years.

I received some trail magic from a nice old man named Rodney. He had no ties to the trail, but just said he enjoyed spending his Saturday sharing his delicious homemade banana bread with hungry hikers. It's just ridiculous how nice people are down here.

I hit the 100 mile mark as I summited Albert Mountain. There's a fire tower on the top that is freaking scary. The wind speed between the bottom and the top must have differed by 20 mph. I made a nice grab of my hat when it got blown off though.

I covered a total of 18.2 miles today as I crossed Beech Gap, Coleman Gap, Mooney Gap, and Glassmine Gap to Rock Gap Shelter, situated in a valley. I arrived pretty late so I attempted to set up my tent as the wind howled down the mountain. It usually takes me about 5 minutes to set up my tent if I do it slow. It took me almost 30 minutes because the only available tent sites were on an incline, too small, and not protected from the damn wind. I didn't expect it to last the night and it didn't.

Our usual group was joined at the campfire by Fireball, who killed it on his backpacker's guitar, Skinny Tall, and Zach Galifinakis.

With temperatures dropping into the lower 30s, I crawled into my precariously pitched tent. You could hear the wind coming like it was gathering up forces for a last charge. Only an hour after I hit the hay, my tent collapsed and flew off with me inside. Stakes were ripped out of the ground and thrown into the night. Rather than try to stumble around in the dark trying to fix it, I just took my sleeping bag out and threw it down on top of the tent and slept cowboy style with no cover. Oh and as I look around with my headlamp, the two groups of over-nighters had slung up their bear bags less than 10 feet from my tent. I mean, come on. Any anger or frustration I had quickly evaporated when I looked up and noticed the brilliantly bright stars in the sky - just beautiful. I actually did sleep pretty well though and only woke up twice when leaves and sticks were blown into my face.

Ah it could've been worse.

DAY 10

Starting Location: Rock Gap Shelter
Destination: Siler Bald Summit
Today's Miles: 8.4
Trip Miles: 114.4

Apr 3, 2016 - Peach and I got up early to try to hitch a ride into Franklin, NC so we could get some food and check out the Lazy Hiker Brewing Company. It took all of 2 seconds - we climbed into the truck bed of a couple on their way to church. Let me tell you it's damn cold sitting in a truck bed flying down the highway at 60 mph in freezing temperatures. After 10 grueling miles, we stepped into the parking lot of the brewery and realized we had 4 hours until it opened. We quickly toured Franklin to realize that literally nothing is open on Sunday. We had to walk two miles outside of town to a Bojangles for chicken and biscuits, which were awesome despite the fact that they are a fast food joint.

After stuffing our bellies, we hitched back to the center of town and waited outside the brewery until it opened. We were eventually joined by Moonshine, Survivor, Zach Galifinakis, and a day hiker named Emily. Six beers later, we called a cab, purchased half of the items on Arby's menu, and returned to the trail to hike 8.0 miles to Siler Bald Summit, our campsite for the evening.

This place was unreal - 5,216 feet above sea level and completely open on the summit (a bald). With a completely clear sky, our group, which included the regulars plus Jukebox (he carried an actual stereo with him),

Little Heater, Voodoo, Blister (he had 18 blisters at the time), Skywalker (whose real name is Hans and he looks just like Luke Skywalker), Mama Cheddar, and Smoky, got a fire going and watched the sun set.

Finally, the stars came out and it was the first night you could see the Milky Way stretched across the sky. I cowboy camped (voluntarily this time) on the summit under the stars and looked forward to an amazing sunrise the next morning.

PRINCESS PEACH, SURVIVOR, MOONSHINE, EMILY AND MYSELF ENJOYING A FEW BREWSKIES AT LAZY HIKER BREWING COMPANY.

DAY 11

Starting Location: Siler Bald Summit
Destination: Wesser Bald Shelter
Today's Miles: 17
Trip Miles: 131.4

Apr 4, 2016 - I hiked a pretty challenging 17 miles today to Wesser Bald Shelter at mile 131.4.

Remember when I ran into Apostle last week? He had told me to look out for a woman named Jewels who was carrying a red Osprey. Today, I passed her and recognized her immediately. Better yet, she already knew I was Mountain Goat!

We discovered during dinner that we can make quesadillas over the fire with foil. Game changer. We also discovered why the trail is nicknamed the 'Green Tunnel' - rhododendron bushes on either side of the trail and overlap above forming a literal brownish green tunnel.

We were so exhausted from our hike today that we were all in our tents before the sun went down.

NOC tomorrow. I'll try to grab some pizza slices or pies, but, frankly, they don't have a lot of pizza down here. It's killing me. Not a single lake yet either...I'm dying for a shower. Actually, we did pass a lake today for the first time, but it was 5.7 miles off trail. Not cool.

DAY 12

Starting Location: Wesser Bald Shelter
Destination: Sassafras Gap Shelter
Today's Miles: 12.6
Trip Miles: 144

Apr 5, 2016 - We're in a bit of a cold spell so the nights have consistently been dropping to around freezing - it's supposed to be 17 on Friday. This motivates me to get my ass moving in the morning when the birds wake me up around 6:30 am. Peach and I dominated a quick six miles in under two hours to make it to the Nantahala Outdoor Center (NOC). The NOC is built on the edge of the Nantahala River and they specialize in water sports.

There, I finally had the opportunity to do some laundry ($3) and take a shower ($2). This is easily the best $5 I've spent in a long time. The stink was so bad that when I got out of the shower, the fumes emanating from my body still caused my nose to wrinkle in discomfort. Hey, it's all relative and the nose does get used to it, believe it or not.

Next up was a delicious meal at the River's End Restaurant. I crushed a 10" personal plain pie (which I'm counting as 5 regular slices, Tim, so my total is now 12), a side of sautéed vegetables (I miss them so much I brought a pound of frozen Brussel sprouts into the woods and just ate them when they defrosted), a "side" of tater tots that was served on a full size dinner plate, and two beers. For dessert, a pint of vanilla ice cream and a block of fudge. I was stuffed. All this and we hadn't even hit noon yet. We relaxed for a bit and soaked our tired feet in the cold river.

Finally, we had our toughest climb of the trail so far to get to Sassafras Gap shelter - 3,000 feet of elevation spread across 7 miles of consistent uphill. It wouldn't have been horrible if I didn't have a brick in my stomach or Peach hadn't pressured me into starting the climb with a very unsatisfying IPA in hand given the circumstances. However, the beer was called Shiva, which called for a Shiva blast right there on the mountain. I turned to music to get me going: Mother, We Just Can't Get Enough by the New Radicals had me climbing swiftly in no time. Once I got past the first mile without making a mess, the rest wasn't too bad.

Survivor was our Good Samaritan of the day - after making the 7 mile climb, he turned back and helped a woman named Barbara make it up the mountain by carrying her pack the last mile. She said she wouldn't have made it without him. Good man.

I met a few more people today including Monkey, Josh, John, Gucci, Twizzler (no he did not have Twizzlers at the time) and Mike, who gets bonus points for being Canadian. Unfortunately, we don't see a lot of these people again because we've been driving at a fast pace. Fortunately, we do get to meet all these great people.

All in all, we hiked 12.6 miles today. Only 22 miles from the Great Smoky Mountains!

A FIRE AT THE TOP OF SILER BALD - OUR HOME FOR THE NIGHT.

DAY 13

Starting Location: Sassafras Gap Shelter
Destination: Cable Gap Shelter
Today's Miles: 15.2
Trip Miles: 159.2

Apr 6, 2016 - Today was a fairly uneventful 15.2 miles with the exception of Jacob's Ladder, which was nothing more than a short, extremely steep section of trail. We discovered that the kid Gucci that we met last night drank directly from the stream and ended up running 7 miles back to the road throwing up the whole way. There have been rumors of norovirus spreading on the trail and this was the first case I heard of.

I snagged a spot in the Cable Gap shelter so I could avoid the rain that is supposed to come tonight. It's always a tough decision: rain or snoring? They're equally bad in my opinion.

I met a few cool, new people tonight: Hot Toddy (she makes whiskey drinks by the same name), Yoshi (he and Princess Peach nearly went at it...but not really), Ankle Weights (a section hiker who brought s'mores), Sushi (he has sushi embroidered gaiters for some reason), Emma and Tony who are sorely in need of trail names, Mardi Gras, St. Nick, Steel, Cheshire, and Nightingale (this is a nice old man who has been accidentally diagnosing all these illnesses and problems the last two weeks), John and Helton.

Survivor rolled into camp last as usual and we had been wondering what was taking him so long. As it turned out, a man in the parking lot 6 miles back lured him into his car and brought him to an all-you-can-eat pizza buffet, food shopping at the nearby grocery store and then returned him to the trail. I nearly lost my shit when I heard this. Ridiculous. That could've been me if I walked just a bit slower.

Fontana Village tomorrow.

DAY 14

Starting Location: Cable Gap Shelter
Destination: Fontana Village, NC
Today's Miles: 5.5
Trip Miles: 164.7

Apr 7, 2016 - Five easy miles brought us near the Fontana Dam. The Killer Quad (it's corny, but I don't care) teamed up with John (Bad Apple) to split a room at the Fontana Lodge five ways. Seeing as the lake near the dam was the first body of water we've seen in 160+ miles, Peach and I stripped to our undies and vaulted over the side of the gangway into the frigid waters. Amazingly refreshing. We had to sprint back up the hill in our underwear to catch the shuttle that had arrived to take our group from the trail to the lodge.

We managed to get there in time for breakfast so we ordered our eggs and breakfast meats. Peach asked the waitress for the beer list. She laughed. No one else laughed. Then she said, "Wait, for breakfast?" We just don't kid about such things.

Fontana Village is a super super small town that is virtually dead in the winter. Without hikers, it literally doesn't exist. They had laundry, a general store, one bar that was also a gas station, two restaurants, a post office, one ice cream shop that was closed for the season, and, oddly enough, a mini golf course AND a disc golf course.

I picked up the gigantic package from my mom that contained an insane amount of goodness. I had requested a small package of baby wipes and she supplied no less than 168. Between the wipes and homemade cookies and zucchini bread, she made all of us very happy.

We ended up hosting a little party on the back porch of our hotel room. Josh, Helton, Barbara, Daniel, John, Firefly (she always hangs around the fire), Fish n Chips (he eats fish but no meat, but he's cool about it), Josh, and another Josh. Then, Trail Magic! The neighbor next door had her son complete the trail last year and they've become Trail Angels. They brought beer and leftover lemon meringue pie. They're just traveling the trail and passing out trail magic because they are caught up in the spirit of the whole endeavor. It's all part of the contagious culture that surrounds the trail. It's a completely different take on life that people live on a daily basis. It's not part of the real world, but it's their world and they love it. Right now and for the next 4 months, I'm a part of that world.

They say time flies by when you're having fun. Well, I'm having an amazing time, but it feels like I've been out here for well over a month. It's an odd feeling.

Tomorrow, it's the Great Smoky Mountains!

DAY 15

Starting Location: Fontana Village, NC
Destination: Fontana Village, NC
Today's Miles: 0
Trip Miles: 164.7

Apr 8, 2016 - Psych! We were completely ready to head out and continue hiking when the weather reports began to reach our ears. Temperatures in the teens, 50 mph winds, and up to a foot of snow in the Great Smoky Mountains. Despite this, the killer quad was still intent on hiking until the military guys waiting with us received orders from their superiors to stay put. It's a lot of fun to test yourself in extreme conditions, but with roads closed and potential rescue unlikely, we decided better safe than sorry. The danger wasn't necessarily the cold, but cold combined with 50 mph tends to bring trees down in an unpredictable fashion. So, we booked another room at the Fontana Lodge and had our first zero.

Ever since Cable Gap Shelter, Princess Peach and I had been talking about Hot Toddy on a regular basis. She was very attractive and definitely a lot of fun to hang out with. So, needless to say, we were both thrilled when we found out she would be arriving at Fontana Dam during our zero.

We filled the afternoon with Hot Toddy, the Warrior Hikers, beers, horseshoes, several meals, and then ended up in a game room that some other hikers discovered. We convinced the manager of the restaurant to go pick us up two cases from the general store that had already closed, and proceeded to play corn hole, air hockey, pool and ping pong. Peach and

Survivor, unaware that we had secured beer already, hitched a ride to Bryson City, NC, 33 miles away to grab a case.

As the beers continued to flow, Hot Toddy made us all Hot Toddys – these delicious whiskey drinks put me over the line. I passed out and missed the brief, naked pool party with Hot Toddy and company. Peach, who must have been a little excited to see Hot Toddy's breasts, fell over the gate to the pool area and walked away with a massive bump on his head.

The entire lodge was filled with hikers and it was basically one really large party. I also met a few new hikers: Liam, Casper (he always creeps up on people unintentionally and scares the crap out of them), Constantine, Tortuga (he actually looks like Steve the pirate from Dodgeball), and Melanie.

DAY 16

Starting Location: Fontana Village, NC
Destination: Mollies Ridge Shelter
Today's Miles: 12.6
Trip Miles: 177.3

Apr 9, 2016 – Saturday morning means one thing at Fontana Lodge: breakfast buffet. Rob Swonson said it best, "There is no sadness that can't be cured by breakfast food". A hangover isn't necessarily a sadness, but the saying still applies.

After breakfast, we hopped on the shuttle and returned to Fontana Dam (unfortunately Hot Toddy was taking another zero in Fontana Dam). The walk across the top of the dam led the killer quad to the southern terminus of the Great Smoky Mountains National Park. Of course, this meant climbing over 3,000 feet of vertical just to get into the Smokies. That's not great for hangovers by the way.

In the Smokies, the policy requires that shelters be completely filled with hikers before tents are set up. Shelters are definitely warmer, but the snoring is unbearable. I ended up tenting about 30 yards from the shelter and I still heard people snoring.

Although 99% of hikers are excellent people, you do see some bad apples. This section hiker we met did nothing but complain about norovirus, the park's apparent lack of effort to prevent noro and openly disrespected the ridge runners who are simply there to help us and because they love the woods. I just know this guy was one guilty of snoring, too, which is definitely his most egregious offense.

JUST JAMMING OUT AT THE ENTRANCE TO THE GREAT SMOKY MOUNTAINS.

DAY 17

Starting Location: Mollies Ridge Shelter
Destination: Mt. Collins Shelter
Today's Miles: 25.5
Trip Miles: 202.8

Apr 10, 2016 - Princess Peach and I had the bright idea to hike a pretty big day in order to situate ourselves 5 miles from Newfound Gap. Tomorrow, from the gap, we would catch a ride into nearby Gatlinburg, TN to check out the Smoky Mountain Brewery (this trip was rapidly turning into a 2,200 mile brewery crawl. However, in order to make this plan work, we needed to hike 25.5 miles today. This was no ordinary 25.5 miles. The Great Smoky Mountains are considered some of the more challenging terrain on the entire AT and it is home to the highest mountain on the AT in Clingman's Dome (6,667 feet). We climbed an estimated 6.000 feet in elevation while summiting Thunderhead Mountain, Silers Bald, Mt. Buckley (which I thought was Clingman's Dome only to realize it was a false summit), Clingman's Dome, and Mt. Collins. All summits were above 5,300 feet.

Even though Clingman's Dome is only 6,667 feet high, you can't help but feel like you're on top of the world when you're up there. It makes it all that much sweeter that I worked to get up there. There's a small parking lot near the summit where people can drive up and walk a few hundred yards to the top of a tower for a view. It's amazing hearing some of their conversations - a younger couple was actually complaining about walking up the paved, gradually inclined path to the summit.

Walking up the mountain allowed me to watch the environment change with the elevation. Above 5,300 feet, the rhododendrons, wildflowers and deciduous trees gave way to strictly pine trees. It's stark and very surprising how abruptly the boreal environment takes over at that particular elevation.

An initial estimate had me thinking that the shelter we were walking to was only 2.5 miles past Clingman's. A sign near the summit indicated that it was actually 4 miles plus another half mile off trail to our destination. This was psychologically devastating. I was crazy exhausted, stumbling and slipping in mud, snow and ice (yes, ice in April) and had already fallen several times. I threw my pole at the sign and swore pretty loudly alarming a few of the lazy people that drove to the summit.

When I finally stumbled into the shelter a half hour before sunset, I realized we hiked too much and I was lucky that I didn't get hurt. I was also insanely hungry. Breakfast, four lunches, snacks, and dinner just wasn't enough. As I tried to fall asleep, I heard something that sounded like someone praying. As it turned out, Moxy and Scout (who I would meet later) were reading to each other before bed in the adjacent tent.

Anyway, another 25.5 miles in the books and I'm over 200 miles!

DAY 18

Starting Location: Mt. Collins Shelter
Destination: Gatlinburg, TN / Newfound Gap
Today's Miles: 4.3
Trip Miles: 207.1

Apr 11, 2016 – As is the case with most of our neros, Princess Peach and I hiked a quick 4.3 miles into Newfound Gap where we hoped to find a ride into Gatlinburg, TN. The First Baptist Church was waiting for us with snacks and fruit. After talking to them briefly, we hopped on their shuttle and went into town.

I had heard rumors of Gatlinburg's extravagance, but just driving 50 yards into this town felt surreal. The closest thing I can compare it to is one of those fake towns inside a Disney or Universal Studios theme park. Still, they had beer and good food, which already exceeds expectations in my book.

We got in touch with Moonshine and Survivor and discovered they were on their way. Peach and I got settled at the Sydney James Mountain Lodge – we took advantage of their laundromat, jacuzzi, pool, and sauna. All of this for only $14 by the time the four of us split the bill.

Next up, two scoops of homemade cookie dough ice cream and a half block of fudge, a foot long corn dog, pizza and a calzone at the Mellow Mushroom, beers at the Smoky Mountain Brewery (our second brewery stop on the 2,189 mile long crawl), and a resupply. I hadn't planned on resupplying, but I also hadn't planned on eating 6 days of food in 3 days.

Unfortunately, on the way to dinner with Monkey (he retrieved his bear bag when it was stuck by climbing the tree), Shovel (he loves shoveling snow), Stumble, Dos Equis (he looks just like the most interesting man in the world) and Emma, Sushi told us in passing that he had just witnessed a local jump off the tower in the center of town and commit suicide. He was decapitated on the way down, which caused the police to close the streets around the tower. Messed up.

After dinner, we aided our digestion with the free tastings at three of the moonshine distilleries in town. It was absolutely delicious. Tim Adams, the pizza slice count is up to 29.

PRINCESS PEACH, SURVIVOR AND I CHILLING WITH OUR CLOWN NOSES OUTSIDE A STORE IN GOOD OLE GATLINBURG.

DAY 19

Starting Location: Gatlinburg, TN / Newfound Gap
Destination: Tricorner Knob Shelter
Today's Miles: 15.1
Trip Miles: 222.2

Apr 12, 2016 - The four of us stocked up one last time on the deluxe breakfast down the street before heading back to the trail at Newfound Gap.

The shuttle back to the Newfound Gap trail head was already full so Peach and I put on our red clown noses that we bought at Walgreens to support a charity and attempted to hitch. An elderly couple were laughing as we climbed into the back of their pickup truck. The temperature was warmer this time (the difference in temperature between Gatlinburg and the mountains near Newfound Gap must have been 30 degrees without exaggeration), but this time we got rained on while in the truck bed.

We ran into a few hikers in the parking lot - it's always weird how everybody flip-flops because everyone hikes different distances on different days. You just never know when you're going to see someone again.

I passed Charlie's Bunion as I continued hiking north. At the start of this short, blue-blazed loop trail, there was a sign warning parents of danger and to keep children close. Naturally, the cautionary sign automatically made the detour worth it. Unfortunately, I was caught in a whiteout as I started to explore, which blocked some surely stunning views from the steep precipice that was Charlie's Bunion.

I hiked 15.1 miles to Tri-Corner Knob Shelter and the place was a mob scene. There must have been about 50 hikers there. It was so crowded that Moonshine, Survivor, and Peach decided to move on to the next shelter 7.7 miles away. No way! I stayed, fell asleep early and planned on catching them with a super early start in the morning.

DAY 20

Starting Location: Tricorner Knob Shelter
Destination: Painter Branch Campsite north of Standing Bear Hostel
Today's Miles: 20.5
Trip Miles: 242.7

Apr 13, 2016 – As I woke up, the only sensation I registered was wetness. I thought I pissed myself while sleeping but I knew that didn't make any sense. It turns out I slept on the mouthpiece of my water hoser and two liters of water filled the bathtub floor of my tent. Ugh. It was before six, so I just packed all my wet equipment into my pack and started hiking to the next shelter 7.7 miles away where I hoped to catch Moonshine, Survivor and Princess Peach before they left.

When I arrived, I found a note pinned to the shelter sign from Peach saying they were still there. Not only had they waited for me, but they also had a small pile of food that two section hikers had donated. The day was definitely looking up.

Another 10 miles and we exited the Great Smoky Mountains. Our permits required that we get through the Smokies in 8 days. We did it in 5 including our nero in Gatlinburg.

Tugboat, a section hiker, was waiting for us at the northern terminus of the national park while he surveyed budding trees. He was a pleasant fellow that looked like Joe Pesci and even more pleasant because he had snacks and sodas for us in the bed of his truck.

On the big mile days, my legs really start to cramp up, like 'amusement park' legs (my made up term for how your legs feel after walking around an amusement park all day) only much more severe. Eating food obviously helps, but Tugboat gave me my first soda, Mountain Dew, in years and it was amazing. Five minutes and it completely erased my amusement park legs. As unhealthy as my diet has become on this trip, I guess I was still subconsciously avoiding sugar due to the paleo diet I had followed for two years. Not anymore. I'm definitely less interested in the ingredients of my food and more focused on the macronutrients the food provides. This includes carbohydrates. It's a necessary evil because I'm burning a ridiculous amount of calories every day.

Probably the only disappointment on this trip so far has been the lack of wildlife. We had just been lamenting this fact to Tugboat and less than 2 miles later, I saw my first elk standing in a stream. It was so satisfying. Next up is a bear, hopefully.

Two miles before our target campsite, we stopped by the Standing Bear hostel because Moonshine needed to pick up a package. The owner, Lumpy, was pleasant enough, but very sketchy. The whole place had a hillbilly feel to it. I wouldn't have been surprised to find a still and a few marijuana plants hidden somewhere especially after I noticed the plants growing in old hiker shoes. Still, we picked up beers, hot dogs and frozen breakfast biscuits that we cooked over the fire later that night.

We took a quick rinse in the stream before a grueling two mile climb to our campsite. There we met a few more hikers: Cheeks (an English woman with cold cheeks), Sailor Pete (a veteran of the navy), Scooter, One Extra, Yellow Jacket, Iwoks (I originally thought this was because of those creatures in Star Wars, but it's not), Southpaw, and Fried Pickles.

Crazy 20.5 mile day, but well worth it.

DAY 21

Starting Location: Campsite north of Standing Bear Hostel
Destination: Walnut Mountain Shelter
Today's Miles: 17.9
Trip Miles: 260.6

Apr 14, 2016 - Today was a fairly uneventful 17.9 miles to Walnut Mountain Shelter. The terrain has certainly changed from ridge hiking in the Smokies to just continuous hills - we go up and then down and then back up all day.

By the time we reached Walnut Mountain Shelter, we were positioned about 13 miles from Hot Springs, NC so we will arrive tomorrow around midday just in time for Trailfest! My first huge hiker Woodstock will finally take place this weekend and should provide a solid preview of Trail Days (the largest festival in Damascus, VA) later in May. There will be a bluegrass band playing, cheap meals, plenty of outfitters and organizations that are sure to have trail magic. I will be partaking in the festivities on Saturday and early Sunday.

Jimmy Kersch, a friend from UD that I traveled to Australia with for a study abroad program, put me in touch with his Uncle Paul who lives down here in Asheville, NC. He'll be hiking south from Hot Springs tomorrow morning with his dogs to meet me on the trail. He has generously offered to take me back to his home in Asheville tomorrow night for dinner, a shower and some beers. I'm pumped to meet him. Thanks, Jimmy, for putting me in touch.

DAY 22

Starting Location: Walnut Mountain Shelter
Destination: Hot Springs, NC / Paul and Catherine Kersch's
Home in Fairview, NC
Today's Miles: 13.1
Trip Miles: 273.7

Apr 15, 2016 - The plan this morning was to leave Walnut Mountain Shelter around 8:30am and meet Paul and his two dogs, Ash and Atlas, as they hiked south along the trail. With about 5 miles left to go before Hot Springs, I saw the two dogs and I sat down with Paul for some lunch. He had an extra peanut butter and jelly sandwich and a few packs of Butterscotch Krimpets (that do not exist in the south - he had bought these during a recent visit north) that I quickly devoured.

Hot Springs is a very small town nestled in a valley with the mighty French Broad River winding its way through the landscape. It's a hiker town through and through with only the basics: two pubs, a post office, a few hostels, a hillbilly market, a tobacco shop, an outfitter, a general store, a school, a bank, and a dollar general.

I picked up the massive and excessive package my mom generously sent me from the post office, sent home a pound and a half of winter gear and took a load off with some Yuenglings near Paul's car with the rest of the killer quad.

Finally, Paul and I took off toward his home in Asheville, NC. From the brief tour I received, Asheville strikes me as a small, walkable city flush with breweries and places to eat. It's also less than an hour to excellent outdoor activities. We stopped at the French Broad Brewing Company and the Catawba Brewing Company to enjoy a couple cold beers and get the (slightly buzzed) feel of the city – the 2,189 mile brewery crawl continues!

Paul's quaint house is just outside of Asheville in the mountains of North Carolina. You can literally look outside his living room and perfectly glimpse the sun rise over the mountains. While it was a small home, it clearly wasn't wonting for anything. I met Paul's wife, Catherine, and then, they just started spoiling me: a shower, a soak in the hot tub, beer, whiskey, home grilled burgers and real vegetables (my special request), corn hole and good conversation.

DAY 23

Starting Location: Hot Springs, NC
Destination: Hot Springs, NC
Today's Miles: 0
Trip Miles: 273.7

Apr 16, 2016 - Paul and Catherine continued pampering me with an omelet made with fresh eggs from the farm down the street, veggies and the remaining leftover hamburger from last night.

Next up was a quick hike to walk the dogs that was surprising beautiful and pleasant since I didn't have a 30 pound pack on my shoulders. We returned to Hot Springs around midday and immediately began exploring Trailfest.

The actual festival was not as large as I expected, but it had a unique small town feel to it. The Appalachian Trail Conservancy (ATC) was handing out thru-hiker goody bags with homemade baked goods, Nutella packets, crackers and hand sanitizer. The event had all of the stands you'd normally have at a town festival only they were subtly or not so subtly geared toward hikers. There was a stand on foraging, which I found interesting, an outfitter stand, an organic energy bar stand, and live music and speakers.

When I reunited with Princess Peach, Survivor and Moonshine, it was evident that I had missed a wild night. Peach "slightly" kissed Hot Toddy (even though she still ended up sleeping with another guy), Survivor hooked up with a nameless 52 year old spawning a secondary trail name in

'Grey Blaze' and Moonshine smoked some weed with the waitress (Sheena) from the Spring Creek Tavern in her apartment upstairs.

The Spring Creek Tavern turned into our hangout spot again that day. Peach, Survivor, Moonshine, Hot Toddy, and the Warrior Hikers each crushed the AT Burger (three patties, cheese, bacon, onion rings and a plate of fries). The tavern had a super small beach / patio next to a creek that we all took full advantage of. While drinking and tackling each other into the stream, we met a few other hikers: Crispy, Legs, Verge, Jingle and Weebles. Just as I thought the festivities were dying down, Peach tackled me into the creek and knocked my glasses off (no, I did not have a spare pair or contacts). Next thing you know, a squad of hikers is in the water combing the creek bed for my glasses. Peach redeemed himself by managing to locate them before they swam too far downstream.

As the day wore on, everyone in town gathered around the creek for the rubber ducky race. The man running the race needed help holding up the net to catch all the floating ducks. So, naturally, a rather drunk Princess Peach volunteered. In front of most of the town, he waded out into the creek in nothing but his boxers carrying a full pitcher of beer. He collapsed several times, but heroically managed to save nearly all of the beer. We continued to play Russian Roulette with beers until dinner, which was offered up for free by the Laughing Heart Lodge.

After a delicious trail magic at the Laughing Heart Lodge (a hostel), Miss Janet rallied all the thru-hikers to play the Appalachian Trail board game. While the game was fun, the real treat was watching Peach and an attractive woman named High Wire have an intensely, public, sexual tension filled, R-rated encounter in front of many small children. Miss Janet also handed out our hiker ties. I guess in 2003, all the thru-hikers wore ties while they hiked and part of the tradition still lives on. I honestly wasn't crazy about mine.

Despite all this action, all the hikers staying at Miss Janet's campsite trekked back across town and started a bonfire. We roasted s'mores and drank a few more beers (as if we hadn't already had enough). I was exhausted and finally slipped off to bed. Peach, on the other hand, somehow mustered enough energy to go back to the Spring Creek Tavern.

DAY 24

Starting Location: Hot Springs, NC
Destination: Hot Springs, NC
Today's Miles: 0
Trip Miles: 273.7

Apr 17, 2016 - I woke up this morning feeling pretty good. The plan was to hike 11 miles past Hot Springs to the Spring Mountain Shelter. The plan never happened.

The bar next to the Spring Creek Tavern was serving a $4 pancake breakfast that included sausage, watermelon, apples, coffee, and snickers. I started talking to Ken during breakfast and he mentioned that someone had slept in the Spring Creek Tavern last night. I immediately wrote this off as ludicrous and continued shoveling pancakes into my mouth. We had an extra seat at our table and an absolutely beautiful girl just happened to stroll in and ask to sit with us. Her name was Training Wheels and she was a music therapist from Kansas City, MO. As she was easily the most attractive person I had seen on trail, I sincerely hoped I would have the chance to hike with her.

After breakfast, Peach, Moonshine, Ken and I walked past the tavern and, sure enough, Daniel was lying on the floor with a roll of paper towels as a pillow! Somehow (we never did figure out what happened exactly), all the employees went home and locked up shop with Daniel still inside. Still shaking our heads with disbelief, we made our way back to the campground and told Bad Apple what happened. He immediately ran to the bar and reached the door just as the first employees were arriving. Apparently, they were mad at first, but they couldn't help but laughing in the end. In fact, they ended up giving him a free t-shirt. This stunt earned Daniel his trail name: Sleeping Beauty. You can't make this stuff up. As we headed back to the campsite, I waved to Training Wheels as she hiked out of town (it turned out I wouldn't see her again for nearly 1,000 miles).

Weebles is the reason we didn't hike today. She inspired a group of us to go tubing down the French Broad River just outside of town. As the Warrior Hikers, Hot Toddy and the Killer Quad (and a few others) started to float down the river (with several cases of beer, of course), we immediately realized we made the correct decision. It was a gorgeous day, the water was immensely refreshing and you just couldn't beat the company. Shortly into the tubing excursion, we hit some rapids and lost control of the tubes – Hot Toddy slammed into a rock wall and the tube completely exploded. Luckily, Peach was there to scoop her up into his tube where they made out for most of the day. Again, you can't make this stuff up. The supposedly 4 hour tubing ride was going on 6 hours when the manager hailed us from the road and told us they had closed an hour ago! He asked us if we could get out and we were too happy to oblige since we were getting pretty chilly.

Our last night in Hot Springs was spent at none other than the Spring Creek Tavern. We had literally cleaned them out of their Russian Roulette beers (a craft beer for $2 – the catch was you got whatever beer the waitress picked out). It was a fitting end to probably the best weekend I had on the entire trail.

DAY 25

Starting Location: Hot Springs, NC
Destination: Spring Mountain Shelter
Today's Miles: 11.0
Trip Miles: 284.7

Apr 18, 2016 - After another deluxe breakfast at the Smoky Mountain Diner, I stopped at the outfitter in town to rearrange my pack. It only cost 69 cents to add a cord so that I could strap my tent to the outside of my pack, which completely changed the way I pack it. Finally, we started hiking again.

As it is with most towns, the trail began with a steep uphill for about two miles. It was damn tough after relaxing (and drinking) for two days. Plus, someone turned up the heat outside, which was exacerbated by the smoke from a nearby forest fire, and that made the going slow. To help me get up that first hill, I turned to music - my pump up song so far on this trip has definitely been Mother, We Just Can't Get Enough by the New Radicals. As soon as it starts playing, my adrenaline slowly climbs until it reaches a peak and there's nothing else for it except to stop and jam on some air guitar using my trekking poles.

One song was enough to get me bounding up the trail in true Mountain Goat form. The next 11 miles was a breeze despite it being almost entirely uphill to Spring Mountain Shelter.

Oh and never buy corn tortillas – they are actually worthless. Hot Toddy met us late at the shelter. I would soon learn that this was to become the new routine along with breaking camp late in the mornings.

DAY 26

Starting Location: Spring Mountain Shelter
Destination: Jerry Cabin Shelter
Today's Miles: 15.4
Trip Miles: 300.1

Apr 19, 2016 - Today was just another day at the office. It was still hot, but I banged out the first 9 miles in less than 3 hours. Heat and exercise are directly proportional to stink. So, yes, after two days, I already smell like poop. And there are still no bodies of water in these damn woods. Anyway, the heat and the bugs are only going to get worse so there's no sense in getting upset about it.

About 4 miles in, I came to a road and saw an establishment within walking distance: Mom's. It had very meager offerings (basically just a bunch of coolers plugged into the walls), but I still snagged a pack of hot dogs for the fire later.

With about 5 miles left, I came across a trail intersection and found two other hikers resting there: Beast and Longstride. The sign at the crossing pointed to the AT, which led up a steep, rocky incline to what looked like a ridge, and to the Bad Weather Trail, which is the blue-blazed, safer, flatter trail in case of inclement weather. Both Beast and Longstride had decided to take the blue-blazed trail because they weren't feeling up to the more difficult trail. I would never say anything to them because I believe the 'Hike Your Own Hike' mantra is important, but, personally, I think those reasons are bullshit. I'm out here to thru-hike the AT - that means every

WHITE blaze, not blue. If I'm tired or not feeling well, I'll set up camp and continue hiking when I feel up to whatever challenge is in front of me. If I take a side trail to see a view or something interesting and there is a cutoff trail that returns me to the AT farther north than the original side trail, I will make a point to return to the same spot on the AT that I left. That may be extreme, but I just don't care.

I arrived at the shelter (300 miles today!) shortly before sunset and hung out with Helton, Chicken Feet (he carried a chicken foot on his bag) and GAMElle (GA - Georgia, ME - Maine, Name = Elle) while I waited for my friends. Chicken Feet and GAMElle are easily my favorite older hikers on the trail. Scavenger was also at the shelter - I know he means well, but he really is a pain in the ass most of the time.

DAY 27

Starting Location: Jerry Cabin Shelter
Destination: Hogback Ridge Shelter
Today's Miles: 15.1
Trip Miles: 315.2

Apr 20, 2016 - It's almost been four weeks out here and I can already feel myself changing a bit. My friends at home will know me as a pretty organized, schedule-driven person. I love planning get-togethers with friends and knowing what I'm doing and when. Well, out here, I have no schedule, no plans, no time constraint, and no monetary constraint (within reason, of course). The freedom is literally infinite. I came out here with the most flexible mindset I could muster and the results have been really rewarding.

The first three and a half weeks of my hike, I just went with the flow and did whatever felt right at the moment. Every day was the first day of high school - I met so many people. Despite this stress free environment, I still developed a bit of a routine. Every morning, I woke up between 6:00 and 6:30 am and was on the trail hiking by 8:00 am. Every night, I was in my tent between 8:30 and 9:00 writing or reading. Subconsciously, it had gotten to the point where I felt I needed to be on trail by 8:00 when, in fact, there was no such need.

Yesterday, I realized my routine caused me to miss out a bit. Ever since Hot Springs, I realized that I finally fell into the beginning of my trail family. As a result, in just one day, the routine was replaced by a ridiculously relaxed outlook. This morning, I slept in until 7:30, had coffee and breakfast with the family and didn't start hiking until 9:30. After we realized the rumors of Trail Magic were not true, we stopped at the new Hiker Paradise hostel and relaxed for almost 2 hours. Afterwards, I realized I was too full to start hiking, so I read my book in a shady spot for a while and Peach caught salamanders in the stream. I took a rinse in a waterfall, tripped and bent two trekking poles, collected some wild onions for dinner, and finished hiking around 7:00 pm. Once everyone arrived at the Hogback Ridge shelter, we shared stories around the campfire until almost 10:00 pm.

It was also 4/20 and Bad Apple shared some hash oil and a few joints with everyone around the fire. Despite several hits of some extremely concentrated hash oil, I swear I don't get high from smoking. I just felt no different whatsoever. This had been true the few times I smoked previously on trail and in college as well.

I also found an awesome faggot of wood that I decided to carve into my new spoon seeing as I continued to break and lose my spoons. I planned to use coals from the fire to hollow out the depression in the spoon.

DAY 28

Starting Location: Hogback Ridge Shelter
Destination: Spivy Gap Campsite
Today's Miles: 15.8
Trip Miles: 331.0

Apr 21, 2016 – The Hogback Ridge supposedly had the nicest privy on the entire trail. It just so happens that this was the first morning I did not have to take a crap. Apparently, I missed out on a beautiful sunrise.

Today, the target was the No Business Knob Shelter about 20 miles away. This would put us about 6 miles from Erwin, TN.

The highlight of the day was easily the summit of Big Bald. A bald is basically a summit that is free from trees and other vegetation. As you can imagine, this open landscape provides for some pretty stunning views. At 5,516 feet, Big Bald is a beautiful, grassy picnic spot with clear, 360 degree panoramic views. I ate lunch up there with a few other hikers and continued on my way.

About 15 miles in to the hike, I arrived at Spivy Gap to find Boomauer performing some Trail Magic. He had Natty Light and Natty Ice beers in a cooler. I haven't had one of those bad boys since school so obviously it was amazing. Slightly buzzed and pretty tired, everyone decided to stop at a campsite just off the road for the night. Sassy, Good Talk and Songbird joined the Warrior Hikers, the Killer Quad and Hot Toddy. Sassy was a fiery, weird blonde from Virginia that I was honestly very attracted to. I just knew she was crazy. Peach and Hot Toddy appear to be moving closer and closer to being in a trail relationship. I'm not sure how I feel about it.

DAY 29

Starting Location: Spivy Gap Campsite
Destination: Erwin, TN / Cantarroso Farm
Today's Miles: 11.1
Trip Miles: 342.1

Apr 22, 2016 - Peach and I were up at the crack of dawn - Erwin had an all-you-can-eat Pizza buffet from 11:00 am to 2:00 pm. FINALLY! After Big Al's disappointment in Hiawassee and Survivor's mystery pizza buffet (he still can't remember the name of the town or the restaurant, so who knows if it even happened), we finally had confirmation that this buffet actually existed.

On nothing but a cup of coffee (Peach is our resident coffee maker in the morning - he uses a tea strainer as a reverse French press and refuses to use bad coffee), we hiked 11 miles in only 3 hours and 5 minutes. We arrived at Uncle Johnny's hostel around quarter after eleven and asked the group of hikers there what the best and quickest way to get to town was. They suggested we sit tight and wait for the shuttle at 12:30 pm. Ha! Those amateurs. Instead, Peach and I set off in the pouring rain and hitched a ride in the back of a pickup truck. Dripping wet and stinking, we walked into that place for our $7 pizza buffet with huge smiles plastered across our faces. Seventeen slices later, I was forced to call it quits, but damn I was satisfied.

I saw Training Wheels sitting at the picnic table at Uncle Johnny's, but didn't have a chance to talk with her at all. When we went back to the hostel, she was nowhere to be seen. At least I got pizza...

We hitched a ride to Wal-Mart for a resupply - I can honestly say the hardest part of this thru-hike so far has been food shopping. After 342 miles, I have yet to purchase the correct amount of food. I just always have too much. Afterwards, Moonshine, Peach, Survivor, Toddy and I went to Cantarroso farm, which had a small cabin that we rented for the outrageous price of $25 per person. Just kidding. I took a dip in the Nolichucky River located directly behind the cabin and relaxed for the rest of the afternoon. Later that night, the Warrior Hikers stopped by and hung out for a bit.

DAY 30

Starting Location: Erwin, TN / Cantarroso Farm
Destination: Johnson City, TN
Today's Miles: 0
Trip Miles: 342.1

Apr 23, 2016 - Today is zero number 4 and it is the first one that I physically need. My feet are starting to get beat up pretty badly despite the fact that I haven't made any changes to my equipment. Both feet have suddenly been plagued by blisters and muscle cramps near the balls of my feet. I'm thinking the causes for the sudden change include that my feet are noticeably swollen and therefore, larger, or they could just be fatigued.

Anyway, the rest today was necessary. I'll keep an eye on my feet and, if the problems persist, I may have to look into insoles.

We were supposed to go whitewater rafting today, but we discovered the business was closed this morning. Instead, we attended a hiker feed in town organized by the church across the river from Uncle Johnny's hostel. This was by far the best Trail Magic we've received so far - they had hot dogs, hamburgers, corn on the cob, five different types of beans, multiple pasta salads and Mac-n-cheese options, fruit, veggies, and an entire dessert table. As if that wasn't enough, they had a separate table filled with food for hikers to take with them when they left. It's pretty unbelievable the trouble these people go through to help us out.

Unfortunately, the killer quad is now the tenacious tripod - Moonshine decided not to take a zero today. He is leaving at the end of next week to attend his friend's wedding in Maine and he couldn't justify sitting out another day. It really sucks, frankly; I enjoyed hiking with Moonshine these past 4 weeks and getting to know him. While we're going our separate ways for now, I find it very hard to believe that we don't meet up again on this trip so I'll remain hopeful. Regardless, we will definitely stay in touch.

After the hiker feed, Peach, Survivor, Toddy, the Warrior Hikers (Bad Apple, Sleeping Beauty, and The Colonel took a cab to Johnson City, TN for a night out on the town. Our brewery crawl continued with stops at the Yeehaw Brewery and the Johnson City Brewing Company. I've been collecting stickers at all of our brewery stops. Later on, wearing our stinky clothes and hiker ties, we bar hopped down main street. Somehow, we ended up in a salon that was giving out free beer and free food. We were pretty sure we weren't supposed to be there, but nobody said anything or commented on our hiker ties. In fact, they filled our beer glasses several times!

Finally, we all ended up at the Electric Cowboy - a country bar filled with an older crowd that just loved dancing. Survivor, of course, had to stay at the hotel because he was only 18 years old. Dancing isn't actually my favorite thing to do, so after a few drinks and a few throwback tunes, I hitched a ride back to the hotel and called it a night.

DAY 31

Starting Location: Johnson City, TN
Destination: Beauty Spot Gap
Today's Miles: 11.8
Trip Miles: 353.9

Apr 24, 2016 - I set out from Erwin today with Survivor to resume hiking north.

Our first mile did not go well. Survivor started to Charlie horse in his shin, then had the trail collapse underneath him so that he fell part of the way down the hill. I reached down to grab his trekking pole and had a different section of the trail collapse. After we both picked up and dusted ourselves off, I Charlie horsed in my thigh. I'm not done yet - my foot cramps kicked into high gear and I had a real difficult time walking.

We both decided to take a break and soak our feet in the cold stream to attempt to recover. We ended up catching crayfish, which we fully intend on boiling later for dinner.

The rest of the day wasn't much better, unfortunately. Plagued by foot cramps, I basically limped 11.8 miles to Beauty Spot Gap. It was very slow going - my usual 2.5-3 mph pace was slowed to less than 2. Good thing there is only about 110 miles left to Damascus where I can get some help from an outfitter.

Princess Peach, Hot Toddy and the Warrior Hikers joined us at Beauty Gap late and set up camp. Beauty Gap is an absolutely gorgeous meadow atop a small hill overlooking the sunset. With good weather expected for the night, nearly everyone cowboy camped and watched the sun go down from the comfort of our sleeping bags.

At the bottom of the hill, a high school student had set up his entire drum set with the sunset as his backdrop. As the sun drooped low in the sky, he jammed out a short drum solo much to our delight. This guy did all the work of bringing his drum set out into the outdoors and setting it up just for a few pictures of him playing in front of the sunset. That's going big rather than going home.

DAY 32

Starting Location: Beauty Spot Gap
Destination: Clyde Smith Shelter
Today's Miles: 14.4
Trip Miles: 368.3

Apr 25, 2016 – Since today was a fairly straightforward, unexciting day, I'm going to take this moment to define the various colors of 'blazing' that exists on the AT:

- White Blazing: This refers to actually hiking the AT by following the white blazes posted on trees rocks
- Yellow Blazing: This refers to using a car or other form of modern transportation to skip sections of the trail
- Blue Blazing: This refers to hiking any of the side trails, easier trails, or shortcuts along the trail
- Grey Blazing: This refers to chasing / hooking up with older women along the trail
- Camo Blazing: A term we made up to describe hiking according to the Warrior Hikers schedule, which is predefined and part of their program (we have been doing this for a while whether it's intentional or not)
- Brew Blazing: This is a term I just made up to describe tailoring our hiking schedule to cater to towns that contain breweries and it's awesome. Peach and I have made it a priority to check out breweries near the trail and try new beer when we see it for sale in town. I guess it could also refer to hiking while consuming beer.

- Purple Blazing: This refers to hiking while consuming wine (honestly not sure about this one, but it sounds appropriate).
- Aqua Blazing: There are actually a few opportunities for hikers to rent a canoe and paddle upriver rather than hiking.
- Pink Blazing: This refers to tailoring your hiking schedule according to a woman's hiking schedule with hopes of some action.
- Peach Blazing: This refers specifically to Hot Toddy putting in big miles to chase after Princess Peach

Anyway, that was just for your edification. Today, I hiked 15.7 miles mostly with Survivor. We were struggling most of the day again. Survivor was dehydrated and my foot cramps were killing me. I am starting to think that they are not, in fact, foot cramps.

DAY 33

Starting Location: Clyde Smith Shelter
Destination: Overmountain Shelter
Today's Miles: 15.6
Trip Miles: 383.9

Apr 26, 2016 - Since the beginning of this trip, we've been hearing about a large, famous shelter in North Carolina that is a renovated barn. Well, tonight, we would finally find out what all the fuss is about as Overmountain shelter was the destination for the evening. However, we had to conquer Roan Mountain first.

At just over 6,200 feet, Roan Mountain was a beast that just kept going up. When I was in the Smokies, I was "ridge hiking". Since the ridge is already at around 5,500 feet, climbing summits above 6,500 feet aren't necessarily as challenging as they seem. Summiting more independent mountains like Roan involve hiking from lower elevations - in this case 4,000 feet. It was actually a pretty rejuvenating climb that only took about 4 hours. Waiting for us at the top was Roan High Knob Shelter, the highest shelter on the entire AT. Peach and I got a fire going and took an extended lunch break while we waited for the rest of the kids to catch up.

On the way down, some day hikers were handing out small bags of Skittles as Trail Magic. These provided the necessary energy to climb two more absolutely beautiful balds on our way to Overmountain shelter. The Skittles reminded me of an anecdote regarding thru-hikers: "A day hiker will come across a stray Skittle (or any other piece of candy) on the ground and just walk past it. A section hiker will pick up the Skittle and eat it. A thru-hiker will pick it up, eat it and then dig for more".

Overmountain shelter did not disappoint. The original purpose of the barn was to dry tobacco as evidenced by the small spaces in between each piece of wood comprising the structure. A while back, it was repurposed as a shelter for hikers along the AT. Complete with picnic tables, fire pits and multiple stories, the barn could easily house upwards of 25 hikers making it the largest shelter on the AT.

Despite these amenities, I still prefer to sleep outside in my tent so I set up in the east-facing meadow next to the barn. I got a fire going and waited for Steel, St. Nick, the Warrior Hikers, Hot Toddy, Peach, and Survivor to join me. We roasted some ramps (wild onions) that we harvested near Roan Mountain and I continued working on my wooden spoon. Tonight, I used coals from the fire to burn a small depression in the head of the spoon burning myself several times in the process.

DAY 34

Starting Location: Overmountain Shelter
Destination: Elk River Campsite
Today's Miles: 15.3
Trip Miles: 399.2

Apr 27, 2016 – I woke up to yet ANOTHER ridiculous sunrise – a little later than usual as the sun peeked out over the mountain to the northeast. As always, coffee and breakfast followed and then the walking began. About 6 miles in, we crossed out of North Carolina for the last time and into Tennessee (the trail actually follows the border between the two states for a while until it finally leaves NC). That's 2 states down and 12 to go.

Just nine miles in, Peach, UConn, and I hit the jackpot – a deep stream in the middle of the woods. Hoping GAMElle (a really nice older lady that has actually section hiked the entire AT) didn't catch us, we all stripped to our underwear and took full baths. Then, we hitched into nearby Roan Mountain, TN for a meal and a small resupply to get us to Damascus, VA in about four days.

Our meal was at the Smoky Mountain Bakers, which was highly recommended by GAMElle. This hole in the wall bakery specialized in brick oven pizza, choice baked goods and bread. Naturally, I got a buffalo chicken pie and crushed the entire thing (Tim, I'm up to 55 slices after Erwin and Roan Mountain). So good.

With our stomachs extremely full, we left Roan Mountain and walked the last couple miles to the Elk River Campsite. I arrived first to find Sushi already set up. However, knowing that I had a pretty large group coming behind me, I noticed that there weren't too many other available campsites. Anyway, I stripped again and took a swim in the calm, waist high Elk River while I waited for everyone else to show up.

The crew arrived to find Sushi and I sitting around the campsite having a conversation when a loud clap of thunder tore through the sky. In no time at all, the rain was pounding and lightning was visibly striking ground in the field just a hundred yards or so from us on the other side of the river from our campsites. Sushi and I flew into our tents, but due to the limited campsites, Peach, Toddie, Survivor and the Warrior Hikers had no choice but to ford the river in the thunderstorm and attempt to set up in the field where I had just seen the lightning strike. From inside my tent, I heard everybody yelling and frantically trying to set up without getting puddles of water in their tents.

With nothing else to do, I lay down and fell asleep with chaos occurring all around me.

LEAVING NORTH CAROLINA!

DAY 35

Apr 28, 2016 - Luckily, the sun came out this morning to help us dry out our gear. I woke up to a nice puddle in the bottom of my tent which wet my pad and sleeping bag considerably. I'm pretty sure this was from a combination of condensation and a tent site that was conducive to pooling water.

It was a slow morning and we didn't get hiking until almost 11. I, of course, went swimming for some time while my stuff tried to dry off. It's amazing how much heavier your pack is when everything is wet.

I crossed mile 400! The terrain was pretty easy today, but between the blister on my toe, which is borderline infected, and the muscle in the bottom of my foot, walking was awful. I can't get this damn blister to go away - I drain, clean, dry, air out, bandage the blister at least twice a day, but I guess sticking it in a filthy sock and shoe every day has its price.

DAY 36

Starting Location: Moreland Gap Shelter
Destination: Black Bear Resort
Today's Miles: 6.7
Trip Miles: 418.2

Apr 29, 2016 - I would consider today a nero - I only hiked about 6 miles to Dennis Cove Road near Hampton, TN. The Warrior Hikers had cabins reserved for them at Black Bear Resort just a half mile west of the trail. Peach, Survivor, Hot Toddy, Toddie's friend Erica (Juicy as she's recently been named because she has a really nice ass), and myself were planning on staying in the cabins. First thing's first, though - I had to hitch a ride into Hampton to pick up an antibiotic prescription for my toe, which is slightly infected and showing no signs of improving. Peach, Survivor and I managed to get a ride from an 81 year old day hiker named Ralph. As nice as Ralph was, the only word to accurately describe this guy is senile. The short trip over the mountain was insane - Ralph was constantly honking his horn, slowing down for no reason, speeding up to catch cars and he never stopped talking. Anyway, glad to be alive, I obtained my prescription and a disgusting amount of McDonalds for lunch. Back at Black Bear, the Warrior Hikers' cabins were very tiny so we just purchased tent sites for $10. Good thing, too, because somehow, just about every hiker 1-3 days ahead of us was staying there that night. The evening turned into a hiker party with what must have been 50 plus hikers. It was an absolute blast.

A combination of the campfire, live music from Sleeping Beauty, and Bad Apple's homemade moonshine led to Sassy and I sneaking away and making out for a while. It was very enjoyable and she's definitely a little crazy as I previously thought. She's also interested in the ladies.

When I finally returned to my tent, it was to find Hot Toddy and Peach getting at it in the tent 2 feet from mine. This was not the first time and, unfortunately, would not be the last time.

DAY 37

Starting Location: Black Bear Resort
Destination: Campsite near Spring south of Vandeventer Shelter
Today's Miles: 16.0
Trip Miles: 434.2

Apr 30, 2016 - With the stress of my infected toe basically alleviated by the antibiotics I picked up in Hampton, I was looking forward to an 18 mile day to Vandeventer Shelter to put myself into striking distance of Damascus, VA!

The first thing I noticed when I got up was that all Survivor's equipment was gone. Apparently, at around midnight, he had the bright idea to leave the resort and hike to the top of the mountain for better service to call his ex-girlfriend. Oh and he was hammered, by the way. All morning during our hike, we couldn't help but comment on the difficulty of the terrain and how much tougher it must have been drunk and in the dark. I gave him a good jab when I finally saw him at lunch for being such an idiot - his trekking pole was literally bent at a right angle. If only I had been awake to stop him.

Well, it turns out that nearly the entire day was uphill so it turned exhausting very quickly. The humidity didn't help at all. I did circumnavigate Wautaga Lake, which provided for some excellent swimming and refreshment before the remaining 9 miles to the shelter.

The second half of the day was beautiful as well until the thunderstorm hit. I crossed Wautaga Dam and started up yet another mountain. This put me on top of an isolated ridge just as the thunder and lightning attacked, which was more than convenient.

I ended up stopping about 1.7 miles south of the shelter at a small campsite near a spring and setting up camp during a lull in the rain because, frankly, I was already exhausted and soaking wet.

If all goes well, I'll be in Damascus in less than 2 days.

DAY 38

Starting Location: Campsite near Spring south of Vandeventer Shelter
Destination: Campsite near Spring south of Vandeventer Shelter
Today's Miles: 0
Trip Miles: 434.2

May 1, 2016 - All did not go well. Halfway through the night, I woke up several times with severe diarrhea, which forced me out of my tent and into the dark and the rain. Just as I thought I was finished, I stumbled out of my tent just in time to vomit over the side of a rock. The throwing up continued through the night and into the morning. A throw up session is also much more likely when you're in a sleeping bag that quite literally smells of shit and you're wearing sweat soaked clothes that haven't been washed properly in 7 days.

Thankfully, Steel made me coffee (which I threw up) and left me some extra toilet paper since I was almost out. She basically saved my life. Also, I did make it out of my tent for each gross event, which is actually a huge accomplishment based on some of the stories you hear out here. . Things could always be worse, though it would've been cool if the new Goo Goo Dolls album was suddenly released 6 days early (as if I could even download it out here).

Drained of energy and dehydrated, I slept through most of the morning and still couldn't keep water down. Between my toe, the foot cramps and norovirus, which I obviously contracted, I was forced to fall behind and spend another zero in my tent. I also realized that I couldn't take my antibiotics because I would just throw them up shortly after.

Sitting in your tent all day is not fun. The sun came out midday and forced me from my stifling tent. It sucks watching other hikers walk by, too, since this campsite is a great spot for lunch and I have to tell them I'm sick and they shouldn't eat here. Norovirus is to hikers as kryptonite is to Superman. Literally. So, now, I'm THAT guy for a few days.

On the bright side, I did have a day of rest for my toe and foot cramps and I did manage to hold down a box of raisins, some water and my antibiotic pill around midday.

So, I would say this has definitely been my low point on the trail so far, but hopefully tomorrow, I'll have enough strength to push halfway toward Damascus at the very least. Never have I wanted to reach a town more.

DAY 39

Starting Location: Campsite near Spring south of Vandeventer Shelter
Destination: Damascus, VA / The Place Hostel
Today's Miles: 35.7
Trip Miles: 469.9

May 2, 2016 – I must have broken my fever in the middle of the night because I woke up absolutely drenched in sweat on a cool night. I woke up at around 6:30 am and felt much better. Damascus was 35 miles away and it's been dangled in front of me for 9 days – a town that finally had an outfitter that could solve some of my foot problems. It also had food, which was something I was very low on at the time. I had sent a message ahead letting my friends know I'd be there on Tuesday, one day later than scheduled. But as soon as I woke up, I knew I'd be there by the end of the day.

At 7:15 am, I just started walking. I couldn't really eat anything other than a small handful of trail mix at a time because my stomach was still doing backflips so I stopped only twice throughout the day for 5 minutes to refill water. I was in zombie mode – I didn't even talk to anyone. I did, however, yell at a few small hills as my exhaustion and frustration boiled to the surface.

The weather was hot and humid as I neared Damascus with an approaching thunderstorm on my heels. At about mile 25, I was so tired, I felt like I was driving home late at night and needed to talk to someone to stay awake. I called both my parents separately to take my mind off the walking and the fatigue. I did cross into Virginia, my fourth state on the AT, which provided a brief positive moment.

I walked for 11 hours and 45 minutes and covered 35.7 miles. I arrived at The Place, a church that opened its doors to hikers and bikers for a small donation. The thunderstorm hit as I was walking through the front door. Finally, things were starting to go my way. I caught up with Peach and co. – it turns out he and Survivor had legged it the 33 miles from Vandeventer Shelter to Damascus yesterday.

By the way, the proprietor of The Place was a man named Bayou who looks and acts exactly like that guy in Office Space that loves his red stapler. However, I saw no staplers of any color anywhere inside.

I unpacked my stuff on a stiff mattress on the upper floor and took my shoes off. I counted 13 blisters and the area under the ball of my foot was a sinister black and blue. After a quick shower, I walked over to Bobo McFarland's for a bite to eat. I ordered three different dishes and as soon as they were put in front of me, I knew I wasn't going to be able to eat even half of it with my stomach in its fragile condition. I ordered with my mind and not my stomach.

Tomorrow, at last, I can rest and figure out my damn footwear situation.

DAY 40

Starting Location: Damascus, VA / The Place Hostel
Destination: Damascus, VA / The Place Hostel
Today's Miles: 0
Trip Miles: 469.9

May 3, 2016 - Damascus is a hiker town similar to Hot Springs in that the trail runs right through the center of town. It's the home of Trail Days, the largest hiker festival that takes place from May 13-15 this spring. Needless to say, I'll be headed back here in about two weeks.

I zeroed again today in Damascus - I am grateful for another day of rest that is not confined to my tent. I began with an everything bagel breakfast sandwich at Mojo's, a very unique cafe situated directly on trail. I wanted the cinnamon roll and the breakfast quesadilla also, but I learned from my mistake last night.

Next up was footwear. I visited all three outfitters in town and finally settled on a pair of Oboz with Superfeet insoles. I had no idea what I was looking for or needed, but the man at Mt. Roger's Outfitter was surprisingly the only employee to actually measure the length and width of my feet and present a trail shoe that fit. I learned that my left foot is actually smaller than my right foot and that my feet have not expanded as I expected. I stuck with my usual size 12s and hoped for the best. The Oboz were definitely lighter and more supportive than my Keens at the very least. It was pretty funny when I took off my Crocs, the employee visibly recoiled and commented on how screwed up my feet were. Yea.

I also picked up a new dry stuff sack for my food bag since my current one had a few holes and suffered a marshmallow fluff explosion. In case you didn't already know, marshmallow fluff may actually be the worst thing to have explode inside a bag. If not the worst, then definitely top 5.

I picked up another massive and much appreciated package from my mother. This one contained my all-time favorite cookies: rich chocolate chip toffee bars. I returned the favor by mailing home a package with smelly clothes and her Mother's Day gift.

Honestly, by 2 pm, I had finished my chores and was wiped. I napped for a few hours and then went to Hey Joe's, a Mexican place for dinner. I still couldn't eat anything other than rice, though. My stomach was still unsettled and I was still experiencing one of the issues that accompany norovirus.

I finished my zero by soaking my feet in Epsom salts and calling it an early night. It was back to the trail tomorrow and I definitely needed all the sleep I could get. The guy from Mt. Roger's Outfitters stressed that I need to let my feet heal before I hit the trail again. It's more complicated than that, though. I could take multiple zeros, but then I am several days behind my trail family. I'd rather just grit my teeth and walk through some of the pain if it means I get to spend my days in the woods with Peach and Survivor.

DAY 41

Starting Location: Damascus, VA / The Place Hostel
Destination: Campsite north of Lost Mountain
Today's Miles: 16.3
Trip Miles: 486.2

May 4, 2016 - Mojo's round 2: this time I did get that cinnamon roll and wow I screwed up yesterday.

Juicy was hanging back in Damascus today since she had to catch a flight later in the week back home. After a tearful goodbye, Hot Toddy, Peach and I got back on trail (Survivor didn't want to stay another night in Damascus so he had hiked out yesterday).

The AT coincided with the famous Virginia Creeper Trail for a few stretches today, which is a popular biking trail. We hiked a fairly uneventful 16 miles to a campsite set in a spruce forest - it's always a pleasure falling asleep on a bed of pine needles with that citrusy scent surrounding you.

We did see a pretty cool black rat snake on one of the bridges we crossed today. We also encountered our first detour: one of the bridges on the AT had been washed out by the river causing hikers to be rerouted on the nearby Virginia Creeper Trail. Since the detour is considered the official AT, we didn't argue.

I was still extremely tired all day so I was more than relieved when we reached our campsite for the night. It's amazing how comfortable my tent has become after sleeping in it for over a month. Any subconscious anxiety

I had about sleeping outside is no longer existent and I would honestly choose my smelly sleeping bag in my tent outside over a bed in a hostel or hotel room.

Another really fun part about camping (sometimes) is hanging the bear bag. Whether it's throwing the rope over a branch with a rock or stick or trying to get the rope down when it's caught, crazy shit always seems to happen. I remember a few mornings ago stepping out of my tent just in time to see Spoon throw a stick like a spear at the bear bags because they were stuck in the tree. Well, tonight Peach and I got the rope stuck while trying to hang the bag. Peach yanked on the rope and a massive branch snapped and came raining down on us. When we surfaced, a 6 foot branch had impaled itself in the ground where we had been standing. Now, we were stuck using Hot Toddy's two tree method, which she's been rubbing in our faces for a few nights now.

I met a few new people today: Salty, Bug Juice, Crisco, and Long Cloud.

DAY 42

Starting Location: Campsite north of Lost Mountain
Destination: Campsite north of Grayson Highlands State Park
Today's Miles: 16.2
Trip Miles: 502.4

May 5, 2016 - Snow in May? Wild ponies? Today was easily the most unique, bizarre, and enjoyable day on the trail.

The day started as expected - a brisk, cold morning with a good chance of rain later in the day. We packed up camp (Helton had to stay back as he came down with norovirus during the night) and set off toward Mt. Rogers, Virginia's tallest peak at just over 5,700 feet, and Grayson Highlands State Park, which is famous for the wild ponies that will lick the sweat off your skin.

Now, remember I sent home the rest of my winter gear in Damascus just two days ago. The only item I still had was my 20 degree down sleeping bag and thank God for that.

As we ascended to Mt. Rogers and increased our elevation, it started sleeting. The sleet turned to snow as continued to climb higher and it just kept coming down. May 5 and it's snowing! Unbelievable.

Predictably, as we crested 5,300 feet, the landscape changed from spring foliage to a dense pine forest. That was when we saw our first two wild ponies. Survivor came running back along the trail with his pack off yelling that two ponies, a mother and her foal, were chasing him. These harmless, beautiful animals were just looking for food and hardly noticed us. We didn't have any sweat for them to lick off anyway since the temperature was down in the 30s and I was hiking in a bathing suit, a t-shirt, and a rain jacket.

The trail skirted the summit of Mt. Rogers by about a half mile and brought us into Grayson Highlands State Park. The gently falling snow had now turned into an all-out blizzard. High winds and thick, wet snow flakes bombarded us as we picked our way across the rocky, exposed landscape. Sure, I was cold, but it was honestly a blast. Near the 500 mile marker, Survivor and I walked past close to 20 ponies.

SURVIVOR AND I HIKING THROUGH THE SNOW JUST BEFORE MULTIPLE WILD PONY SIGHTINGS

We were not allowed to make camp within the state park and the shelter was full, so Survivor and I quickly crossed the boundary and set up camp in a dense thicket of rhododendrons to give us some relief from the wind. All through the night, we heard the loud clumps of snow falling off the branches and onto our tents. That night, the 20 degree bag that smells like it was stored in a bucket of human waste was the most comfortable thing I've ever experienced after freezing all day. It's really tough to convey how wonderful that thing is without experiencing it firsthand.

Princess Peach, Hot Toddy and Brandon managed to find us and set up alongside our tents. Peach singing "I want a rich, dumb, young nymphomaniac" (our perverted marching song) at the top of his lungs was more than enough to herald his approach.

DAY 43

Starting Location: Stealth Campsite north of Grayson Highlands State Park
Destination: Stealth Campsite north of Trimpi Shelter
Today's Miles: 23.6
Trip Miles: 526

May 6, 2016 - Crawling out of my sleeping bag seemed impossible with absolutely frigid air blowing under my rain fly, but somehow I managed to extricate myself and begin packing up all of my gear. Most of it actually stayed pretty dry - I've got my system down to such a routine that it's actually fairly easy to keep everything dry even when setting up and taking down in inclement weather. The trick is to do everything inside your tent. Then, when it's time to get out, all I have left is my wet tent, which takes about a minute to pack up.

Today, the goal was to push ourselves about 23 miles so a short hike tomorrow would allow us to hitch into Marion, VA for a quick resupply. The weather finally started to warm up around mid-morning and the sun was definitely doing its best to come out. When it finally did, the sunshine was short lived and it started to rain again. This teasing cycle continued a few times throughout the afternoon and evening. Frankly, this is a pain in the ass because you're constantly putting on your rain jacket and then taking it off. Finally, after the third time, I just said screw it and let it rain on me.

Honestly, the highlight of today was the release of the new Goo Goo Dolls album 'Boxes' so I continually checked for service until I could download the new songs. The album definitely made the rain more bearable.

I also made a long overdue call to the foot doctor, Dr. Wallack, whose office is across the way from my Dad's office. I explained the issues I've been having and how the new shoes and insoles have definitely helped with the pains near the ball of my left foot due to better arch support. However, I am still experiencing some discomfort and occasional stabs of pain down there. His cell phone diagnosis is that the small bone in that region of my foot is broken. That's comforting. Seriously, though. I would very much prefer that to a muscle or tendon issue. This is just pain and that can be dealt with.

We missed Trail Magic at one of the road crossings, but still caught the Trail Angels in time for some conversation. One of the ladies actually has a triple crown under her belt, which means she thru-hiked the AT, the Pacific Crest Trail (PCT) and the Continental Divide Trail (CDT). That's pretty unfathomable at only 530 miles on the AT.

I mistakenly set up camp at a premature campsite to the one we were aiming for so everyone else grumbled while they set up in the adjacent spots. The site had a stream running right next to it and enough flat spots. The campsite we were supposed to stay at ended up being like 200 yards up on the left. Whoops!

I split my Pecan Log (an incredible dessert that I've been missing my whole life) with Survivor and then proceeded to make some dinner. The day before a resupply is great because you can binge on everything in your food bag and binge we did. Survivor and I split a homemade Thai noodle dish (Ramen without the seasoning packet mixed with peanut butter, olive oil and hot sauce), a bag of loaded mashed potatoes and some hot chocolate. Delicious.

DAY 44

Starting Location: Stealth Campsite north of Trimpi Shelter
Destination: Partnership Shelter
Today's Miles: 6.2
Trip Miles: 532.2

May 7, 2016 - Resupply day! A short 6 mile hike brought us to the Partnership Shelter near Marion, VA. This shelter was similar to the Fontana 'Hilton' shelter near Fontana Dam in that it had a sink and shower with solar heated water and a nearby bathroom. Unfortunately, there hasn't been sun in about 3 days so my shower was ice cold.

St. Nick, Princess Peach and I had all these plans for a fast food crawl of Hardee's, Taco Bell, Wendy's, and Sonic when we noticed a Chinese menu on the picnic table. Buffet from 11 am to 2 pm. Hell yes! St. Nick and I hitched a ride in a back of a pick-up truck from a gentleman named Mike and soon found ourselves with loaded plates of the good stuff. We were only on our third plate when the rest of the gang joined us. Our favorite anecdote dish was the 'Cucumber Salad', which was just a tray full of gross looking, sliced pickles.

I resupplied at the adjacent Ingles supermarket and Wal-Mart. Everyone agreed to pitch in and get a meal and beer for later that night at the shelter. We had Bubba burgers courtesy of Survivor, corn on the cob courtesy of myself, hash browns courtesy of Peach, baked beans courtesy of Songbird, and s'mores courtesy of Hot Toddy. There was plenty of craft beer from Trouble brewing company to wash it all down. Peach also impulse purchased this game called Zombie Dice at Wal-Mart that turned out to be a blast. It was an excellent meal that we cooked over the fire and definitely made the 6 mile day worth it.

DAY 45

Starting Location: Partnership Shelter
Destination: Crawfish Trail Campsite
Today's Miles: 18.4
Trip Miles: 550.6

May 8, 2016 - Mother's Day! I made sure to check for service today so I could wish my Mom well on her day. She's helped me more than anyone on my trip and her packages have been game changers. The sun actually managed to come out today though that may have been due to Songbird's sun dance. We're still not sure.

Our plan on this magical day was to push 26 miles to Knob Maul Shelter. That was before we received no less than 4 instances of trail magic. The first was about 8 miles in - we had just taken lunch when we realized that a family had set up a table outside an old one room school in a country lane with sandwiches, chips, sodas, salads, cookies and homemade banana pudding. There was also a loaded hiker box with literally anything you could need.

On full bellies and with food comas setting in, we hiked through the small town of Atkins, VA. Peach and I stopped in at an Exxon to get a coffee to counteract the effects of the postprandial somnolence. When we walked out, Bad Apple and Sleeping Beauty pulled up out of nowhere in a stranger's pick-up truck. Some guy that gave them a hitch just gave them a truck for the day and said bring it back before 9 the next morning. They couldn't even tell us the stranger's name. They had just purchased a case of beer and were planning on stashing them in the woods for other hikers when they saw us. Naturally, we stopped, had a few beers and caught up with the Warrior Hikers who were taking a zero today.

We managed to tear ourselves away only to find sodas stashed along the trail less than a mile later. We weren't done yet - less than a mile from there, someone left a big bag of cookies on the hood of their car with a nice note. Since we were so stuffed, we decided to take some for the campfire later.

In the end, our 26 mile day turned into just over 18, but honestly, that's impressive considering our late start and the ridiculous string of Trail Magic that eats into the day (no pun intended). Another super enjoyable day - they never end out here.

DAY 46

Starting Location: Crawfish Trail Campsite
Destination: Chestnut Knob Shelter
Today's Miles: 17.3
Trip Miles: 567.9

May 9, 2016 - We had big plans for miles yet again today as we left our campsite. Survivor and I left camp early and nearly had 12 miles done before noon (unfortunately, this hasn't been as easy as it used to be since Hot Toddy has delayed our usual morning routine). My only regret that morning was not swimming in a river that we passed so when I saw a second river around lunch time, I had no choice. I stripped and belly flopped off a little ledge into the refreshing water. Beast, St. Nick, and Sassy were alarmed for a second until I got out completely covered in mud. Getting dirtier was not what I had in mind so I crossed to the rockier side of the stream and properly cleaned myself off.

Later on that day, Survivor and I were walking through the woods when we were startled by the deafening sound of what I subconsciously thought was an incoming missile. We both reacted on instinct and threw ourselves down behind a nearby rock with our heads down. When we chanced a glance upward, we saw a fighter jet fly by just above the tree line less than a football field's length above us. The trees actually swayed and split apart a bit due to the force of the jet stream. It was freaking awesome - I couldn't stop talking about it all day. While Survivor and I were set on walking more miles, Sassy had brought up a good point - we needed to catch a hitch into Damascus for Trail Days in two days. It's tough to catch a hitch in the middle of the woods so we needed to position ourselves near a major highway. Bland, VA was the best place to do this, but it was only 20 miles away. Because of these hitchhiking logistics, we ended up stopping about 7 miles short of our original goal at Chestnut Knob Shelter.

The shelter was one of the only completely enclosed shelters on the trail because it was situated on top of a bald. I set up my tent on a grassy patch overlooking a beautiful valley filled with farms and completely enclosed by mountains. Honestly, the view we had was like one of those backgrounds they put behind you at one of those mall photo shoots. It just didn't look real. The campfire that night was a hell of a good time. Sushi, Sassy, Songbird, Chicken Feet (a hysterical, old Vietnamese man that retired the day before he started hiking), Hot Toddy, Princess Peach, Survivor, and St. Nick finished up some s'mores from our party at Partnership shelter and played some more Zombie Dice.

DAY 47

Starting Location: Chestnut Knob Shelter
Destination: Laurel Creek Campsite
Today's Miles: 15.1
Trip Miles: 583

May 10, 2016 - The revised, pre-Trail Days plan was to walk a pleasant 15.1 miles to a campsite by Laurel Creek, about 7 miles from Bland. As I left Chestnut Knob Shelter, I heard a crash in the woods off to my right. I had scared a pretty medium sized black bear that took off running through the trees. Still, my first black bear on the trip. A moose is still number one on my list, though.

I'm a very fast hiker. I mean when I get going full speed, I have not had a single person pass me in about 600 miles regardless of the terrain. That was until today. I was on cruise control when I heard snapping twigs behind me and immediately thought there was a large animal behind me. Nope. It was Nature Boy, this tall, lanky hiker with the smallest pack I've seen on trail. He didn't just pass me, he flew past me and even jogged every few steps. Needless to say, that was the last I saw of him. The rest of the hike was uneventful as I finished 15.1 miles in 5 hours flat.

I arrived at the Laurel Creek campsite early in the afternoon and I was very glad I did because the river was perfect for swimming and laying out in the sun. I quickly set up my tent and doubled back to the stream to take a bath, swim and try to even out my severe hiker tan. I was soon joined by Sassy,

St. Nick, Chicken Feet, Sushi, the Tenacious Tripod, Hot Toddy, and the Goon Squad (Sundance, Muffinman, Q-tip, Romeo, and Scarecrow).

I wasn't the only one (I usually am) interested in swimming and sun-bathing today. As other hikers joined us, Chicken Feet, Survivor and I started catching crayfish in the stream. Chicken Feet was trying to show Peach how to catch them, but Peach kept pulling his hand away – he was afraid of getting pinched by the small claws. Chicken Feet let him know, too. The sight of a small, Vietnamese man standing in a river in his underwear yelling "He's scared!" with his heavy accent is one of the funnier things I've seen thus far.

We were also joined by this kid named The Gatherer. His reputation has preceded him – he never stops talking. As this was the first time I met him, I had a little trouble keeping a straight face. The Gatherer made the Scavenger look like the most amicable guy on the trail. As soon as The Gatherer rolled into camp, Sushi left the campfire and went to bed because he can't stand the kid.

DAY 48

Starting Location: Laurel Creek Campsite
Destination: Bland, VA / Big Walker Motel
Today's Miles: 6.9
Trip Miles: 589.9

May 11, 2016 - A loud clap of thunder woke me up this morning a half hour earlier than usual. Bland, VA, our destination before Trail Days, was only 7 miles away so I got up, packed up in the pouring rain, took a very wet dump, and started walking. Of course, the rain stopped only 20 minutes after I left the campsite, which means I could've done without the puddle in my tent's stuff sack.

In just over 2 hours, I arrived in Bland to find Trail Magic waiting for me in the form of bananas, Powerade and a ride to the center of town about 3 miles away. Richard is a repeat thru-hiker from Alabama that simply remembered how hard it was to hitch into Bland and wanted to help.

Richard dropped Sundance and myself off at the Dairy Queen in town (my only two options were that or Subway). I pounded some breakfast food, chicken tenders and a blizzard while I waited for the rest of the group to arrive. I also set up my tent in the lawn so the sun could begin drying it.

Ken, Husker, Survivor, Hot Toddy, Princess Peach and I decided to split a motel room for the night because it was right next to the interstate and we were going to hitch one hour back to Damascus for the trail festival early the next morning. A motel was a perfect opportunity for a shower, some bath tub laundry, and some beers. Despite the rain that morning, it ended up being a beautiful day as we relaxed outside at the motel with our neighbors: Beast, Sassy, Lino, Buckeye, and Bobsled.

Tim, the pizza count is up to 56. Sorry, but it's been a while.

DAY 49

Starting Location: Bland, VA / Big Walker Motel
Destination: Damascus, VA / Tent City for Trail Days
Today's Miles: 0.0
Trip Miles: 589.9

May 12, 2016 - I used the top of the pizza box from last night to make a sign to help Survivor and I catch a ride down to Damascus for Trail Days (Hitchhiking is a lot easier in pairs). We made our way back to Dairy Queen for some breakfast. Another former thru-hiker named Parks must have noticed my sign and just straight up offered us a direct ride. I had expected to be hitching various rides all morning to get to Damascus, but I didn't even get to use my sign. Trail Magic strikes again.

Trail Days is the largest hiker festival period. It was estimated that about 20,000 people would visit the humble hiking town of Damascus (population: 800) this weekend. The festival is like a Trail Magic smorgasbord: showers, laundry, multiple hiker feeds, resupply items, raffles for gear, gear repair and most of it is free.

Parks dropped us off at Tent City, which is a field and an adjacent wood where all the hikers could camp for a one-time payment of $5. This place was jam packed with probably over 1,000 tents. No exaggeration. Survivor and I even had the honor of helping Miss Janet set her tent up.

Since the festival technically started on Friday, the rest of our day was spent running errands, seeking out free food, drinking beer, and catching up with all the other hikers we hadn't seen on trail in a while. Peach and I walked to the Damascus Brewery around dinner time to check it out and continue Brew Blazing (I added another sticker to my collection). The brewery was literally a 50 gallon system with a super friendly atmosphere and unique, tasty beer. Definitely worth it.

Later that night was our first experience of Miss Janet's drum circle - a massive fire pit (maybe 20-30 feet in diameter around which hikers ceaselessly dance and play drums. It was like one of those Native American celebrations you see in the movies.

DAY 50

Starting Location: Damascus, VA / Tent City for Trail Days
Destination: Damascus, VA / Tent City for Trail Days
Today's Miles: 0.0
Trip Miles: 589.9

May 13, 2016 – The first official day of Trail Days was an early one. As usual, I woke up around 6:30 and headed straight to Mojo's for round 3. I was hoping I'd beat the crowd and I did. Unfortunately, they had a special Trail Days menu so I couldn't get the breakfast quesadilla, which I had been craving – the cinnamon bun and a breakfast platter were more than enough, though.

After breakfast, I just wandered around town watching the gear and food vendors setting up until I found myself back at Tent City. I walked right into Moonshine! It was great seeing this guy again. We found another hiker feed for lunch, entered every raffle we could find to try to win Survivor a new pack (his was literally falling apart and currently completely held together by carabiners – the gear repair guy was visibly taken aback).

I was in the market for a warm weather sleeping bag to temporarily replace my 20 degree down bag. It's true that I do have a 40 degree synthetic bag at home, but it's too small in the shoulders, the zipper sucks and it's not down. If this bag is going to be my bed for 3 months, I wanted to be comfortable. Jacks R Better offered a 40 degree 800 fill down quilt (basically a down blanket that you can wrap around you and loosely secure like a sleeping bag) for $190 that was only 18 ounces! That's a no brainer that would reduce my pack weight by over 2 lbs! I couldn't wait to test it out.

Moonshine, Constantine, Walking Bear, Fireball, and I then proceeded to purchase a few cases of beer and headed down to a hidden waterhole on the river we heard about from a former thru-hiker. We swam, shot gunned a few brewskies and had probably the most fun I had all weekend.

Next up was the hot dog eating contest. When I signed up in the morning, I was the only one on the list, but over 30 people had enlisted. Since there were only 5 spots, I was very unfortunately not chosen to compete. Stretch took down 7.5 hot dogs in only 3 minutes. I still think I could've done that.

The rest of the afternoon was spent in Tent City hopping from campsite to campsite and catching up with all the other hikers. I also met many new people, but the sheer quantity of trail names became overwhelming. Here are the few I remember: Chunks (he blew chunks early on in the trip after drinking too much), Stripes, Mother Theresa of the Forest Animals (she rescued an abandoned dog who is now at home waiting for her to finish the hike), Navigator, Finch, Fern, Thin Mint, Timon (crazy jealous), Pocahontas (this got me crazy excited as she is one of my top Disney princesses), Jingle, Hoodlum, Wildcard, Bartender, Tony Good Looks, and loads more that I just can't remember.

For a few weeks now I've had other hikers tell me there is another Mountain Goat on trail, a female Mountain Goat. I finally caught up to her in the Chinese buffet in Marion when I literally sensed her walk through the door. Well, thinking it would be fun to have a showdown, or "Goat Roast" as I called it, on Trail Days, I challenged her to the best of 7 tasks for the status of Alpha Goat. Since I was ahead of her on trail, I wrote the challenges across 4 shelter registers to build up the excitement. Here were the proposed challenges:
1. Fastest to climb a hill with a pack on
2. Fastest to hang a bear bag
3. Fastest to hitch a ride
4. Fastest to set up and take down a tent

5. Guessing the weights and prices of common resupply items chosen by a third party
6. A Chopped camp cooking showdown with ingredients chosen by a third party. Judges to be determined.
7. Fastest to eat a 7 lb can of chocolate pudding we found at Food City with two partners of the contestant's choice.

However, when I saw the other Mountain Goat at Trail Days, she basically shot me down - she said she enjoyed reading the messages, but seemed totally uninterested in the showdown. Needless to say, people were bummed. Peach and I even lost all interest in eating the can of pudding, which we knew would be disgusting but had been excited for anyway.

Anyway, later that night, we headed to Bobo's in town for karaoke. Now, if you know me well, my two biggest fears are the ocean / sharks and singing karaoke. While there was no way in hell I was singing, it turned into a damn good time. Sassy and High Wire performed a duet together that, no doubt, turned on every guy in the bar. It was almost disturbingly sexual and hot.

Finally, all hikers assembled at the drum circle for at least 5 hours of shenanigans. The last thing I remember at 4 am was the cops shutting the thing down. Otherwise, I don't know that it would have ever stopped. I also remember very nearly hooking up with the other Mountain Goat. There was flirting, touching and she even told her friend to leave. I made a move and she turned me down again! I just can't catch a break with this girl.

RIDICULOUS SHENANIGANS AT TRAIL DAYS IN DAMASCUS WITH HOT TODDY, PRINCESS PEACH, HELTON, AND TWO STRANGERS.

DAY 51

Starting Location: Damascus, VA / Tent City for Trail Days
Destination: Damascus, VA / Tent City for Trail Days
Today's Miles: 0.0
Trip Miles: 589.9

May 14, 2016 - I woke up with an insane hangover as I fell out of my wet tent into a pile of mud. I headed straight to the pancake breakfast across the street, took a shower, then went right back to bed for the rest of the morning. I just couldn't function as was evidenced by the multiple syrup stains on my thru-hiker tie.

When I finally came to, I headed to the park in town where all the gear and food vendors were set up. I needed something greasy and I found it in a plate of deep fried gator bites, which definitely improved my state of mind.

Next, I had my picture taken for the thru-hiker yearbook then quickly headed to the south side of town where hikers were assembling for the Trail Days parade. This parade had no floats, but was just a large mass of hikers walking from one end of town to another while spectators shot at us with water guns. A few of us had acquired our own water weapons so we could retaliate in kind.

The crowd dispersed after the parade and Peach and I took one more lap around town to see if anything else was going on. We saw several men wearing dresses and carrying handbags. Schnicklefritz informed us that the dresses were for the hiker prom, which was taking place that night.

Apparently, the guys are supposed to "dress up" and the best dress is actually voted on.

Peach and I went straight to the thrift store and picked out two blue dresses and two handbags, which were actually necessary since we no longer had any pockets – it turns out balloon cleavage isn't enough to actually hold anything. All this buildup and we didn't even end up going to the prom. It was sponsored by the brewery so when we bought our wristbands and beverages, we simply went straight to the brewery to redeem our beers. Of course, people there were not expecting dresses so we stuck out like a sore thumb. I even caught a few people trying to sneak photos.

The night ended just like every other night during Trail Days: at Miss Janet's drum circle. I swear there was an added fervor to the circle on this last night of Trail Days and the bonfire raged long into the morning.

DAY 52

Starting Location: Damascus, VA / Tent City for Trail Days
Destination: Stealth Campsite 3 miles north of Bland, VA
Today's Miles: 3.0
Trip Miles: 592.9

May 15, 2016 - This morning, the hangover wasn't too bad, but I was exhausted.

Three straight days of drinking, slack packing (walking without a pack, or I guess just walking to a normal person) around town, eating and not sleeping will do that to you though. Survivor and I had to find a ride back to Bland so we could resume hiking. Princess Peach elected to stay behind with Hot Toddy and perform some volunteer trail maintenance for two days. And just like that, the Tenacious Tripod became the Dynamic Duo. It was a sad moment as I realized I may not see my good friend for the rest of the trail. I'll be honest: I was bitter. Hot Toddy was not my favorite person and she had stolen Peach from us. Moonshine may catch us in a week or two, but I'm not sure about Peach.

Another thru-hiker suggested that we walk to the north end of town and try hitching there rather than in the center of town or in the parking lot. I crossed the bridge on the edge of town and stuck out my thumb. Before I even had a chance to look behind me, a car was already pulling over. Kelly and Joe's destination just happened to be Bland, the small, insignificant town where we had paused our thru-hike. This hitching thing is just too easy. Not only did Kelly and Joe drive us to Bland, but they gave us chocolate frosted donuts, brought us to the supermarket to finish resupplying, and gave some of their leftover food from the weekend. Ridiculous. Kelly was also playing some very relaxing music that caused Survivor, Joe (who was also exhausted) and me to fall asleep. I know I'll have a harder time hitching as I move north, but so far my luck has been outstanding.

Back at the trailhead in Bland, we ran into Sassy and started hiking with her. All three of us didn't feel like doing anything, especially hiking. We all had that itchy, uncomfortable sweat that oozes out of you after a night of drinking excessively. We loaded up on water and stealth camped a whopping 3 miles into the woods. As the three of us sat around our small campfire, I slipped my arm around Sassy. Survivor noticed and slipped off to bed a little earlier than usual. Sassy and I continued talking and kissed for a while before heading to bed ourselves.

And so ended a weekend I will certainly remember for the rest of my life.

Tim, the pizza count is at 74. I did better this weekend.

DAY 53

Starting Location: Stealth Campsite 3 miles north of Bland, VA
Destination: Dismal Falls Campsite
Today's Miles: 17.2
Trip Miles: 610.1

May 16, 2016 - The temperature dropped into the low 40s last night and, despite how amazing my new quilt is, I got quite cold. However, I pulled my fleece on in the middle of the night and that was enough to get me to the sunrise.

Sassy, who contrary to me, actually knows where she wants to hike to each day, mentioned a campground near Dismal Falls. At about 17 miles, that seemed just about right for a first day back from vacation. Plus, how bad could camping next to a waterfall be?

The hike was honestly freezing today - it was that uncomfortable temperature where putting a jacket on is way too hot, but a t-shirt is just cold. Our solution was to move quickly and stop at Trent's Grocery (basically a gas station with a lot of common hiker resupply items and treats) for some warm food.

I passed mile 600 today after about 6.5 weeks on trail. This isn't as far as I thought I'd be (unfortunately, I'll have to miss an off trail camping trip in Assateague, MD over Memorial Day weekend), but based on the average hiking pace of my fellow thru-hikers, I'm still moving at a pretty good clip.

I'm also in no rush and am enjoying the hell out of this trip so I don't really care if I'm a little behind in miles.

Trent's Grocery hit the spot, as most hot comfort food will undoubtedly do. On our way back to the trail, we found Sassy staring across the road at the trailhead and taking a break. She had attempted a thru-hike last year and Trent's Grocery was the furthest she got until she slipped, fell, and broke her arm. It seemed like a pretty important moment for her. It's crazy to think that one slippery rock or a patch of slick mud can end a thru-hike in less than a second. I mean I fall all the time so it's a scary thought.

Dismal Falls was only 2 miles from Trent's Grocery and was definitely worth the hype. Survivor and I got a campfire started and then ran into the pool of water at the base of the falls. Holy shit it was cold – as close to a polar plunge as you can be without breaking through a sheet of ice. The breath was knocked out of us and the cold made our heads hurt. Still, it's a chance to clean myself and I've been in just about every body of water I've seen so far.

I love Survivor, but damnit did I miss Princess Peach. Songbird, Shaman / Foot, and the Colonel joined us in time for dinner and we caught up on stories from Trail Days.

DAY 54

Starting Location: Dismal Falls Campsite
Destination: Stealth Campsite 5 miles south of Pearisburg, VA
Today's Miles: 19.4
Trip Miles: 629.5

May 17, 2016 – I woke up to rain and, as I've already mentioned, not much is worse than taking down camp in the cold rain of morning. The best thing to do is just start walking as quickly and as soon as possible.

The rain continued unabated for the entire day. However, it did warm up so the rain ended up being quite refreshing especially since we had our first climb of over 1,000 feet in a while (Virginia is definitely not flat, but it is indeed flatter than the previous states – everything is relative).

Hiking today (and most days in the rain) kind of sucks – wet leaves and branches continually spraying you with water, my shoes sinking into piles of mud until my socks are soaked through, slippery rocks, unstable footing, slick patches of mud that make hiking hard and dangerous (especially on downhill slopes), pooping and wiping with wet toilet paper, my glasses fogging up due to condensation or just becoming covered in droplets of water making it difficult to see, a heavier, wetter pack, sometimes a wet sleeping bag and pad, chafing, and just being wet all day with no way to dry off. On the bright side, I don't notice my sweat in the rain and it can feel good when you're climbing mountains and working hard.

Survivor and I did stop quickly at Woods Hole Hostel a half mile off trail because it has such an excellent reputation among hikers. The hostel was a beautiful wooden home with an adjacent farm and bunkhouse. I looked at the chalkboard on the front porch and when I saw that rain was forecast for the next 3 consecutive days and all the patrons were having homemade lasagna for dinner, I was very tempted to purchase a bunk for the night. The place had a feel that made it seem like hikers were just staying at Grandma's house for the evening. That's how at home this place made you feel. I settled for a homemade blueberry smoothie and a homemade loaf of bread that I packed out for dinner. Both selections were gourmet to say the least.

We ended up stealth camping again about 5 miles from Pearisburg, VA because I need to pick up a package from Mom tomorrow. I may also find myself at the Chinese buffet, but we'll see. Actually, I will definitely be there. I may also try to do some laundry. It has been 13 days since I've washed my clothes in an actual machine rather than the bottom of a bathtub. Thankfully, the rain stopped long enough for us to set up our wet tents.

DAY 55

Starting Location: Stealth Campsite 5 miles south of Pearisburg, VA
Destination: Rice Field Shelter
Today's Miles: 12
Trip Miles: 641.5

May 18, 2016 - Rain, rain, rain. This morning is the second in a row with rain pouring down as I take down camp. It's cold rain, too, with temperatures in the 40s, which makes it very difficult to get moving in the morning. My quilt isn't enough in these cold, wet temperatures and I have been uncomfortably cold for the second night in a row.

I only had 5 miles until I hit the road crossing that led to Pearisburg, but it was all straight downhill in some of the slickest conditions I've seen on trail. No less than three times I found myself on the ground with my ass and pack covered in mud. It was not fun. Exacerbating the trail conditions was a flare up of the IT band on the outside of my left knee. Mild pain began yesterday, but on the downhill this morning the pain was excruciating. The pain would build then shoot down my lower leg causing pins and needles in my foot. Something to keep an eye on I guess, but pain in the IT band can't be good at this point.

Despite all this, my Mom's package was waiting for me at the post office and the bag of chocolate chip toffee bars waiting inside was far better than Aleve. Following the cookies, I stuffed my face at a Chinese buffet and I was ready for some more hiking.

Another 7 miles uphill brought me to the Rice Field Shelter where I could rest my knee. Zebra brownies left at the trailhead helped fuel my climb and ignore the pain in my knee, which was definitely getting worse. During the ascent to the shelter, I had to stop a few times because the pain built to a point that forced me to stop walking. I was forced to call it a day as soon as I reached the shelter. I know I stopped walking north, but I still had to walk 0.3 miles to get water, which was a real ass-kicker given the pain I was experiencing. Survivor decided to push on for another 3 miles so he could sleep in.

Joining me that night at the shelter was Sassy, Good Talk, Clovis (finally, Ken got a trail name), Puma, Ragwort (a type of flower), Easy, Crumb Cakes, Little Rhino and Lolligag. We basically commiserated together about the rain (it's only been two days but it honestly feels like a week because there's just no escape from it. Plus, the forecast that night was rain until next Tuesday, which was 6 days away). Good Talk showed me some stretches for my knee.

DAY 56

Starting Location: Rice Field Shelter
Destination: War Spur Shelter
Today's Miles: 25.3
Trip Miles: 666.8

May 19, 2016 - The morning was cold and wet again. It took me a little longer than usual to pack everything up and set off across the field north of the shelter in dense fog. I hadn't gone 20 feet before I completely lost sight of the shelter behind me. My knee felt much better this morning once I got going.

It turns out Survivor went rogue. I didn't see him camped anywhere along the trail for several miles. Finally, I reached the first shelter 12.5 miles into my hike - the trail register said, "Somehow ended up staying here last night. Look alive Mountain Goat. -Survivor". That means he hiked 12.5 more miles starting at around 6 pm. That's nuts.

Now, I was kind of stuck between two bubbles of the hikers I usually hang out with, one ahead and one behind. I decided to push and catch the group ahead of me. So, I just kept walking. I used the notes left in shelter registers as clues to try to guess where my friends would stop to camp for the night.

I was able to deduce that Survivor was trying to catch Steel (Survivor and Steel hooked up at Trail Days much to everyone's surprise), Bad Apple, St. Nick and Sushi among others. If I was to catch Survivor today, I needed to do 30 miles which was not going to happen. However, the sun did manage to come out and assure us that it is, indeed, still there. So, I just decided to keep walking until around 6 pm.

It was a pretty quiet 25.3 miles as I was hiking alone for most of it, but at the same time, very peaceful. I rolled into the War Spur Shelter around 6 pm and joined Ragwort, Splinter, Boyardee, Homer, Trail Talk, Ghostbusters, and Chupacabra.

Despite the wet conditions, I labored at making a fire because I had an entire log of pork roll fresh from Jersey that I wanted to sear. It took almost a half hour to dry out enough wood to get it going, but the heat was worth it. I used long strips of dry bark to support my bread, cheese and pork roll on top of the coals as they were cooked to perfection. With a little hot sauce donation from Boyardee, I felt like I was at home eating a deli breakfast sandwich. Phenomenal. The pork roll was a hit with the others at the shelter, too, as none of them had ever tried it before. Splinter lives in New York City, too - I told him he needs to get out more.

DAY 57

Starting Location: War Spur Shelter
Destination: Pickle Branch Shelter
Today's Miles: 28.1
Trip Miles: 695.1

May 20, 2016 - My goal today was to finally catch the group in front of me. Looking at the trail guide, I determined that I needed to push over 28 miles to get to the shelter where I figured they'd be staying. Ugh that's a long day. I started early and just kept walking - when I do big days like that, I stop as little as possible and only to refill on water or grab a snack.

Morning sunshine gave way to overcast skies before noon and it threatened to rain again. There was nothing wrong with the rain except that it began as I was walking along the exposed ridge and clambering over massive, slanted rocks. The rocks became wet and made the scramble much more difficult.

I arrived at the Niday Shelter 18.2 miles into my hike at around 3:30 pm and decided I had enough left in me to push the extra 10.1 and complete the comeback. Brush Mountain was the only thing standing in my way - nearly 2,000 feet of vertical spread across 2 miles. Despite the continual, but bearable, ache in my knee and general fatigue, the climb wasn't bad. As I stood covered in sweat on the summit, it started to pour and it actually felt wonderful.

I passed Keefer Oak, which is the largest tree on the AT in the south. It's 18 feet in circumference and over 300 years old. The rest of the hike was just downhill for 5 miles into Pickle Branch Shelter where nearly everybody was waiting: Bad Apple, Survivor, Steel, Husker, and Finch. Only Sushi and St. Nick were still ahead of us. I triumphantly walked into camp and then collapsed at the picnic table and made some dinner in the rain.

I made it! While it's nice to hike alone, I'd still prefer to hike with friends. It was nice, too, because I hadn't seen everyone since Trail Days at the very least. The plan was to rest tomorrow at Four Pines Hostel and go to the Homeplace restaurant for dinner – an all you can eat buffet of homemade southern comfort food. Since we were near Virginia Tech, I texted my friend, Robbie Lajeunesse, and asked him if he ever ate there while at school. This is his response verbatim: "GO THERE RIGHT NOW YOU WILL NEVER REGRET IT EVER FOR THE REST OF YOUR LIFE". That ecstatic response certainly agrees with the rumors we've heard of the place on the trail. Hell yes.

DAY 58

Starting Location: Pickle Branch Shelter
Destination: Catawba, VA / Four Pines Hostel
Today's Miles: 6.7
Trip Miles: 701.8

May 21, 2016 - It violently rained for the entire night as far as I could tell, which was sure to make for some muddy hiking as the trail had already been in bad shape. Still, only 6.7 miles until we reached the Four Pines Hostel. The Dragon's Tooth was on the way - a massive, jagged rock that protrudes from the top of a ridge.

After a rugged climb to the ridge line, we scrambled up and down boulders for a couple miles until a short side trail brought us to the tooth. Fog obscured any view of our surroundings but the Dragon's Tooth was still a pretty cool sight. Steel actually scaled the seemingly unscalable monolith and posed for a picture at the top.

The descent from Dragon's Tooth was challenging and enjoyable, but also kind of dangerous. The trail was almost entirely rocks for about a mile and it was so steep that the trail builders actually drove steel rings into the rocks at certain sections so hikers could ascend and descend safely. The fact that all surfaces were wet and muddy from the rain last night didn't help.

A mile down from the tooth the trail leveled out a bit and we crossed mile 700! Finch carved a '700' in the dirt and we reveled in our small accomplishment for a few seconds until we again realized the enormity of the distance still to go.

Four Pines Hostel was a half mile east off trail - the owner, Joe Mitchell, was out front putting a fence around his garden when Survivor, Steel, Finch, and I walked up the driveway. Joe and his wife had gotten married at Trail Days a week earlier at a Trail Magic feast hosted by Four Pines. It was very obvious this guy had his beautiful, sprawling property paid off and he opened a donation-based hostel simply so he could hang out with hikers all the time.

He transformed his 3 car garage into a glorified man cave where hikers could stay. It was complete with fridge, shower, bathroom, beds, cots, couches and chairs strewn across the room. The place was pretty clean for hikers, which would probably still be considered filthy in the real world. Hikers could also tent outside or sleep in the barn up the hill. This place was surreal - the only rule was to treat the place like it was your own home. Everybody there pitched in to clean the place every morning and then just continued to hang out in the hiker paradise. Chickens, guinea fowl, dogs, cats, and the largest turkey I've ever seen ran (well, the turkey was so fat he actually couldn't walk more than 5 feet) haywire around the property.

The shuttle (the Dragon Wagon - just like the Scooby Doo van, but with dragons) driver, Eddie, soon brought us to the Homeplace Restaurant. There were seven of us: Puma, Survivor, Doc, Scooter, Husker, Laser and myself. When the hostess asked for our last name so he could call us, I just said "Goat" without thinking. Before you know it, the table for "Goat - party of 7" was ready and we mentally prepared ourselves for southern goodness. Unlimited fried chicken, roast beef, Virginia ham, corn, slaw, mashed potatoes, baked beans, green beans, biscuits, ice cream and cobbler, and sweet tea did not disappoint. It was easily the best meal any of us had eaten on the trail so far.

The rest of the evening was spent resting, showering, doing laundry, drinking beer, and playing chess and corn hole. During a pretty intense game of chess with Scavenger, the door opened and lo and behold, Princess Peach walked into the hostel! With the chess game forgotten, I jumped up and gave my hiking partner a hug. He hurriedly gave us an update: after finishing the 2 day trail maintenance event with Hot Toddy, Peach was pushing her to catch up to us. Several nights without me and Survivor made him realize he made a mistake staying behind. Finally, tired of the big mile days, Hot Toddy actually decided to stay behind while Peach pushed ahead to Four Pines where he knew we'd be located.

"The tables have turned, Mr. Powers..." – Dr. Evil

STEEL, BAD APPLE, SURVIVOR, FINCH AND MYSELF AT DRAGON'S TOOTH.

DAY 59

Starting Location: Catawba, VA / Four Pines Hostel
Destination: Catawba, VA / Four Pines Hostel
Today's Miles: 0
Trip Miles: 701.8

May 22, 2016 - While the Whipporwill remains my arch-nemesis, the Rooster may be a close second. They started their loud, signature calls at 5 in the morning and wouldn't stop until the sun was up. I exited my tent and made my way to the garage to cook myself some freshly laid, complimentary eggs on top of the stove. I supplemented these with Mama Survivor's delicious, homemade banana bread and apple fritters.

Joining the Tenacious Tripod at Four Pines that day was Husker, Good Talk, Clovis (Good Talk was pissed because Clovis put a 7 lb rock in the bottom of his already heavy pack), the Goon Squad, Flannel, Stardust (I gave her a lot of shit for not having read the book OR seeing the movie), Pokey, Lupine, Two Souls, Lemonhead, Waterboy, Steel, Finch, Pluto, Bee's Knees, the other Mountain Goat, Iceberg, Blazer (he is not a Globo Gym Purple Cobra), Wander, Puma, and I think that's it.

We spent about 15 minutes cleaning the hostel, but the rest of the day consisted of nothing but corn hole, chess, beer, and a short trip to the grocery store so we could get ingredients for a homemade dinner. It was, in fact, a true zero because we actually rested. I made sure to ice my IT band as much as possible throughout the day and hoped it wouldn't give me any more trouble. Steel, Finch, and myself decided to make two pasta dinners and garlic bread for ourselves and share the leftovers with everyone. We actually incorporated healthy foods for a change, such as asparagus, spinach, eggs and tomatoes. However, I definitely counteracted this brief healthy streak by attempting to eat a half gallon of ice cream in preparation for the Half Gallon Challenge coming up in Pine Grove State Park. I failed pretty miserably and realized I had a lot of work to do.

DAY 60

Starting Location: Catawba, VA / Four Pines Hostel
Destination: Stealth Campsite on Tinker Cliffs
Today's Miles: 15.2
Trip Miles: 717

May 23, 2016 – Mama Mountain Goat is driving down to meet me in Buena Vista, VA, this Friday, which means I needed to hike about 105 miles in 5 days. That wasn't too bad – I just hoped my knee would be able to handle that workload. Princess Peach, Steel and I were headed to the Hay Rock Campsite about 20 miles away. Survivor, unfortunately, decided to stop at McAfee's Knob, about 10 miles short of our destination due to his shin splints. It was an emotional, temporary goodbye – we had no doubt he'd catch back up to us eventually. It was finally a sunny, warm day and the hike was refreshing after a day off. My IT band wasn't too bad, just a continual ache that was aggravated primarily on steep downhills. We reached McAfee's Knob, which is one of the most famous and photogenic spots on the entire AT. A large slab of granite juts out over the cliff at the top of the mountain providing for ridiculous views of VA below, the next 5 miles of our hike along the ridge line, and the Tinker Cliffs across the valley. It's traditional for hikers to creatively pose for a picture at the tip of McAfee's Knob. The classic picture is of hikers hanging their legs off the cliff as they look out over the valley. After Steel captured my classic picture, she called for my "next pose". With about 15 other friends and strangers resting and eating on the cliffs around me, I took off all my clothes and took my position at the tip of the knob. It was perfect. I did apologize to the three college students who unexpectedly received a full frontal, but they thought it was great. Check it out!

MY POSE AT MCAFEE'S KNOB...HIKING DOES GREAT THINGS FOR YOUR ASS

We ran into Q-tip, Sundance, and Wander on the trek to Tinker Cliffs and began hiking with them. I was about 2 miles away when I made the mistake of reaching down and massaging my IT band. It exploded with pain and I couldn't take two steps without stopping. I had to stop and rest for about 20 minutes and when I finally got moving again, I slowly and painfully limped to Tinker Cliffs. The views were absolutely gorgeous so we decided to make camp right there on the cliffs despite having less than a liter of water each. Honestly, I was so relieved to stop walking, I would've set up camp with no water.

After dinner, we all sat with our legs dangling over the cliffs and looked out over everything the sunlight had for us on display. A quick shower passed over and we were lucky enough to watch it traverse the valley before us - a curtain of rain varying in density and slowly moving away from our location. The dark clouds were moving slightly southeast and they cleared out just in time for the sun to set. I was pretty down on myself and frustrated while my knee inhibited my walking (especially since there are no signs of this problem going away), but if it hadn't forced me to stop, then I would've missed out on one of the top campsites of the trip so far. It's also extremely liberating to be able to change plans so quickly and abruptly. Whatever we do out here, the only thing we know for sure is we don't want to have any regrets and that is why I took my clothes off.

DAY 61

Starting Location: Stealth Campsite on Tinker Cliffs
Destination: Stealth Campsite near Curry Creek
Today's Miles: 19.1
Trip Miles: 736.1

May 24, 2016 - Unfortunately, I slept right through the sunrise this morning - I just didn't wake up at my usual time. No worries, though - today, we would be passing through Daleville, VA. I didn't need a resupply, but they did have a BBQ place called Three Little Pigs that sounded excellent.

Peach and I walked the 10 miles to town as quickly as possible and arrived just around lunchtime as intended. As we were coming down the last hill into town, can you guess who we ran into sitting on the side of the trail? If you guessed the injured Survivor that supposedly stayed behind at Four Pines, then you would have been correct. Frankly, we were shocked, but delighted, of course, to see the kid. Apparently, yesterday, instead of doing an easy day to rest his shin splints, he pushed 27 miles all the way to Daleville looking for our campsite. The reason he didn't find it was because he took a wrong turn and actually walked under the Tinker Cliffs rather than over them. Several hikers had made this same mistake while we were looking over the cliffs, but we never saw Survivor. Anyway, he ended up getting a hotel room and just waiting for us all morning at the trail head.

The BBQ joint did not disappoint - Peach and I split a vinegar base BBQ sauce sandwich and a tomato base BBQ sauce sandwich and I ordered a small sampling of their wings. The best part of the meal for me was watching Hot Toddy and Steel, a long time vegetarian and pescatarian, order an entire rack of smoked ribs and sink their teeth into the greasy, tender goodness. Meat is truly a beautiful thing.

After our meal, I headed back out on trail, but was soon hampered severely by my knee again. It seems that as I get near 15 miles or so, my knee sort of gives out and walking becomes very difficult. My friends graciously stopped 3 miles short of our original destination for the second day in a row and made camp near Curry Creek. Steel surprised us with marshmallows around the campfire and I grilled up some Brussel sprouts using tin foil and the coals.

DAY 62

Starting Location: Stealth Campsite near Curry Creek
Destination: Campsite at Cross Jennings Creek
Today's Miles: 19.6
Trip Miles: 755.7

May 25, 2016 - As you know, I enjoy swimming and have eagerly taken nearly every chance I've gotten out here. So, in the trail guide, when our destination for the day was actually noted as a "great swimming hole", I was pretty pumped. I was hoping my knee could handle the 21 miles required to get there.

Steel and I hiked together for most of the uneventful day. It was extremely hot in the sun, but the canopy of trees consistently provided much needed shade. The terrain today was a mix between woods and open areas that had a distinct desert feel to them. We arrived at the swimming hole early around 4:30, which meant we had plenty of time to enjoy it.

While I thought there have already been many better swimming spots than this one, it was undoubtedly refreshing after sweating our asses off all day. We cleaned ourselves and then dried off in the sun. Many fishermen had left dead squid and fish heads in the water, which made it difficult to relax.

Peach soon arrived along with Two Souls, Lemonhead, Waterboy, Tanto, Iron Will, Waldo, Carjack (an adorable dog that was named for jumping into stranger's cars in the hopes of a joyride) and Fire Starter. Apparently, there was a campground down the road that offered free shuttles for some hot food. All of us rushed to squeeze ourselves into the bed of the pickup truck that served as the shuttle. As we were moving, the door of the truck bed snapped open and luckily the three of us leaning against the door caught ourselves before falling out.

A double cheeseburger and a plate of fries later, the shuttle brought us back to the swimming hole where we set up camp. The trip was definitely worth it especially since we ran into the Warrior Hikers who we hadn't seen in too long.

My knee held up for the day, but it continues to cause me some serious discomfort. I still can't picture any scenario where the pain will go away. I can only see it getting worse without several weeks of rest. I was able to obtain some ice from the campground, but it's honestly not doing much.

DAY 63

Starting Location: Campsite at Cross Jennings Creek
Destination: Stealth Campsite near Big Cove Branch
Today's Miles: 24.5
Trip Miles: 780.2

May 26, 2016 - Thursday morning brought a small shower of rain before the sun came out and continued baking everything. I had two days and 38 miles to reach Mama Mountain Goat, which meant that today needed to be a pretty big day.

Unfortunately, I just did not feel like hiking today. It was probably because of the heat the past few days, but I was exhausted. Just like in the real world, sometimes it's just one of those days. Regardless, I kept trudging along slowly and taking plenty of breaks.

I passed this cool part of the trail called "The Guillotine". Originally, I assumed it was just an incredibly steep section of downhill, but it's actually a large boulder that was caught in midair between two larger rocks. Very cool.

Finally, as I was ascending the last big climb of the day with sweat pouring off me, the skies opened up and it started pouring. At the summit, I just sat down, took off my hat and let myself get soaked - it felt wonderful.

However, the rain wore out its welcome 2 hours later when it was still coming down hard. With saturated shoes and blisters starting to form, Peach and I bowed out at 23 miles, 2 miles short of the shelter we were aiming for. We found a quaint campsite near a small stream just as the rain stopped.

Hot Toddy joined us as we were finishing up dinner and I retired early as I was still exhausted. I cannot describe to you how good it felt to lay down and crawl under my quilt.

DAY 64

Starting Location: Stealth Campsite near Big Cove Branch
Destination: Lexington, VA / Hotel
Today's Miles: 15.3
Trip Miles: 795.5

May 27, 2016 - I looked at the elevation profile first thing this morning and groaned. We had to climb up no less than 3 massive inclines during our 15 mile trek: Little Rocky Row, Big Rocky Row, and Bluff Mountain. In total, these inclines summed to over 3,000 feet of elevation on an incredibly hot day. On the bright side, Mama Mountain Goat would be waiting for us at the end of it with an air conditioned car, Taylor Ham, egg and cheese bagel sandwiches fresh from Jersey and cookies.

Peach, Toddie and I got off to an early start this morning and approached the James River footbridge, which is the longest footbridge on the entire AT. Hiker tradition requires that you jump off the bridge into the James River. However, it's a $120 fine if you're caught by the park ranger.

Of course that didn't stop us - Peach swam out in the river to make sure it was deep enough. Safety first! We then took turns jumping. I'm not sure why, but Hot Toddy was actually egged on by an elderly woman to jump naked. She obliged.

The climb up Little Rocky Row may have been the toughest climb of the trail yet. It certainly wasn't the steepest or the longest incline, but other factors, such as the extreme heat, the pain in my knee, and general exhaustion made it very difficult. At the top, I threw down my pack and gulped down some water. That's when I realized I had less than half a liter of water for the next 7.5 miles with two significant climbs. Shit. Not good.

Another thru-hiker, Beast, met us at the top of the mountain and lamented that he was thinking about leaving the trail. His primary reason was the heat and how he didn't feel like he could carry enough water to stay hydrated. I suggested he focus on something else and give his body time to adjust to the heat. However, if he's allowing those types of thoughts to enter his mind only 800 miles into this trip and before summer has even started, he doesn't have the mental toughness to succeed on this trip. I honestly thought I would think of quitting quite often before I started, but it hasn't even remotely crossed my mind. Every single hiker on trail right now is hurting in one way or another or, at the very least, battling some sort of issue. That doesn't mean you quit, though. You grit your teeth, try something new, depend on each other and focus on the positive. No rain, no pain, no Maine!

Anyway, I was in a little bit of trouble with this water situation. All of my friends were just as low as I was, too. I was sweating buckets and I had two very difficult climbs ahead of me spread across 7.5 miles. There was nothing for it except to suck it up and push forward. As dehydration began to set in, my saliva dried up, the muscles in my legs tightened, and I started to feel weaker and slightly dizzy. It was no joke as I slowly progressed through all the symptoms of dehydration that I had learned about in my Wilderness First Aid class. Believe it or not, the worst part was actually getting to the water source and then sitting there waiting for the water while it was treated.

I finally made it to the road crossing where my Mom was supposed to pick us up. It turns out she was at the wrong Robinson Gap Road. It took her over an hour to finally find our position on the gravel road. Still, it was a joyous meeting - I gave her a big hug then immediately devoured the 8 hour old Taylor Ham, egg and cheese bagel sandwich she brought me. Yes!

My Mom brought us to our hotel where we showered, did some laundry and took a load off. Then, we drove (I forgot how amazing it is to have a car at your disposal) into Lexington, VA, for some dinner at The Southern Inn Restaurant, which was excellent. After dinner, I soaked my feet and knee in a warm bath of Epsom Salts. Soon enough, we were all so tired, there was nothing else we wanted to do except sleep.

Love you, Mom.

DAY 65

Starting Location: Lexington, VA / Hotel
Destination: Lexington, VA / Hotel
Today's Miles: 0
Trip Miles: 795.5

May 28, 2016 - Despite the day off today, I still woke up around 6:30 and went downstairs to get coffee from the hotel lobby. Breakfast was in full service so naturally I indulged. After I was satisfied, I had major plans to take a long, relaxing Epsom Salt tub in my room. Epsom salts have been very effective in helping my feet heal during short rest periods, so I thought I would try soaking my knee. While the bath was certainly relaxing and my feet were already showing signs of improvement, the warm water seemed only to aggravate the pain stemming from my IT band.

The rest of the morning consisted of a trip to Walmart to finish my resupply. Then my Mom drove Steel, Peach, Survivor, Hot Toddy and myself into the center of Lexington to walk around and explore the city. My Mom and I had a quick, but good lunch at a bakery and then we all headed back to the hotel to change into our bathing suits.

The plan was to return to a spot on the river that we had passed on the way to the hotel from the trailhead the previous day to do some swimming. We sat on the soft grass next to the river in the sun and shade alternatively and floated in the water when we needed to cool down.

The riverside spot also offered up some excellent people watching of a couple atrocious, redneck parents. This one father actually encouraged his younger son to punch the older one in the face. The sun, the shade, the plush grass, the cool water and the people watching made for an incredibly relaxing afternoon.

My Mom and I went across the street to the Italian place for dinner since it looked like they actually had some good pizza. The pizza was New York style and they didn't do a half bad job. We quickly realized that we should've gotten the cheesesteak, though – no less than 7 people ordered it while we were there. One man actually ate one for dinner and then ordered another to take home.

Finally, Mom and I just hung out in the hotel room and watched a movie on television. It would be an early return to the trail in the morning so none of us really wanted to do anything crazy. A zero is honestly meant for doing nothing anyway.

DAY 66

Starting Location: Lexington, VA / Hotel
Destination: Cow Camp Gap Shelter
Today's Miles: 14.4
Trip Miles: 809.9

May 29, 2016 - Mom got us all moving pretty early as she had a 7 hour drive back and wanted to get started. She dropped us off back at the trailhead and we grudgingly started walking again.

The first 10 miles were full of beautiful, relatively easy terrain. I recently started listening to an audiobook of the Count of Monte Cristo, which has kept me very entertained.

We did have a large climb today of about 3,000 feet. Just as I was crossing the road to begin this climb, I noticed three gentlemen providing Trail Magic. Two of the gentlemen were photographers and had actually set up a photo booth to snap pictures of thru-hikers for their blog. They noticed my tie so I obliged them by putting it on and posing for a few official snaps. They have my email so pictures should be coming soon.

The third gentleman was Tom - Tom had been waiting for his girlfriend, Terrible Lizard, on Friday afternoon in the same spot we were waiting for my Mom. We had told him we hadn't seen her on our hike and there was no way she'd reach the gap by today. He had already hiked up the mountain looking for her. As it turns out, he had realized she must have thought they were meeting up Saturday instead of Friday. So, he drove around to the footbridge over the James River, hiked in and found her at the shelter 15 miles back. While we had thought she genuinely ditched Tom and truly earned the trail name "Terrible Lizard", it was actually just an honest mistake. Today, Tom was waiting for Terrible Lizard to finish a slack pack and, in the meantime, getting rid of all his beer and food to other thru-hikers before his ride back up to Albany. I was the first to arrive and only left 11 beers later when all the beer had gone. Whoops.

Except for those itchy alcohol sweats, I swear those beers made the climb up to the shelter much easier. Because the shelter was a half mile off trail, our usual group and Husker were the only hikers there. Since I positively knew that no one there snored (Survivor moans consistently, but we have no idea why) and rain was forecast, I decided to sleep in the shelter. That's only the third time on the whole trail I've slept in a shelter. I made Taylor Ham and cheese bagel sandwiches over the fire with the resupply my Mom had provided.

The climb up to the shelter had another major significance: Princess Peach broke up with Hot Toddy! While I feel sort of bad for Toddie, I had been waiting for this moment since they started dating back in Hot Springs. The relationship had lasted from mile 273 to 809 - the reign of Hot Toddy was officially over!

MY ON-TRAIL PROFESSIONAL HEAD SHOT.

DAY 67

Starting Location: Cow Camp Gap Shelter
Destination: The Priest Shelter
Today's Miles: 16.8
Trip Miles: 826.7

May 30, 2016 - Today was another easy day - a 16 mile ridge hike to The Priest Shelter. Hot Toddy did elect to stay behind and stop hiking with us. Not much else happened, honestly, with the exception of a short detour to climb Spy Rock. This monolith was just off trail and provided a fun opportunity to take off the pack and do some rock climbing. Once at the top, I sat for a while and gazed out at the surrounding wilderness. I actually felt very out of place among all the day hikers seated up there. I was alone, covered in sweat, and surrounded by a veritable cloud of flies who were delighted this smelly piece of trash decided to sit there. All the day hikers actually smelled clean as I walked past them - it's amazing how I notice that now when I never did before. It's all relative.

The Priest Shelter is pretty famous on the AT because hikers write their confessions into the shelter register, which, as you can imagine, make for some pretty funny reading. Here are some of the things I learned:
-An alarming number of hikers have shit themselves on trail
-Many people do not dig cat holes that are the required 6-8 inches deep
-Many hikers have yellow blazed portions of the trail
-Olive Oil does not actually carry olive oil
-One hiker took a revenge dump in the road, then felt bad and packed it into the woods.

Just to give you an idea of what some of the entries are like. As to my own confession, that is between me and the Priest ("I have failed to close on multiple occasions. I resolve to change this").

The Priest is actually a mountain and is widely known as one of the 7 hardest climbs on the AT. Luckily, tomorrow we would be hiking down the Priest rather than up.

DAY 68

Starting Location: The Priest Shelter
Destination: Devils Backbone Brewery
Today's Miles: 15.5
Trip Miles: 842.2

May 31, 2016 - Just as my mother came to visit me this past weekend, Peach's parents were driving down this afternoon. The meeting place was Devils Backbone Brewery, but that meant Peach and I had to hike 16 miles before 2 pm when they were scheduled to arrive. This wasn't just any 16 miles though - we had a steep, 3000 foot descent spread over 4 miles and, immediately after we reached the bottom, an almost identical 3000 foot ascent also spread over 4 miles. The 3,000 foot descent was called The Priest as I explained in my previous post.

We managed to get out of camp at 7 am on the dot and hiked with great speed. We didn't stop for a break until about 10 miles in when we were halfway up the monster. The day was hot and humid with temperatures in the high 80s or low 90s. With sweat dripping annoyingly on my glasses, my clothes saturated, and my hands slipping from my poles, I finally reached the rocky summit. I sat down, took my pack off and reached for a snack. Only then did I bother to look around me and proceed to groan with despair. I was on a false summit and the actual summit was looming over me like a big bully. I gloomily packed everything back into my bag and mentally prepared myself for another climb. As always, once I finally did get to the top, the climb didn't seem so bad. Plus, I only had 4 more easy miles to go before cold beer (which you learn to appreciate when you're used to warm beer in the woods).

Peach and I completed our 16 miles in less than 6 hours and were seated at the air conditioned bar with cold pints by 1 pm. In retrospect, of course, the climb definitely seemed a lot less difficult than it had 2 hours earlier. The brewery also let us camp on their property so we set up our tents and went back to the bar. As the afternoon wore on, several other hikers joined us: Bee's Knees, Pluto, Golden Boy, Sweets, Jingle, Ummgahwah, Cheddar, Chef Tumbleweed O.G. (Original Gangster), Fire Starter, Husker, Pharmacist, Steel and Survivor.

Peach's parents arrived in the middle of the afternoon with his sister and dog, Scoober, who would be joining us for the rest of the thru-hike. Scoober made his debut by peeing on Cheddar's pack. Papa Peach was gracious enough to pay for dinner, discreetly pick up my tab and drop off most of the necessary ingredients for us to make Taylor Ham, egg and cheese bagel sandwiches in the morning. I did convince the bartender to sell me a dozen eggs, which was pretty awesome.

The rest of the day was spent consuming beer, socializing, and making s'mores by the campfire when the brewery closed. Again, not a bad life...

DAY 69

Starting Location: Devils Backbone Brewery
Destination: Waynesboro, VA / Town Campsite
Today's Miles: 19.1
Trip Miles: 861.3

Jun 1, 2016 - I awoke to hear the sizzle of grease on a frying pan. Other than sexually, I don't think there is any better way to wake up. Peach had started frying that Taylor Ham and those eggs. I went straight to the large paper bag near the propane stove and selected my New Jersey everything bagel in preparation for my much anticipated meal. Peach added the cheese and I toasted my bagel by placing it in the flame of the spare burner. And then the bagel sandwich was complete and in my mouth. I actually pitied all the other hikers who were paying to have the brewery cook them breakfast.

Peach also made me coffee, but when I went to the bathroom, I came back to find my coffee gone. Survivor had thought I was done with it so he poured it in his cup. Unforgivable. It will be a long time until I let him forget this transgression.

Anyway, Peach's parents drove us back to the trail head - we had 19 miles to go to reach Waynesboro, a rather large hiker town. The morning passed swiftly enough and I noticed a new sound: Scoober panting. The dog certainly looked happy as he basically did wind sprints up and down the trail. He quickly learned to tone it down as he was exhausted at the end of the day. It was fun to try to prevent him from passing me. I discovered that

Scoober, while adorable, is very rude. He completely ignores trail etiquette and doesn't give a shit about anything except himself. It's hysterical.

Survivor's shoes had finally failed him and were literally being held together by a zip tie. He insisted that he was going to try to make it to Harpers Ferry, which is 200 freaking miles away. Steel, Peach and I resolved to pitch in and buy him a new pair from the outfitter in Waynesboro.

A quick lunch break had me looking at the guide book and I noticed a movie theatre in Waynesboro. Steel and I immediately resolved to crush the remaining 12 miles and catch the 7 pm showing of Captain America: Civil War. Finally, a movie theatre. Well, we crushed the 12 in a little over 4 hours and immediately got a hitch from John, who, contrary to most drivers, actually insisted I sit my smelly, sweaty ass in his backseat rather than the truck bed.

John gave us a quick tour of town and then dropped us off at the town campground, which offered free tenting to AT thru-hikers. Steel and I then hurried to the YMCA to take free showers and do some quick shower laundry (we literally wash the clothes we're wearing while we take a shower and then wear them until they dry). Next up was another hitch from Tony and Emily (a lovely elderly couple) to the movie theatre.

With an hour before game time, the two of us bought tickets, pounded a burrito from Moe's and then walked a half mile to the grocery store to purchase some cheap candy and wine. The movie might have been legendary – I especially enjoyed the Spider-Man reveal.

When the movie ended, we noticed a man sitting up front by himself. We asked Cornbread (this was his nickname as a comedian) for a ride back to the campsite. Not only did he give us a ride, but he bought us milkshakes, too. I mean, how much better could the night have gotten?

DAY 70

Starting Location: Waynesboro, VA / Town Campsite
Destination: Blackrock Hut
Today's Miles: 20.7
Trip Miles: 882

Jun 2, 2016 - John had suggested Weasie's for breakfast and I fully intended to go there this morning. It did not disappoint - I gorged on 2 pancakes, 1 gigantic cinnamon bun, 3 slices of bacon, 2 hash browns, and 3 scrambled eggs. Damnit, I LOVE breakfast food.

Since the outfitter didn't open until 10 am, Peach and I started to work on a hitch back to the trail head. Steel had some errands to run in town and would stop at the outfitter to purchase Survivor's new trail shoes. Speaking of Survivor, he was probably still sleeping through all of this. I couldn't wait to see the look on his face later when the three of us surprised him with new shoes.

One mile into my hike, I passed into Shenandoah National Park. I completed the self-registration as required and attached the slip to my pack for the next 101 miles. My goal today was the Blackrock Hut 21 miles out from Waynesboro.

As I walked through the national park that paralleled the famous Skyline Drive, I couldn't help but notice that it looks like most of the other woods I've been in for over 2 months. I guess when I pass into a national park so celebrated for its beauty, I expected something grand and different. The same thing happened in the Great Smoky Mountains. However, both parks appear to be just ridge hiking with more camping restrictions than we're used to. Don't get me wrong – the park and literally all the woods I have walked through are absolutely beautiful. The national park just didn't live up to the pedestal I had unconsciously put it on.

About 6 miles from the shelter, a thunderstorm rolled in and it started to rain. I put my pack cover on and kept walking as I usually do in this situation as I expected it to pass within an hour. I could not have been more wrong. The rain intensified until it was a deluge – my glasses were so covered in water I could barely see anything. It was easily the hardest rain I've ever hiked in and it went on for close to 3 hours before the storm transformed into a light rain.

I walked into the shelter soaked to the bone. I setup my tent in the rain and as I went through my stuff, I realized the trash compactor bag I use to waterproof my bag had several holes. Puddles of water coated everything. Thankfully, my stuff sacks kept my clothes and sleeping quilt dry.

At the shelter, I ran into Verge and Legs, who I hadn't seen since Hot Springs. Also there was Sleeping Beauty, Dolly, Farmer, Tree, Storyteller, Diatom, Mola, New Hampshire Bob (I'm quickly learning this 66 year old with a thick Boston accent is very crazy in a good way...can't wait to drink with him in town), and Miles. I actually passed New Hampshire Bob in the rain – he had been huddled under a tree and I couldn't help but thinking that his choice of shelter was very poor given the intensity of the rain. It turns out he was just trying to keep his Snickers bar dry.

Peach had stealth camped 6 miles back and I had no idea what happened to Survivor and Steel. I guess I wouldn't be able to see Survivor's face when he saw his new shoes after all.

DAY 71

Starting Location: Blackrock Hut
Destination: Stealth Campsite on summit of Hightop Mountain
Today's Miles: 21.4
Trip Miles: 903.4

Jun 3, 2016 - While the rain did finally stop in the middle of the night, none of my stuff had started to dry. My shoes actually had a puddle of water in them. Packing up wasn't so bad, but getting dressed was awful. Pulling my dripping wet clothes on, wringing out my socks, which could be considered lethal to someone not prepared for the smell, and pulling on my shoes with an audible squelch was not fun at all. However, all I could do was start walking.

I tried not taking Aleve in the morning for my knee to see how I would feel. That was a mistake. While I had felt that the Aleve wasn't really helping, I could not have been more wrong. I barely made it a mile before I literally could not take another step without burning, shooting pains making their way down my leg. I just sat down and waited for the pills to kick in. I usually hate to take pills at home, but doing something unnatural (like hiking 2,200 miles with 30 lbs on your back) requires some outside help.

Shenandoah National Park has small restaurants called waysides every 20 miles or so that hikers can stop at for a bite to eat. I had decided to stop at the camp store near the wayside and wait for Peach behind me. I ended up waiting there almost 3 hours (I did take a shower and do some laundry). Verge and Legs were also there and I had a chance to catch up with them after 600 miles. I forgot just how delightful they were. After no sign of Peach, I pushed on.

Rain had been forecast again for tonight, but as I walked through the afternoon, the sky only became clearer. After another 21 miles, I reached the Hightop Hut (shelters are called 'huts' in the national park for some reason) at the late hour of 7 pm only to have a ridge runner turn me away. She claimed that the shelter was too full and I should push on another 0.6 miles to the top of Hightop Mountain where I would find a spring and a handful of other hikers she had already turned away. So, already exhausted (and disappointed – I had spotted Training Wheels sitting at the table in front of the hut. The ridge runner deprived me of the chance to see her again after nearly 600 miles), I climbed another half mile to the top. I found a spring, but only one other hiker (Living Proof – this guy had brain cancer for 38 weeks and survived) and almost no camping sites. I just found a leafy spot in the middle of the woods, cleaned off in the spring and ate a quiet dinner on a rock ledge while I gazed at a spectacular view of the sun setting over the mountains. Living Proof joined me for the last bit of the sunset.

I collapsed onto my sleeping pad and almost immediately fell asleep. I had been a little peeved at being turned away from the shelter, especially with my knee screaming at me. It all worked out though as I was treated to a nice water source and yet another ridiculous sunset. I also passed 900 miles which felt pretty damn good. I think tonight is the only night on trail I camped by myself.

Mountains are better than the beach.

DAY 72

Starting Location: Stealth Campsite on summit of Hightop Mountain
Destination: Elton, VA / Harrisonburg, VA
Today's Miles: 3.4
Trip Miles: 906.8

Jun 4, 2016 – Elkton, VA was only 2.7 miles away and I had forwarded the package containing my new JacksrBetter quilt to the post office there. Plus, Survivor's Mom was driving down to meet him for the afternoon and I was invited along with Steel of course.

I caught a fairly tough hitch near the entrance to the park from a religious guy named Johnny. I've got nothing against the religious folk down here, but sometimes it's hard to talk to them when every single sentence is punctuated by references to the good Lord. Still, Johnny was nice enough and was obviously giving me a ride into town.

Of course, when I made it to the post office, the package hadn't arrived yet. I had to forward it yet again to Harper's Ferry where maybe I would have more luck. I had several hours to kill before Survivor, Steel and Survivor's Mom were supposed to arrive. This is a dangerous situation when I am in a town surrounded by food joints. I started with McDonalds: a coffee, 3 hot cakes, 1 hash brown, 1 sausage biscuit, and 1 sausage burrito. Still not satisfied, I walked to Dairy Queen: 1 large peanut butter cookie dough blizzard and a basket of 6 chicken fingers, fries, and Texas toast. Honestly, I still wasn't full, but it wouldn't have been right to continue.

Shawna arrived around 2 pm at the Dairy Queen to pick the 3 of us up and take us to a hotel room she so graciously bought us. Steel was literally covered in poison ivy and needed the break. Back at the hotel, I met Shawna's boyfriend, Matt, and Survivor's two little sisters, Sophia and Emily. Sophia was especially adorable - she drew me a picture of my face that I put in my pack so that I could keep it.

Steel had a bad case of poison ivy that she apparently got from snuggling too closely with Survivor in his one person tent. Imagine sweating profusely and not showering for more than 5 days and then cuddling / having sex with your significant other in a tent that's barely large enough for one person. It's gross. Maybe I would feel differently if I had a significant other, but I think I would just wait to fool around until a town day when I'm relatively clean.

The afternoon was spent relaxing, showering, doing laundry and other chores associated with a nero. Dinner was to be at Golden Corral. I had never been to a Golden Corral, but I was pretty stunned when I walked in. Literally every single type of American comfort food lined the front of the building in one of the more impressive buffets I've ever seen. It was nearly too much to handle - I only headed back to the table after I realized food was actually falling off my plate because there was so much on it. Three plates later, I had the usual stomach pains that follow an enormous buffet, but no regrets whatsoever.

Following dinner, Matt drove us to resupply at Wal-Mart. Since I still had food from when my Mom drove down a week ago, I only bought some carrots, apples and wine for the rest of the night. Watch out - Survivor came away with a smart phone.

Steel, Survivor, and I watched The Martian, crushed the wine and had an excellent night of sleep. Actually, Steel did not have a great night - her poison ivy nearly drove her crazy. Fortunately, I've never had poison ivy and can't really imagine what she was going through, but watching someone normally so calm and happy become so frustrated and uncomfortable really put things into perspective.

DAY 73

Starting Location: Elton, VA / Harrisonburg, VA
Destination: Rock Spring Hut
Today's Miles: 20.5
Trip Miles: 927.3

Jun 5, 2016 – The hotel breakfast actually wasn't too bad – hard boiled eggs, muffins, English muffins, and coffee. We packed up pretty quickly and had Shawna and Matt drive us back to Swift Run Gap so we could resume hiking. I had to average 20 miles a day for 6 straight days in order to reach Harpers Ferry on Friday, June 10. Ben 'Studley' Dudley would be meeting me there.

While I was sheltered from the storms last night, I had no such shelter to look forward to this evening. The forecast for this afternoon and into tonight were high winds, thunderstorms, and possible hail. I started booking it as soon as I started hiking around 10 am with the intention of hiking 21.5 miles before the storms hit.

About 9 miles in, I stopped in at the Lewis Mountain Campground for a snack and to meet up with Princess Peach. We had been separated three nights ago during the thunderstorm because Scoober had cracked his paw. He had to take it slow until Scoober healed up a bit. Our reunion was consummated in the most appropriate manner: with a beer.

Peach and I continued hauling ass and reached the Rock Spring Hut at around 5 pm, literally just as the rain started coming down. However, despite the harsh forecast, it drizzled for about 20 minutes and then the sun came back out. It ended up being a beautiful evening and we were all afforded a perfect view of the sunset.

I actually slept in the shelter for only the fourth time all trip due to the supposedly impending weather. Joining me was Verge, Legs, Peach, Scoober, Happy Feet, Napster, Pharmacist, and Cheeseweasal. Steel and Survivor showed up after the shelter had already been filled.

Mice regularly roam the shelters at night – you can always hear them scurrying and scratching as they search for food. Apparently, Pharmacist carries mouse traps with him to kill mice at the shelters. Before tonight, he had slayed 19 mice, with 6 being the most in any given night. However, everyone knew tonight might be the night he set a new record as his first two traps coated in peanut butter each killed 2 mice at the same time! After about 2 hours of continually resetting the traps, Pharmacist had caught no less than 15 mice, his new record! It was a very entertaining show. Somehow, it was my job to put any mice the traps didn't kill out of their misery.

DAY 74

Starting Location: Rock Spring Hut
Destination: Stealth Campsite near Spring
Today's Miles: 17.6
Trip Miles: 944.9

Jun 6, 2016 - Scoober woke me up just before 6. I guess he was uncomfortable so he just hip checked my leg out of the way and lay down on my sleeping pad (he really is a bully). I think he likes me, but I'm definitely not sure because every time I pet him, he growls AND wags his tail. It's almost like he's purring.

In order to hold to the plan of arriving in Harpers Ferry by Friday, we were looking at another big day to maintain our 20 mile per day average. The only problem was Scoober - he was obviously exhausted since he had gained weight during the first half of the trail and didn't have his hiking legs yet. The fat was still very obviously jiggling on his hind legs as he trotted along.

Peach, Scoober and I were walking from the shelter back to the trail when we were stopped by a large black bear. The bear didn't even seem to notice us as he moseyed across the trail.
Shortly after we resumed hiking, we were forced to stop into the Skyland Resort and Restaurant when we smelled the food they were cooking as it wafted onto the trail. And it turns out, we hit the jackpot - breakfast buffet! The only problem with a buffet is hiking immediately afterward with a full stomach, which is, of course, exactly what we did.

We ended up stopping 17.6 miles into our hike at a stealth spot next to a spring. Survivor rolled in to camp a little later with the news that Steel actually got off trail and went to the hospital because her poison ivy was so bad. She planned on slack packing the next day to catch back up to us.

As it continues to get hotter out, the bugs are becoming pretty unbearable. We actually all sat in our tents and chatted with each other after dinner since fires are not allowed in Shenandoah. Otherwise, we would've been eaten alive.

DAY 75

Starting Location: Stealth Campsite near Spring
Destination: Tom Floyd Shelter
Today's Miles: 21.3
Trip Miles: 966.2

Jun 7, 2016 - Today would be our last day in Shenandoah National Park. The bears have definitely been my favorite part of the park so far - I have seen 13 already including two cubs the size of cats, which were obviously adorable. Usually, they will just sit there and stare at me with their ears up as I walk past. My favorite interaction was this morning when Survivor, Scoober, Peach, and I caught up to an older gentleman named Grey Ghost. He was stopped on the trail staring down a mama bear just a couple yards off the east side of the trail. Grey Ghost informed us that two cubs had already run down the hill on the west side of the trail so that continuing would place us between mama and her cubs.

Scoober started to bark a bit, which seemed to only provoke the bear. Mama bear mounted a log and hit the log with his paw - you could tell she was thinking about attacking, but 5 against 1 aren't good odds even for a bear. The bear ultimately turned away and we proceeded to hike north.

Another bear encounter I heard about occurred to another thru
-hiker named Jelly and his dog Peanut Butter. The bear had charged from behind unprovoked and tried attacking the dog. PB is pretty quick, though, and successfully dodged the attack. Jelly stepped in and started yelling and clacking his trekking poles together until the bear ran away. Scary stuff.

Anyway, we took advantage of the Elkwallow Wayside before we left the national park by purchasing breakfast sandwiches. We hiked 21.3 miles to the Tom Floyd Shelter just outside the northern boundary of the national park. A sign on trail identified the shelter as a 'wayside' so we got pretty excited until we realized there were definitely no double bacon cheeseburgers there. Also, the water source was about a half mile down a steep hill, which is always pretty demoralizing.

Tomorrow, Survivor and I will be attempting the 24 challenge. This challenge requires that you drink 24 beers and hike 24 miles within a 24 hour time period.

DAY 76

Jun 8, 2016 – Today, I completed the 24 challenge! It was mostly fun, but also very not fun, especially towards the end. Peach, Survivor, Scoober and I left the shelter at 7:15 am – the official start of the challenge. Survivor and I would be attempting the challenge while Peach planned to take a short day to allow Scoober to rest.

Just a reminder, the challenge is to consume 24 beers and hike 24 miles within a 24 hour time period. So, there are literally a hundred different ways to complete the challenge.

We hiked a quick 3 miles to the road crossing for Front Royal, VA. Bill gave us all a ride to the Food Lion where we could acquire beers for the challenge. I chose a 24 pack of Yuengling while Survivor went with PBR. I also had to run to the post office quickly to pick up a package from my Mom containing a knee brace and some food to get me through a few days.

The four of us then grabbed Slurpee cups from 7-Eleven and commenced drinking right there on the sidewalk. Our strategy was to pound about 6-8 beers right away and then resume hiking. This would reduce the weight we would have to carry (24 beers weighs around 19 pounds). Then, we would focus on drinking around 1 beer per hour while hiking. Finally, we would finish off the remaining beers once the 24 miles was completed. We also picked a day with forgiving terrain and abundant water sources since it would be difficult to stay hydrated.

All was going according to plan until we reached the shelter at 14 miles. Survivor was drunk and had something close to a nervous breakdown (he lost a trekking pole somehow). Needless to say, he bailed and decided to stay behind with Peach and Scoober. I was looking at 10 lonely, difficult miles with around 10 beers left.

I reached the stream that marked 24 miles at 9:20 pm. All of my beers were gone - I did it! However, now it was dark and I needed to find a stealth campsite. I stumbled (slightly buzzed) on in the dark by the light of my headlamp for nearly another mile before I decided to just camp in the middle of a side trail I came across. The side trail led to some locked cabin in the woods, but after about a quarter mile, I gave up and settled for the dirt trail. Screw night hiking, by the way. A waxing crescent moon obviously provided no help and 24 beers may have made the experience a bit worse than usual, but it was not fun at all.

I was exhausted and fell asleep as soon as I had set up my tent. I didn't even eat dinner. While the challenge was certainly difficult, I never doubted I would finish. However, I definitely do not want to do it again.

The half-gallon challenge at Pine Grove Furnace State Park is next...

DAY 77

Starting Location: Stealth Campsite on Trail west to Myron Glaser Cabin
Destination: Campsite north of Roller Coaster
Today's Miles: 14.7
Trip Miles: 1006.1

Jun 9, 2016 – I knew as soon as I opened my eyes that today was going to be an extremely long day. Hungover was an understatement. After I got my bearings and confirmed I could stand, I prepared a greasy breakfast of Taylor Ham and cheese, which definitely helped a little. I looked around me while I ate and realized the cabin was about 30 yards farther along the trail, which I hadn't noticed it in the dark.

My woes continued as I started hiking because today I was to tackle the 'Roller Coaster', which is 13.5 miles of straight up and then straight down on repeat (the elevation profile in the guidebook did indeed look exactly like a roller coaster). Luckily, it was a beautiful, breezy day and I was in the shade for most of it. I quickly sweat out the alcohol from the previous day, but seemingly could not stay hydrated and my head continued to pound.

I saw two bears during my hike today. It's pretty funny to see a powerful, 400 pound killing machine run away from me when he hears me approaching on the trail. If they don't run, most of the time they just stare at you with their ears up looking like a cuddly teddy bear.

With about 3.5 miles left in the roller coaster, I met two older section hikers named Old Hoosier and Hopalong. They informed me there was a restaurant called the Horseshoe Curve 0.3 miles west along the road we had just crossed. I asked if I could join them and they honestly seemed happy to have some company.

While I chatted with them over lunch, they revealed that they originally had a third companion named Bernie. During their hike through Shenandoah, he felt ill. They aided him to the next shelter and when help came, the paramedics realized that his aorta artery split and he was bleeding out from the inside. He was rushed to the hospital via helicopter – he had requested a priest to perform last rites and called his family because he genuinely thought he was going to die. After two weeks in the hospital, he is almost fully recovered, but I can't imagine how scary that must have been on the trail. They had been almost 3 miles from the nearest wayside when Bernie started showing symptoms. If it had happened even 1-2 miles farther away, he'd probably be dead.

There's a new blazing term that I heard recently: Platinum Blazing. Basically, this refers to someone paying others to slack pack them along most of the trail. The reason this came up was because Beast, who I have mentioned in the past, has been slack packing very often.

Anyway, I finally finished the Roller Coaster, passing 1,000 miles and finishing Virginia in the process. Even though I struggled for most of the 15.1 miles today, it was extremely satisfying to realize that I've hiked such a large distance. It's also nice to have the 550 mile state of Virginia out of the way.

DAY 78

Starting Location: Campsite north of Roller Coaster
Destination: Harpers Ferry, WV (188 High Street)
Today's Miles: 17
Trip Miles: 1023.1

Jun 10, 2016 - Steel and Survivor had arrived at my campsite during the night and were up early with me around 6 am. I'm pretty shocked no other hikers stopped at the campsite - it was beautiful, just off the trail and had a very clean and accessible spring.

Steel made me a cup of coffee which I was sorely missing yesterday morning without Peach. It was instant, but I cannot describe to you how glorious it tasted. Standards don't exist out here.

I hobbled out of camp just after 7 and decided I needed some music to get me going. A Day to Remember and, of course, New Radicals got my legs pumping and before I knew it, I was flying. The goal for the day was 16.5 easy miles into the quaint town of Harpers Ferry, WV.

I didn't stop once. With about 9.5 miles left, I thought about stopping at the shelter to grab some water, but then I found a stash of sodas and bananas left by the side of the trail. I grabbed a soda and a banana and just kept trucking.

At 12:15 pm, I finally reached the side trail that led to the ATC (Appalachian Trail Conservancy) headquarters in Harpers Ferry, WV. Thru-hikers traditionally stop outside the headquarters and get their picture taken next to the sign. The picture is then stored in the ATC's records - I was hiker #564 passing through this unofficial halfway point.

However, before I stopped at the ATC, I went straight to the pizzeria down the street (Mena's Pizzeria) and ordered a large pepperoni pizza. While I waited for that, I picked up my package from the post office. Mom really outdid herself this time with venison jerky, Polish sausage, peanut butter cups, Taylor Ham, and more.

When I got back to the pizzeria, the waitress verified that I did, in fact, want a 'large' pizza. I assured her I was very hungry and then crushed the entire pie. She was visibly impressed, shocked, or disgusted. Maybe all three. I don't know and I don't care. It was delicious. Tim, the pizza count is up to 87.

Back at the ATC, I waited for the rest of my trail family. Steel's uncle, Cliff, was on his way into town and had reserved a three bedroom apartment for the four of us. This place was ridiculous - 3 bedrooms, 2.5 bathrooms, a deck overlooking the Potomac and Shenandoah rivers, and a genuine musket and bayonet that Peach used to great effect on the balcony to the amusement of restaurant patrons below.

Thankfully, Cliff arrived after we had all showered and completed laundry because we stunk. It had been 6 days since I showered and there have been no bodies of water to jump into. He treated us to breakfast foods from the grocery store for tomorrow morning's feast and then we headed to dinner at the Potomac Grill downstairs. Fish n chips hit the spot. Wine and sitcoms polished off a really nice afternoon. With two zeros to rest my knee and a visit from my long-time friend Ben Dudley to look forward to, this weekend was shaping up pretty nicely.

DAY 79

Starting Location: Harpers Ferry, WV (188 High Street)
Destination: Harpers Ferry, WV (188 High Street)
Today's Miles: 0
Trip Miles: 1023.1

Jun 11, 2016 - After an incredible night of sleep on the couch downstairs, the sunrise cast its rays through the window and woke me up. The breakfast feast was indeed a feast. Steel and I cooked up eggs, potatoes, bagels, bacon, Taylor ham, avocados, and orange juice with LOTS of pulp.

Ben showed up around noon and added some Duck Donuts to the smorgasbord. I ate 7, which I later regretted even though they were delicious. After catching up over a few beers, we caught lunch at Coach House Grill just below and down the street from our ritzy apartment. Lauren, Ben's friend from work joined us for some Grown Up Grilled Cheese sandwiches.

Ben graciously drove me to Wal-Mart to get a few supplies and beer for shenanigans later that night (Cliff was totally on board). My mustache is rapidly growing wild and needs to be tamed before somebody gets hurt. I picked up some Old Spice 'stache wax to help me in this monumental task. The beard is filling in nicely and needs no further direction.

Ice cream from the Coffee Mill followed Wal-Mart and we ate as we walked around the town a bit. Harpers Ferry, WV sits on a small hill overlooking the Potomac and Shenandoah rivers. The two rivers join at the base of the hill and become the Potomac. Across the Shenandoah River is Virginia and across the Potomac River is Maryland - it's a beautiful and significant view as the town was a strategic holding during the Civil War.

Naturally, I went swimming in the river, which was incredibly refreshing on the sunny, humid, 90+ degree day. The current was surprisingly strong so I had to anchor myself against a rock to prevent myself from drifting downstream.

The rest of the afternoon was spent doing nothing as a good zero demands. We ordered pizza for dinner and then cleared a spot in the apartment for shenanigans - Tim, the pizza count is at 95 slices. I did work this weekend.

For shenanigans, I had the pleasure of teaching everyone how to play relay race, the greatest drinking game ever played. Relay race helped prep us for a party down the street at Tumbleweed's house. At the party (this place was true hiker trash - 20+ packs littered the porch. The excess of food and beer at this place was alarming and the house was a mess.) we met a few new people: Duckbat, Brief Thief, Admiral, Happy Feet, Shotgun, Pockets, Odie (the hiker yearbook guy), Frodo (yes, he was carrying a ring and yes, he is going to "cast it into the fires of Katahdin from whence it came"), and Tank.

Peach and I stayed long enough to crush two teams in beer pong before we headed back around midnight.

DAY 80

Starting Location: Harpers Ferry, WV (188 High Street)
Destination: Harpers Ferry, WV (188 High Street)
Today's Miles: 0
Trip Miles: 1023.1

Jun 12, 2016 - This morning was a repeat of yesterday's breakfast feast minus the Taylor ham (happy, Tim? You have to understand that as a New Jersey resident I am an ambassador for Taylor Ham to the rest of the unfortunate country that is deprived of such goodness. It is, in fact, pork roll, so that is what I call it out here. Of course I call it Taylor ham when I order it at home.).

When I say the rest of the day was spent doing absolutely nothing, I mean it. I sat in the air conditioning and watched three movies and eventually game 6 of the Stanley Cup Finals. While I missed most of the playoffs, the hockey gods were merciful enough to present the Stanley Cup on a day when I was in town and in front of the television. I only left the apartment to obtain ice cream (this happened several times during the day – the half gallon challenge was later this week and I wanted to be prepared) and grab a few beers with Steel and Cliff down the street.

Peach made some pulled pork in the crock pot so we made sandwiches complete with coleslaw, macaroni salad, cheese, and barbecue sauce. In the crock pot, Peach just wrapped the pork in foil and turned it once throughout the day. I'll have to remember that because it just doesn't get any easier.

After an extremely restful weekend, I was definitely ready to get back on trail.

DAY 81

Starting Location: Harpers Ferry, WV (188 High Street)
Destination: Pine Knob Shelter
Today's Miles: 22.9
Trip Miles: 1046

Jun 13, 2016 - I needed to get to Boiling Springs, PA (mile 1023) by next Friday for two very important reasons: I was finally getting my replacement JacksrBetter quilt (it's been a painful process thanks to the post office - however, Jack has been more than accommodating) and I was receiving my replacement pack from Boreas. A few days ago, the internal frame on my Boreas pack crumbled. I gave Boreas a call and, once they understood that I was thru-hiking, they told me to email the manager. I explained my situation to Amanda and she immediately said she would send me a new one - no further questions asked. I'm ecstatic. Both Jack and Amanda will be receiving thank you postcards.

This meant an average of 20 miles a day until Friday. My goal for the day was 22.9 miles to Pine Knob Shelter. The terrain looked pleasant, the weather was gorgeous (sunny, 75 and breezy) and I had no knee pain for the first time in almost 400 miles. I'm not sure if it was the rest, the stretches and exercises I've been doing, the IT band brace my Mom sent me or a combination of all three, but I don't care. It was a glorious feeling as I once again bounded up, down and over the terrain. As we approach the infamously rocky PA portion of the trail, the number of rocks on trail has noticeably increased. Consequently, my shoes are rapidly deteriorating and my feet are a bit more sore than usual at the end of the day, but I'm not complaining.

Peach, Scoober and I took our time as we enjoyed the beautiful day. The first few miles were on a flat stretch of trail along the edge of the Potomac River. On our left, was a series of old, disused canals, which was certainly interesting.

Every time I stopped to pee or tie my shoe, Scoober would run back and stare at me with his tongue out until I started to move again. Then, he would immediately run back up trail. He obviously loves the pack mentality and it made me feel good to see him waiting for me.

A pleasant 22.9 miles later, we arrived at Pine Knob Shelter to find Husker and Great P with a nice fire going. Recently, Peach, Survivor and I have been carrying some extra cook wear with us. Peach carries the pizza pan we found at Tom Floyd Shelter, I carry a spatula and Survivor carries an oven mitt. However, Survivor has been showing up to camp very late, which creates issues when we try to cook quesadillas and various meats. Tonight, we lost a piece of Taylor Ham because we couldn't get the pan off the fire quickly enough. Loss of such a life demanded that Survivor immediately have his oven mitt privileges taken away until he could prove to be more responsible with his time.

Steel, Survivor, Tumbleweed, Splinter, Boyardee, Jingle, and Sweets joined us shortly for a pretty nice night by the campfire. We were also treated to some free entertainment - Great P spent nearly 20 minutes trying to hang his bear bag after telling us how good he was. When he finally got it over a tree branch, he realized the rope was too short. He opted to hop onto our bear bag line, but when we were pulling the bags up over a large, healthy limb, the entire limb snapped off and came crashing down. We all barely got out of the way. This is the fourth time someone has almost been crushed by a falling tree limb. Who would have known hanging a bear bag would be probably the most dangerous thing we do out here.

DAY 82

Starting Location: Pine Knob Shelter
Destination: Falls Creek Campsite
Today's Miles: 18.6
Trip Miles: 1064.6

Jun 14, 2016 - Steel, Survivor, Peach, Scoober and I got moving early again this morning so we could make coffee and share breakfast together at the Annapolis Rocks overlook about 1.5 miles north of the Pine Knob Shelter. The view on this gorgeous, clear and cool day was worth it and definitely made the coffee taste a little better.

Peach, Scoober and I made quick work of the remaining miles and arrived at Pen Mar County Park. Legs had sent me a text saying her Mom, Goldberry, was doing Trail Magic there. (By the way, I realized recently that Legs has a Trail Journals blog also: trailjournals.com/loon if you'd like to check it out.) Verge and Legs are a hell of a lot of fun and I really hope we stay in the same bubble for many more miles. Their parents, Goldberry and Bombadil were also hiking the trail this year. They had just passed mile 1200 when Goldberry needed to leave the trail to return to her job as a cardiac nurse. However, she was visiting Verge and Legs this week before she made her way back to Massachusetts. Oh and [Tom] Bombadil and Goldberry are hands down my favorite trail names out here - if you don't understand the reference, you're doing it wrong. Also, she actually referenced a 'babble fish' in normal conversation. Amazing. Again, if you don't get the reference, you're missing out.)

Anyway, Goldberry was offering up chips, fresh strawberries, sweet potatoes, and sodas while she slack packed Legs and Verge. Another woman, Vicki 'The Real Deal' had found Legs' blog and also showed up to compound the Trail Magic we were receiving. She brought fresh apple pie and fudge (and some weed for those that smoked), which was out of this world. Goldberry also gave a few of us a ride to Wal-Mart to grab garlic bread and s'mores for the campfire later that night.

Another mile along the trail and we crossed the Mason-Dixon Line into Pennsylvania (6 states down!) which was pretty cool considering how much history is intertwined with this boundary. All in all, we hiked 18.6 miles to the Falls Creek campsite where, of course, I swam in the river (more like assuming the push up position and dunking myself under) and got a nice campfire going. We played some Coup (a card game Ben left with me) and ate to our heart's content.

Hot Toddy was also at the Falls Creek Campsite - it was the first time we had seen her since the break-up. She definitely made it a little awkward by conspicuously staying away from the campfire, but Peach, to his credit, was perfectly civil to her.

DAY 83

Starting Location: Falls Creek Campsite
Destination: Quarry Gap Shelters
Today's Miles: 19.9
Trip Miles: 1084.5

Jun 15, 2016 – I woke up around 6 again and packed up my stuff. It was perfect timing as it started to rain just as I pulled the drawstring on my pack. Peach, Scoober and I hiked through a few hours of rain, which wasn't too bad. Peach did, however, start to chafe pretty badly. I have been lucky to not experience chafing on the trail yet, but it sounds awful. Around mile 100, I had considered discarding my Gold Bond into a hiker box, but Peach said, "Never get rid of Gold Bond". Nearly 1,000 miles later, I gave him my unused slick stick and he applied liberally. Funny how that works out. However, I would now have to pick up another slick stick because that is one pack item that cannot be shared. Once chafing sets in, that slick stick gets rubbed in and around the most disgusting parts of the body without pause.

The morning had us scrambling over some pretty challenging boulder fields until we hit a road crossing about 15 miles in. We struck west and arrived at a small lunch place for some cheesesteak and burgers. While there, I checked my phone and discovered Legs had informed me of Goldberry's Trail Magic round 2 at Caledonia State Park a half mile north. There we added hot dogs to our stomachs, played some more Coup and shared stories for a while.

Scoober started barking and for good reason. Moonshine had finally caught us! Ironically, he was being picked up by his Dad for his second off trail excursion that same evening, but it was still great to see him and catch up for a while.

Two miles north on the trail brought us to Quarry Gap Shelters, which was nicer than my Mom's gardens. Flowers hung from the shelter and magazines, games and a swinging bench were at our disposal and a spring was directly in front of the structure. It was maintained beautifully and ranks up there with Overmountain and Partnerships shelters. Peach attached a piece of paper to the wall with a fake WIFI and password to drive other hikers crazy.

Tomorrow, we cross the AT midpoint and attempt the Half Gallon Challenge!

DAY 84

Starting Location: Quarry Gap Shelters
Destination: Campsite north of Pine Grove Furnace State Park
Today's Miles: 19.6
Trip Miles: 1104.1

Jun 16, 2016 - It started to pour when I woke up this morning around 6. JJ Don't Play was already gone - he really doesn't play around. His hike must be lonely though seeing as he doesn't stick around long enough to get to know anyone due to his consistently long days.

Peach and I took our time making coffee and chatting with Tumbleweed (notorious for peeing out of his tent without getting out), Jingle, Husker, Buff and Little Red. We didn't leave camp until the rain stopped around 8. However, we walked quickly today knowing the Half Gallon Challenge awaited us. The sky threatened rain all day, but, luckily, we managed to avoid literally all of it.

Around 17 miles into our hike, we entered Pine Grove Furnace State Park - home of the Half Gallon Challenge. Thru-hikers traditionally purchase a half gallon of ice cream and attempt to eat it all in one sitting. Oddly enough, the general store doesn't really care about the challenge at all - all they do is accept money in exchange for ice cream, have a notebook on the counter for hikers to sign and allow hikers to grab a small wooden spoon with a pitiful stamp on it saying "Member of Half Gallon Club". They don't even keep the spoons behind the counter so any hiker that fails the challenge can still take one.

Anyway, I chose chocolate chip cookie dough for my challenge and completed it easily, to be totally honest. I proceeded to order chicken fingers and fries afterwards. The ice cream alone was 2850 calories so, needless to say, I ate a lot. The only person to fail the challenge was Tumbleweed and yes, we gave him a lot of crap for it. Husker was on point with Eye of the Tiger whenever someone had a few bites left. Great P actually ran over to the grass - we thought he was going to throw up, but he merely slammed the empty carton against the ground triumphantly.

I don't know if I've explained my spoon issues yet, but I broke my 9th spoon (I lost some, too) on trail today on the still frozen ice cream. This includes plastic spoons, wooden baking spoons and a homemade spoon that I actually carved out with hot coals from the fire. Until I could obtain a metal spoon, my solution was to purchase a pack of 24 heavy duty plastic spoons from the General Store for my pack.

Peach and I tried to wait for Steel and Survivor, but after nearly 5 hours, we needed to hike the remaining 2.5 miles to our campsite. Our schedules are completely off so I haven't hiked with Survivor in several days.

As I set up camp tonight, I was so hot, sweaty, and filthy that I had a difficult time accepting it mentally. It's only been 4 days without a shower or laundry, but the humidity from the last two days has been stifling despite the fact that the sun hasn't even been shining. My situation is bound to get worse as the summer approaches. During moments like tonight, I can either freak out or just calm down and accept how gross I am. I just tell myself that it can and will get much worse. Even as the rain pelts my tent, I remind myself how much fun I'm having, how beautiful and comfortable the woods are even in a thunderstorm, and that I could be setting my alarm for work in an office building tomorrow. If this experience is teaching me anything, it's to appreciate the moment where you are no matter the circumstances.

WE ALL SLAYED THE HALF-GALLON CHALLENGE!

DAY 85

Starting Location: Campsite north of Pine Grove Furnace State Park
Destination: Backpacker's Campsite / Boiling Springs, PA
Today's Miles: 16.5
Trip Miles: 1120.6

Jun 17, 2016 – The morning began with a liquid rich crap in a muddy hole. Other than that, we had a pretty easy and pretty boring 16.9 miles into Boiling Springs, PA. Jingle joined Peach, Scoober and I for most of the day.

The terrain did present a smaller, rockier version of the roller coaster that I hiked hungover after my 24 challenge. This one was much easier as I was feeling excellent. The roller coaster ended with the start of the blessedly flat Cumberland Valley that brought us through sunny fields lined with mulberry trees and wild strawberries (which are much much smaller than the strawberries you see in the grocery store).

While we thought Boiling Springs was named for a hot spring, it was actually named for around 30 natural springs that fed the large manmade lake in the center of town. The ice cold water was incredibly clear.

Just south of Boiling Springs was a campsite near the train tracks reserved for thru-hikers where I setup my tent. My chores were next: I went to the post office to pick up my new pack and quilt and to mail the damaged ones back to the manufacturer. Next up was a quick stop at the Boiling Springs Tavern for a beer, which was indescribably satisfying after walking through those hot fields. Jingle and I then walked to the grocery store for a resupply. However, on the way, we were blindsided by Benny's pizzeria – so we each crushed 4 barbecue chicken slices and then continued to the grocery store. It's never smart to shop hungry anyway especially with the appetite of a thru-hiker. Following the grocery store was a stop at the town pool for a $2 shower. Since it was Friday, the normally $12 pool access was knocked down to $5, which included a shower. That's a no brainer if I ever heard one. Jingle and I passed the next hour swimming and repeatedly going on all the legit water slides they had. Finally, I showered and returned to the campsite.

Goldberry, who left this morning for Massachusetts, had one more trick up her sleeve and surprised everyone by leaving more Trail Magic near the campsite in the form of cherries, cupcakes, chips and bubbles (as I continue to get to know the Harveys, the bubbles were very characteristic of their wonderfully unique personalities).

Tonight was Legs' 21st birthday party so all the hikers met up at the tavern for some drinks. The tavern was actually a very nice restaurant so I felt a bit ashamed of my footwear: one croc and one sandal (I lost a croc and bought a pair of sandals at the Goodwill in Front Royal. I threw one sandal away since I liked my crocs better. I figured one croc is better than none at all).I was actually stuffed for once so I didn't get any food, but had an excellent time socializing and celebrating.

On the walk back to the campsite, I accompanied Legs and Great P. As I've mentioned before, the social aspect of the trail is very similar to high school. This remained true as I listened to the gossip passing between Legs and Great P: apparently, Training Wheels had a falling out with her romantic interest, Treebeard, who we coincidentally saw night hiking with Slam a few moments later. Despite having not seen her in close to 1,000 miles, I was somehow excited to hear that Wheels and Treebeard weren't getting along. I also realized that Great P and Legs were looking for some time alone so I made myself scarce. They did, indeed, hook up that night.

DAY 86

Starting Location: Boiling Springs Campsite / Boiling Springs, PA
Destination: Duncannon, PA / Red Carpet Inn
Today's Miles: 26
Trip Miles: 1146.6

Jun 18, 2016 - Our original plan was to hike 25.6 miles from Boiling Springs to Duncannon today because Peach had a friend meeting him. His plans ended up falling through, but Duncannon was still the goal for the day.

Peach and I were up early as usual and continued traversing the Cumberland Valley, a 17 mile stretch of probably the flattest miles on the trail. We picked up large coffees in town and strolled through the woods with them on this warm, beautiful morning. We had no idea how long or crazy our day would be. It's funny watching Scoober in the morning because he has the same hiker hobble we all have - he'll basically limp for about 100 yards before his muscles start to operate as they're supposed to.

A few miles into our hike, we noticed a cooler and two chairs set out at the end of someone's driveway. Intrigued, we opened the cooler to find cold beers so we knew the seats were for us. Trail Magic! We sat there for a while, drank, signed the homeowner's logbook and even chatted with her for a while when she pulled into the driveway right next to us.

We continued hiking with our roadies until we came to the crossing for route 11. Our continued efforts to Brew Blaze whenever possible demanded that we hitch to the Appalachian Brewing Co. for a few beers. An older gentleman by the name of Don obliged us with a ride. The beers were pretty good, but the brewery reminded me of the Smoky Mountain Brewery in Gatlinburg - everything just felt too touristy.

We expected hitching back to the trail would prove to be much more difficult, but Corey and John quickly pulled over in their large, red pickup truck. When we climbed into the backseat, we had already started moving when we noticed they were both drinking beer since they had just left the Harley Davidson factory where they worked. These guys were crazy. They thought we stunk and they let us hear it. On the bright side, they did get us some more beer for the trail, but they stopped at their house first. At the time, we were convinced they went inside to do some drugs so Peach texted his friend the address of the house in case we were never heard from again. While we waited, John's kid came out of the front door with an aerosol pistol aimed at the car and approached. It turns out he was just fetching something from the bed, but this was starting to get surreal.

Corey and John finally brought us back to trail, forced some pretzels on us and peeled away with fresh beers in the center console. As soon as I hit the trail head, I realized I forgot my phone in their car. Shit. I'll have to deal with that later.

Also at the trailhead were Steel and Survivor who had finally caught up. We hiked a short way and ran into Splinter, Boyardee and Great P next to the Juniata River. Since it was so hot, we all stripped down and sat in the shallow river while we watched Scoober chase rocks through the water. The water was clean and refreshing.

When we had cooled down sufficiently, Peach, Scoober and I hiked the remaining 12 miles or so into the center of Duncannon. The Doyle hotel in the center of town is famous as far as the trail is concerned. Known for their excellent food and drinks, the hotel itself was known in a much more negative manner. The place was run down with broken windows, no AC, exposed electric wiring, and sagging, leaking ceilings. Seeing as it looked like some of the abandoned buildings near where I used to live in the ghetto of Jersey City, I had no desire to stay there. For the same price, we grabbed two adjoining rooms at the Red Carpet Inn up the road. It was the first time I paid for lodging in almost 500 miles, but it was necessary.

Peach, Scoober and I rolled into the Doyle around 8:30, which was, unfortunately, after they stopped serving food. We did get a Yuengling to soothe our parched throats and restore some life into our tired limbs. A few other hikers were there also: Jelly, Croc, Olive Oil, Treebeard, Slam, and Tink Tank.

When Steel and Survivor arrived, we crossed the road to the only open eating place left in town: Sorrento's pizzeria. As usual, I ordered a pie and crushed it. The pizza up here is finally similar to New York style so I can't get enough. Tim, I'm up to 107 slices.

Finally, we caught a ride to the hotel and after a glorious shower, I passed out on the floor. Scoober took up too much of the bed for me to be comfortable.

Looking back, today was incredibly long and we did so much. Sometimes, it feels like we're living lifetimes inside moments out here.

DAY 87

Starting Location: Duncannon, PA / Red Carpet Inn
Destination: Clarks Creek Campsite
Today's Miles: 16.1
Trip Miles: 1162.7

Jun 19, 2016 - I woke up and started watching Hoosiers on the television. It looked as if it was going to be another scorcher today so it was tough to leave the comfort of the air conditioned room. Peach and I shared a load of laundry - thank God.

My first order of business today was to recover my phone. The phone itself isn't a big deal, but all the pictures, contacts and journal entries that hadn't been backed up were invaluable. I called Trail Angel Mary who lived in town to see if she could help me. She agreed to drive me 30 minutes back to Corey and John's house to find my phone. It would cost $35, but seeing as a cab would have been close to $80 and a new phone probably around $200, I was happy to pay her for helping me fix my mistake.

Mary pulled up in front of the hotel in her van very reminiscent of Miss Janet's. We drove back to Mechanicsburg to the house Find My iPhone directed us to. I knocked on the door and found John and Corey sitting on the couch. They had my phone and it was fully charged. Corey had a pretty nice shiner on his face that was not there yesterday...I didn't ask. While they seemed totally ready to give it back to me, it was a little puzzling that they neglected to look at the clearly visible message on the home screen that told them to call Peach's number if they found the phone. Regardless, I got the phone back and all was well with the world again.

Mary brought me back to the center of town around noon and I immediately resumed hiking north. The trail wound about a mile through town until it went over the Juniata and Susquehanna Rivers. I walked the mile through town and just as I approached the bridge, I realized the actual trail had made a left some distance back and was actually on the street parallel to the one I was on. A battle raged in my head - as a purist, I needed to go all the way back to the Doyle and follow the trail correctly. It would have eaten away at me otherwise. So, grudgingly, I turned around and hiked another mile back to town in the sweltering midday sun to retrace my steps and pick up the trail. As much as it sucked, I'm glad I did it because I have still seen every damn blaze on this trail and it's going to stay that way.

Anyway, I continued hiking up the hill that led out of town and walked along the ridge line for a while. Survivor and Steel stopped at the shelter a few miles back - I didn't know it then, but that would be the last time I saw the two of them for the rest of the trail.

A gentleman in town had suggested a stealth campsite near Clarks Creek. Rather than stop at the campsite near the spring, Peach, Scoober and I pushed on another mile and forded Clarks Creek to a cool, little section of land surrounded by the creek on three sides. I setup my tent on a bed of pine needles (my favorite), Peach got a fire going to ward off the bugs, and I dunked myself in the stream to cool down. The campsite was unique and was well worth the extra mile.

DAY 88

Starting Location: Clarks Creek Campsite
Destination: Stealth Campsite south of PA 72
Today's Miles: 17.6
Trip Miles: 1180.3

Jun 20, 2016 – Due to the combination of the workload and the heat of the past two days, I managed to sleep until nearly 7 this morning. The morning was actually cool so it just felt so good to stay under my warm, down quilt. A fisherman was only about 20 yards away casting his line into the creek.

I had a relaxed breakfast and started up the first hill of the day. There were only two today, but with a high of 91 degrees, I was not looking forward to either of them. All three of us pushed 16 miles without stopping to another stealth campsite near a stream. Personally, I would camp near a stream every single night in the summer if I could. Rinsing my body off and cooling down in the water is immensely satisfying at the end of the day.

While we walked along yet another ridge line, I heard Peach start to run and call for Scoober to follow him. A Timber rattlesnake was in the bushes just off trail and Peach was trying to get Scoober away. I saw the rattler sticking into the trail a bit so I just walked around the snake and continued without any trouble. It was the first rattlesnake I've ever seen.

We arrived at the campsite around 2 in the afternoon which meant we had about 7 hours until the sun set. We got a fire going to ward off the bugs and just lounged around honestly. Scoober really needed the rest - while he appears happy and full of energy during the hike, he's basically dead when we stop for camp. At one point, with Scoober completely sprawled on the ground, Peach called him to come near the fire and eat some food. He merely looked up, slowly widened his eyes as if to say, "What have you done to me?!" and then fell back down into his prone position.

Croc, Joker, Journeyman, Backscratcher, Can Do and Boyardee joined us throughout the day. Croc, Peach and I swam in the creek for a while and then played some Coup, that card game that Ben left me in Harpers Ferry.

DAY 89

Starting Location: Stealth Campsite south of PA 72
Destination: Hertline Campsite
Today's Miles: 18.4
Trip Miles: 1198.7

Jun 21, 2016 - Although the summer solstice, the point at which Earth's northern hemisphere is tilted most toward the sun during its orbit, was officially yesterday, thru-hikers generally celebrate this event on June 21. How do we celebrate? We traditionally hike completely naked for at least a portion of the day. I didn't actually know this, but June 21 is actually known as National Hike Naked Day.

It was an odd morning. I changed into my hiking clothes, but then prior to leaving camp, took them all back off and hung them on my pack. And then I just started walking...naked. I did between 3 and 4 miles with no clothes on, which is very uncomfortable by the way. I fell once resulting in a nice raspberry on my butt, but unfortunately (or fortunately...I'll let you decide) I didn't run into any other hikers. The only people I saw were two cars driving in opposite directions at a road crossing. I simply waited for the cars to pass and noted the shocked look on the drivers' faces. It was hysterical.

Peach and I set the phone up on a timer to catch an image of our smooth / hairy backsides, respectively, before putting our clothes back on. The timer was activated by yelling "Cheese" and Scoober, who had no idea what was going on started barking and freaking out during every attempt.

When we finally captured a suitable photo (Scoober had to be tied to a tree before this was possible), Peach and I resumed our hike. Again, the ridgeline hike was very uneventful and much the same as most of the days in PA. This entire state has been just hiking across the top of rocky, flat ridges with the occasional down and up associated with the transfer to from one ridge to another.

NO CAPTION NECESSARY

About halfway through the day, we stopped at the 501 Shelter, one of the more sophisticated shelters on trail with a shower, board games and a pizza delivery service.

I felt guilty about ordering a pizza until it was in my mouth. It was so worth it. I even packed out a few slices for dinner.

After 18.4 miles, Peach and I called it quits at the "Hertline Campsite and picnic table". There was no picnic table, but there was an unmarked swimming hole with a rope swing that was damned up. The water was super clean even though there was some type of sediment clouding it up. Of course, I rinsed off, but I couldn't shake the feeling that the creature from the Lake Placid movie was about to emerge from the eerily still water.

Once the campfire was going, Journeyman, Olive Oil and Hawaii joined us for a relatively quiet night. The heat of the day dissipated and a cool breeze made sleep incredibly enjoyable.

DAY 90

Starting Location: Hertline Campsite
Destination: Pavilion at Port Clinton, PA
Today's Miles: 18.5
Trip Miles: 1217.2

Jun 22, 2016 - Another early morning had us hiking before 7 - we had a ton of fun stuff to fit into this day. Another easy, yet annoying 18.5 miles along a flat, rocky ridge line brought us to Port Clinton, PA. The descent into the town of Port Clinton was so steep that I needed to walk sideways to avoid sliding down the mountain. I saw two section hikers at the bottom and simply wished them good luck because the ascent must have been hell.

Port Clinton, PA is an incredibly small town with an unusual assortment of shops. For instance, they had an old school barber shop, a post office, a hotel / bar, a fire house, two car dealerships, and a candy store. That's it. Hikers hang out at the barber shop where Frank and Rocco provide cookies, coffee and somewhere to sit. When I say old school, I mean this barber shop is straight out of the 1920s. There was an old man playing live music when I first walked in. A simple men's haircut took nearly 45 minutes because the barbers talked so much. It was a very unique place.

I checked out the candy shop, but quickly realized I needed to leave before I spent $100 on the goodies in there. I just couldn't handle the amount of amazing, homemade candy and I wanted everything.

Peach, Napster, Michael and I got a ride from one of the barber shop's customers to nearby Hamburg, PA for food, a visit to the largest Cabelas in the world and a resupply. The Cabelas, which I've been to before, is extravagance personified. This place has an entire taxonomist display of animals, an aquarium, a restaurant, and a fudge shop where I purchased three blocks of delicious fudge.

Dinner was a Chinese buffet, which should speak for itself. After a quick resupply, a stranger gave us some Hot Pockets. Then, Peach and I caught a ride from Rebel Yell, who actually thru-hiked the trail last year, to Peace Rock. Peace Rock is a 40 foot cliff jump near Port Clinton. It was right up there with the James River footbridge as far as cliff jumps go, but much more crowded. When Peach jumped, Scoober literally flipped out and had a breakdown - his face so clearly said, "What the hell just happened?" Then, he sniffed around looking for him until he just sat down and started whimpering.

Our original plan was to camp near Peace Rock, but since it was so crowded and the area was very dirty (as are most of these types of places, unfortunately), we walked back to town along the train tracks. We were sidetracked at the bar where we shared a beer with Journeyman. Journeyman is 63 years old and will be spending some time off trail with his wife so this would be the last we'd see of him.

After an already overloaded, enjoyable day, Peach and I finally made it to the Pavilion at the north end of town. This was simply a pavilion situated next to the river that hikers were allowed to use as a shelter. Somebody had left a box full of Trail Magic there for us to enjoy and I splurged on the Double Stuf Oreos. Joining us at the Pavilion was Training Wheels (finally), who I hadn't seen since Hot Springs, Jingle, Sweets, Great P, Boyardee, Splinter, and Even Keel. Everybody caught up for a while over a few six packs and slowly made their way to the Pavilion for bed.

It turns out that Peach and I had somehow passed Training Wheels at some point along the trail. After her supposed falling out with Treebeard, she hiked 37 miles in anger and caught up to us. Thank you, Treebeard.

DAY 91

Starting Location: Pavilion at Port Clinton, PA
Destination: Cowboy Camping on The Pinnacle
Today's Miles: 9.5
Trip Miles: 1226.7

Jun 23, 2016 - Hiking was not the first event on the agenda today - Yuengling Brewery had that honor. Peach, Training Wheels, Jingle and I would be touring the oldest brewery in America. As it turned out, the brewery was just the beginning of another ridiculously enjoyable day.

A shuttle picked us up at the Pavilion around 8:30, but not before we watched the largest black bear I've seen on trail so far moseying around the lawn before he retreated towards the privy. Luckily no one was taking care of business at the same - imagine wiping your dirty ass and then opening the door to find a black bear staring you in the face...

Pottsville, the home of Yuengling's first brew house, was a quick 30 minute drive. We had some time to kill before our 11 am tour so we enjoyed coffee and a small breakfast at the Sage coffee house down the street. I finally learned a bit about Wheels and her graduate studies in music therapy. She was between semesters and though hiking the Appalachian Trail would be a good idea.

JINGLE, TRAINING WHEELS, PEACH AND I AT YUENGLING BREWERY

When the brewery tour started, our tour guide walked us across the street from the gift shop and opened an old, large sliding door that led down into a dark cave below the brew house that extended into the side of the mountain. At that moment, the tour became the coolest brewery tour I've ever been on, although Dogfish Head in Delaware remains a close runner up. Since Yuengling has used this particular brew house since 1831, the hand dug cave was used to store the beer at a constant 52 degrees. Moreover, the natural spring at the back supplied the water used to make the beer. Keg machines and barrels over 100 years old littered the floor of the cave and served to preserve Yuengling's history. I won't get into all the details, but, suffice it to say, I was a satisfied customer. Brew Blazing!

With the tour over and several beers in my belly, the shuttle returned us to Port Clinton so we could resume what we all came out here to do. But wait...just 5 miles in, Tom Coughlan and Matt Georgov, two good friends from the University of Delaware, met me on the trail for some Trail Magic and to do some hiking. I was a little late so I literally ran some of the 5 miles uphill and realized that I am in fantastic shape. I don't mean to brag, but I was all out leaping up boulders with a 30 lb pack on like it was a stroll in the park. It felt good.

Tom and Georgov killed it with regards to the Trail Magic: 6 Little Caesar's pizzas (they alone understand the nostalgia those crappy pizzas bring back from my college days), Klondike Kate's wings (still my favorite wings ever and the greatest gift they could have brought me), toilet paper, a metal spoon, baby wipes, a Life Straw, chips, ice cold beers, and jerky. A bunch of hikers stopped by and were able to enjoy the magic also.

Both Tom and Georgov were a bit appalled by how badly I smelled. It was pretty funny - as soon as the hikers started touching the food, they were done. They clearly stood upwind of us and did not touch anything that had been touched by a hiker. Tom attempted to try my pack on, but couldn't get his second arm through the shoulder strap before the smell forced him to put the pack down. We are filthy human beings out here and they finally understand how filthy, I think.

When all the food and beer was gone, Tom and Georgov joined me for a 4 mile hike up the rocky incline to the Pinnacle, a rock outcropping overlooking. It was dark by the time we reached the top and I was little afraid they would have trouble finding their car again since the terrain was pretty difficult, but everything turned out wonderfully. Thanks again for coming, guys - all Trail Magic aside, it really means a lot for you to drive all the way out here to see me and I appreciate the hell out of it.

There weren't really any good camping spots up at the Pinnacle, so Legs, Great P (the sexual tension between these 2 was palpable), Peach and I cowboy camped right there on the rocks maybe 2 feet from the cliff's edge. The breeze coming off the cliffs was incredibly comfortable and kept the bugs away. If the weather cooperated, we were in for a fantastic sunrise tomorrow morning.

DAY 92

Starting Location: Cowboy Camping on The Pinnacle
Destination: Bethlehem, PA / Lehigh Furnace Gap
Today's Miles: 25.1
Trip Miles: 1251.8

Jun 24, 2016 - We were indeed treated to an absolutely ridiculous sunrise this morning. All we did was sit up in our sleeping bags and watch the warm sun crest the horizon.

Princess Peach lived in Bethlehem, PA for 2 years and planned on taking a zero there tomorrow. He invited me. I accepted. That meant 25.1 miles to Lehigh Furnace Gap by 4 pm where my Dad would pick us up and take us to Bethlehem. Plus, this way I could see my Dad for the first time in 3 months and catch up over a rare steak.

The hike itself sucked. The first 12 miles was just an endless pile of rocks - it put me in a very bad mood that only increased every time I slipped or had a jagged rock stick into my foot. I would pick up sticks and smash them against trees as an outlet for my frustration and to provide a distraction from the painful monotony of the rocks. To add insult to injury, my only water stop for the day was a 0.3 mile walk straight downhill over more rocks to a buggy, stagnant spring.

For the second half of my hike, I put my headphones in and 'Hakuna Matata' was the third song on shuffle. Before you know it, I'm through the entire Lion King soundtrack and onto the Frozen soundtrack. I can't help but be in a good mood listening to Disney.

Peach and I stopped briefly at a restaurant immediately next to the trail for a beer and then continued on only to find Trail Magic 3 miles from Lehigh Furnace Gap. The Allentown Hiking Club was out with burgers, dogs, snacks, desserts, supplies and good conversation. Scoober, though he too enjoyed some hot dogs, seemed to just give up and lay comatose on the ground. When Peach tried to get him moving again, he wouldn't get up until Peach started to leave. He too was defeated by the heat and the rocks.

I met Dad at the gap and gave him a big hug – it was good to see him again. We went to Emeril's steak house in Bethlehem that night where I downed the porterhouse. After dinner, Dad headed back home and I went out with Peach at Joe's on the north side of town.

DAY 93

Starting Location: Bethlehem, PA / Lehigh Furnace Gap
Destination: Bethlehem, PA / Lehigh Furnace Gap
Today's Miles: 0
Trip Miles: 1251.8

Jun 25, 2016 – I actually opted to sleep outside last night since Leah's apartment was so hot. Little did I know that a woman in a neighboring apartment started laughing the most horrible laugh I've ever heard...and it never stopped. I was forced to move inside to the floor in an attempt to get some more sleep.

When I woke up at 10, I was still exhausted. Peach and I walked over to the steel stacks that make Bethlehem famous. A few years back, the town installed a catwalk that allowed people to walk past the steel stacks and learn about their history. Up close, the massive operation was fascinating and trying to picture the steel mills in action was pretty tough. The rest of the area had been turned into a nonprofit music stage, which regularly hosted artists for the town's pleasure. The balance the city struck by preserving the history of the steel stacks and simultaneously turning the area into a social gathering place is unique and very enjoyable.

Peach's old roommate, Hudson, gave us a ride to the nearby LL Bean so Peach could finally replace his trail runners after 1251 miles. He managed to get new shoes for only $30 since they were still under the 6 month warranty. It's kind of backwards seeing as they outlasted their expected use by about 800 miles, but it is what it is.

The rest of the afternoon was spent bar hopping around the north side of the city and meeting Peach's various friends. We hit up McCarthy's, Fegley's Bethlehem Brew Works, and Joe's. The Brew Blazing continues.

Following the bar tour, we headed back to Leah's apartment for a Mario Kart tournament. I was not very happy with my performance and I'll just leave it at that.

Tim, after this weekend, I'm up to 131 pizza slices.

DAY 94

Starting Location: Bethlehem, PA / Lehigh Furnace Gap
Destination: Leroy A. Smith Shelter
Today's Miles: 21.1
Trip Miles: 1272.9

Jun 26, 2016 - From Lehigh Furnace Gap, I was a mere 42 miles from the Delaware Water Gap and the PA - NJ border. Leah gave us a ride back to Lehigh Furnace Gap and Peach and I resumed hiking at midmorning on a clear day with temperatures well into the 90s. Scoober was sent back home because he was clearly miserable and showing no signs of improving - "dead" was still a relatively accurate term.

About 5 miles into our hike, we crossed the Lehigh River in Palmerton. On the bridge, I looked up and saw a sheer rock face littered with boulders. This rock face was the Palmerton Superfund site - years ago, a nearby zinc smelting site incurred an environmental disaster that killed all of the vegetation on this particular section of the mountain. The result was a vertical boulder field that proved to be a challenging, but very enjoyable climb. Several sections required the use of my hands as well as my feet so I would throw my trekking poles up over a few boulders and then climb up to retrieve them. While we would have preferred to have hiked this at any other time than the hottest portion of the day, you won't hear any complaints from me. Peach and I sipped beers he packed out as we surveyed the surrounding lands from what felt like the top of the world.

The next four miles of the hike were completely exposed to the sun. Multiple blackberry bushes helped me get over the heat as I gorged on the small, fresh fruits. Water, on the other hand, was scarce - the environmental disaster had contaminated the few water sources near the Palmerton site and the two springs later in the hike were unreliable and, consequently, not worth the long deviation from trail. All of this meant 21.1 miles of hiking on the 4 liters of water I packed out from Bethlehem. Needless to say, I was parched when I finally reached the Leroy A. Smith Shelter, though heartened by the sign that said only 20.2 miles to the Delaware Water Gap.

Between the hot sun, the lack of water and the fact that I hiked over 21 miles along rocky terrain, bedtime was well before the sun set tonight. I still hung by the fire for a bit and chatted with two thru-hikers from last year who were just out for the night. Of course, this was mostly with the hope that they would toss me some food (I felt like a dog waiting for my owner to toss me a biscuit), but they did turn out to be pretty interesting.

DAY 95

Starting Location: Leroy A. Smith Shelter
Destination: Delaware Water Gap, PA / Stealth Campsite south
of Hiker Parking Lot
Today's Miles: 20.1
Trip Miles: 1293

Jun 27, 2016 - Another rocky, miserable 20.7 miles along the ridge line brought me to the top of Mt. Minsi overlooking Route 80 and the Delaware River. I won't go into any more specifics regarding the hike - suffice it to say that it was hot, painfully rocky and dry. My shoes were utterly destroyed. The soles were literally flapping with every step and my right heel had a hole completely through the sole that you could stick your finger through.

Across the river, I could see one of my favorite mountains - Mt. Tammany. I had hiked 1294 miles from Georgia and had finally reached my home state of New Jersey. The feelings coursing through me as I gazed upon the familiar features of home were intensely nostalgic and stimulating. The subsequent adrenaline rush was all consuming and I couldn't contain it any longer. As soon as I saw a pair of day hikers, I couldn't help but blurt out my accomplishment, which is honestly very unlike me.

Anyway, tomorrow I would be going home to my parent's house, but tonight a bunch of thru-hikers were walking down into the town of Delaware Water Gap, PA for a few drinks at the Sycamore Grill. Training Wheels, Boyardee, Splinter, Peach, Treebeard (unfortunately, Training

Wheels was openly flirting Treebeard even though he very clearly was not having it), Waterfall, Olive Oil, Legs, Verge, and Sweets all ordered some food and libations. We all stayed and socialized for a mere 7 hours or so. Happy hour really helped us out with $2.25 Yuenglings. I had intended to order dinner in the restaurant, but I spied a stack of black and white cookies behind the bar before I had a chance to place my order. By the end of the night, dinner had been forgotten - I consumed all four black and white cookies comprising that stack. It was good to be home.

Get-togethers like this are my favorite part of the AT experience. The trail is unavoidably a social experience and it's the people that make it what it is. Others may not associate restaurants or bars with what is 'supposed' to be a quiet, remote hike through some of the most natural areas on the east coast, but, a thru-hike, just like everything else in life, is all about balance. I've come to appreciate all aspects of the Appalachian Trail and that includes the people, the relationships and the communities surrounding it.

DAY 96

Starting Location: Delaware Water Gap, PA / Stealth Campsite south of Hiker Parking Lot
Destination: Pequannock, NJ (Home) / Kitattiny Visitor Center
Today's Miles: 1.3
Trip Miles: 1294.3

Jun 28, 2016 - An extremely short walk through the town of Delaware Water Gap brought me to the bridge that crosses the Delaware River into New Jersey. Just like yesterday, some crazy feelings were coursing through me as I crossed the border into my home state after hiking 1294 miles from Georgia.

Mom and Courtney (and my godson, Chase) drove to the Kitattiny Visitor Center to pick me up and a few other thru-hikers for a nero at my house. Originally, I had told my Mom it would probably just be Peach and I. But, gradually, that number grew to 6 hikers, then to 8, then to 10 and finally to 11 - let's just say things escalated quickly. Needless to say, my Mom was freaking as usual and was worried she didn't have enough food. Plus, her dryer had broken literally yesterday - isn't that ironic?

So, we managed to cram 11 hikers (myself, Princess Peach, Training Wheels, Sweets, Olive Oil, Treebeard, Waterfall, Boyardee, Splinter, Great P and Jingle) and all of our packs into two cars for the hour long ride back to the house. Everything had worked out perfectly so far.

The rest of the afternoon was spent tackling the smorgasbord of homemade and fresh food - cookies, brownies, cake, fruit, cinnamon rolls, bagels, burgers, dogs, ribs, kielbasa and kraut, grilled veggies, lasagna - and a cooler full of beer. My Mom really outdid herself as she washed all of our clothes and offered showers to everyone. Her peak came when she found out it was Boyardee's birthday. Boyardee insisted he didn't like the texture of a classic cake so my Mom went out and bought him an ice cream cake. Mom - 1, Boyardee - 0.

We all swam, played a few beer games and did nothing all day, which is exactly what a nero should be. My friends from home even stopped by after work and really capped off an amazing day. Tim, Jacquie, Sean, Johnny Steyh, Paula, Kunj (he brought me his Mom's homemade Dhokla, a delicious Indian dish - hell yea!), and Steve surprised me with visits and argued over which is more epic: my beard or Sean's crazy long hair.

I had planned on sleeping outside with my fellow hikers, but after everyone insisted that I sleep inside in my own bed, I was persuaded. I sat down with my parents and watched a quick episode of Parks and Recreation with them.

THE GANG AT MY PARENTS HOUSE (FROM LEFT TO RIGHT, BACK TO FRONT: OLIVE OIL, GREAT P, TRAINING WHEELS, SPLINTER, ME, TREEBEARD, SWEETS, PRINCESS PEACH, JINGLE, BOYARDEE, AND WATERFALL)

Thanks for everything Mom – everyone was extremely impressed and grateful. By the way, counting my friends from home, you fed 18 people (including 11 thru-hikers) and still had leftovers without making any more food. Remember that for next time.

DAY 97

Starting Location: Pequannock, NJ (Home) / Kitattiny Visitor Center
Destination: Brink Shelter
Today's Miles: 23.5
Trip Miles: 1317.8

Jun 29, 2016 - This entire trip, I have been an ambassador for Taylor Ham (pork roll) to other hikers. Now that I had kidnapped 10 other hikers and had them trapped at my house, it only seemed right that I feed them the sandwich that I've been raving about for so long: Taylor Ham, egg and cheese on an everything bagel with salt, pepper and ketchup. I ordered 13 sandwiches (I fully intended to pack one out) and my Dad graciously picked them up from Bagel Heaven down the street. The breakfast sandwiches went over wonderfully as I expected, of course.

My parents drove us all to the Delaware Water Gap around mid-morning and our hike resumed. We all made it a few miles to Sunfish pond before we broke for a break and a snack. It's always tough to get back into the groove after a zero. We couldn't resist a swim in the beautiful and super refreshing Sunfish Pond.

The rest of the day was a casual hike through the thankfully less rocky NJ terrain. I mean I can't tell you how happy we all were to leave the rocks of PA behind us. Unfortunately, Wheels asked me to snap a picture of her and Treebeard as we passed 1300 miles. I obliged, and, as I talked with

Treebeard throughout the day, realized that he actually seemed like a pretty cool dude.

I had intended to stop at a campsite 20 miles in, but the water source was extremely stagnant. I hiked on over Rattlesnake mountain because there was supposed to be a reliable spring on the other side. However, the spring was dry – the lack of water in PA followed us through the first part of NJ. I would have loved to cowboy camp on top of the breezy summit of Rattlesnake Mountain, but I just didn't have any water.

Dehydrated and parched, I pushed onto the shelter where I completed my 23.5 mile day.
When I finally made it to the shelter tonight, it was obvious there was a large crowd already there. Obnoxiously loud laughter and yelling emanated from the wooden lean to while I filled and treated my water. I walked a little closer to check out the source of all the noise and found 12 young people horsing around with small piles of garbage and beer cans littered everywhere. I asked if they were thru-hikers and they enthusiastically answered in the affirmative. However, one look at their gear, their countenances, and their general attitudes proved they were definitely not thru-hikers. Sorry, but thru-hikers don't wear Timberland boots or sound like that after 8 pm at a shelter.

People like this are why thru-hikers and the Appalachian Trail are starting to get a bad reputation. The trail is supposedly transforming into this out of control party atmosphere. I strongly disagree with this. We thru-hikers may drink often, smoke a lot (not me, but it is definitely part of the culture) and otherwise have an incredible amount of fun, but the thru-hikers I know only have one goal in mind and that's Mt. Katahdin. The trail is, without a doubt, a social event, but just like anything else in life, it's the people and the relationships with those people that make something worth it. We continually put in our miles, respect each other and respect the trail and all the various constituents that make the AT such a unique place. The key to hiking the AT and doing anything else in life is balance: we work when we have to and we play when we can.

I ended up camping with only Treebeard, Waterfall and Olive Oil. The others must have stopped to camp earlier.

DAY 98

Starting Location: Brink Shelter
Destination: Rutherford Shelter
Today's Miles: 15
Trip Miles: 1332.8

Jun 30, 2016 - Tim and Johnny Steyh had taken off work today so they could come out and do some hiking with me. The plan was to meet them at 10:30 am near at the Route 206 crossing about 4 miles into my hike. I had planned on waiting at the Appalachian Sunrise Deli with a Taylor Ham, egg and cheese bagel sandwich, but the place was closed for good!

I decided to walk a mile south along 206 and hang out at the Jumboland Diner, which would also serve to satisfy my NJ diner aspirations while in my home state. Tim would pick me up there on the way to the parking area. This place was legit - it actually had a drive through window. I sat down with Treebeard, Waterfall and Tink Tank who were just finishing up. I ended up eating quite a bit of food: two scrambled eggs with cheese, hash browns, toast, a short stack of pancakes and a plate of disco fries.

Tim picked me up and drove to the parking area where we met up with Johnny Steyh. Tim was planning on staying the night with us, but Johnny Steyh had to go to work in the morning. Tim had a tent that rolled up to the size of a small adolescent so I told him to leave it in the car because he would just sleep in the shelter.

The three of us hiked 5 miles to the top of Sunrise Mountain where we took a break in the beautiful pavilion that's built up there. Oddly, my first thought when I reached the pavilion was that it would be a ridiculously beautiful place to propose, if done at sunrise, of course. Despite the no camping restriction, it would be a phenomenal cowboy camping spot in the winter. Johnny Steyh turned around and headed back to his car while Tim and I pushed on towards the Rutherford Shelter.

TIM AND JOHNNY STEYH ON SUNRISE MOUNTAIN

Before we reached Rutherford, we stopped in another shelter for a short break and to load up on water. A post in the shelter register from yesterday read that while people were setting up, a snake fell from the ceiling causing everyone to pitch their tents elsewhere. Needless to say, Tim and I checked all the crevices in the ceiling before getting too comfortable. We chatted with a ridge runner named Stan for a while who was very helpful and informative. Their job might seem amazing from the outside looking in (they essentially get paid to hike), but it's a pretty thankless job and they have to deal with a lot of assholes.

When we finally reached the shelter with Training Wheels, Sweets, Boyardee, Great P and Jingle, I set Tim up in the shelter with my sleeping pad. Fires were not allowed, but, frankly, it was necessary to keep the swarms of mosquitos away. We played a verbal puzzle game called Contact for a while before the usual, early bedtime of 8:30 pm.

DAY 99

Starting Location: Rutherford Shelter
Destination: Sparta, NJ / Wallkill River Parking Area
Today's Miles: 14.2
Trip Miles: 1347

Jul 1, 2016 - Tim and I managed to get out of camp by 7 - I slept surprisingly well considering Satan's birds, more commonly known as Whipporwills, were hanging around and that I slept on the ground with no sleeping pad. We had about 15 miles to hike by 1 pm so that Tim's mom could pick us up before the thunderstorms struck in the afternoon. Tim had already hiked 12 miles yesterday so I was curious to see how he would handle the workload today.

The first stop on our hike was High Point, the highest point in New Jersey - go figure. Although it was 0.3 miles off trail, I had never been to High Point and felt, as a resident of New Jersey, that it was time. A 220 foot tall pinnacle was situated at the top. The view from the top at the base of the pinnacle was pretty stellar with panoramic views of PA, NJ and NY. However, we climbed to the top of the pinnacle and were disappointed to find that it was just a stuffy room with four small, foggy windows. Oh well, we did it.

The rest of the hike was fairly flat with only 2 significant inclines. Ripe blackberries, raspberries and sorrel made the trek much more enjoyable. Tim was killing it, though the last hill kind of took the wind out of his sails a bit. When we arrived at the Wallkill River where we were supposed to get picked up, he nearly fell asleep right there on the grass. It was also amusing to see that he already had the infamous hiker hobble we're all afflicted with.

Mrs. Adams and Trish, Tim's sister, picked us up at the agreed to location and took us back to Tim's car. AWOL's coordinates for the parking area were not correct so we lost about 40 minutes during the drive. Of course, the car ride was a lot of fun as the Adams have a habit of enjoying everything all the time. Mrs. Adams treated us all to lunch at an awesome Greek place near Dingman's ferry. The gyro platter was a nice change of pace from the food I usually eat.

Once we obtained Tim's car, he helped me pick up a resupply at Wal-Mart as well as a new Platypus, a bug net, and a new shirt - my wool shirt was littered with holes to the point where I was conscious of how much I looked like a hobo at lunch. Hiker trash!

I showered and threw some laundry in at Tim's house and then we hopped in the car to meet Jacquie and Sean at Angry Erik's brewing company in Lafayette. I ate pizza slices 132 and 133 on the way to my next Brew Blaze. Angry Erik's was a super small brewery but I definitely enjoyed the beers. We grabbed growlers and headed back to Jacquie's house for the rest of the night.

I caught up with Mr. and Mrs. O'Rourke for a bit before heading downstairs where we played some beer games for old time's sake. Relay race with the three of them was an absolute blast. Unfortunately, hiking over one thousand miles completely erased the alcohol tolerance I spent four years carefully crafting at the University of Delaware. Though it hurts to admit, I am now a lightweight.

DAY 100

Starting Location: Sparta, NJ / Wallkill River Parking Area
Destination: Furnace Brook
Today's Miles: 19.7
Trip Miles: 1366.7

Jul 2, 2016 - Despite drinking more than I expected last night, I felt pretty good in the morning. Tim graciously continued ferrying me around by stopping at the deli for some much needed coffee and then taking me all the way back to the Wallkill River so I could resume my hike.

Today's hike was pretty unique - it started with a long, flat walk around a nature preserve. Then, I hiked up a fairly steep hill and cracked a Mountain Dew (Trail Magic!) when I reached the summit. It was an unbelievably cool and breezy day so I was in extremely high spirits. The next part of the hike brought me to a 0.6 mile long boardwalk over a swamp, which I recognized from a picture in the ATC headquarters. As it was a Sunday, there were many tourists out and about, most of which looked at me like I was a zoo animal on the loose. It's funny because people either have no idea what the AT is, in which case I'm basically a dirty, unkempt, smelly weirdo or people recognize me as a thru-hiker and treat me like a celebrity. One man asked me to pose with a garden gnome that his wife sells in the hope that it would go viral and help his wife's business. Another man told me that my legs looked like telephone poles. Others don't even respond to my salutations - rather, they seem slightly alarmed or taken aback that the unkempt beast spoke to them.

Following the boardwalk section of the trail, I took a lunch break and met up with my friend Carolyn who wanted to hike a bit with me. She picked a pretty gnarly section of trail seeing as we would immediately be hiking up the Stairway to Heaven, a steep, rocky section that could appropriately and most accurately be compared to a staircase. It had been awhile since I had seen her so it was great to catch up and share a nice afternoon in the woods. We took a snack break next to a pretty beautiful stream where she met some of my Trail Family. I also showed her what the shelters were like.

After Carolyn went back to her lake house, I continued hiking until I crossed the border into NY – that's 8 states down and 6 to go! I crossed over Prospect Rock, the highest point on the AT in NY. An American flag was raised on the top. Thinking I was alone and feeling pretty jacked up, I screamed "'Merica!". A few section hikers that I hadn't seen nearby laughed but fully supported the yell.

Down the hill, I set up camp after 19.7 miles with the usual crew next to Furnace Brook. It was buggy again, but bearable. I fell asleep to the sound of fireworks over nearby Greenwood Lake.

DAY 101

Starting Location: Furnace Brook
Destination: Fingerboard Shelter
Today's Miles: 21
Trip Miles: 1387.7

Jul 3, 2016 - Nick Vetere, my hunting buddy and one of my Dad's oldest friends, was parking in the lot on Arden Valley Road in Harriman, NY and hiking south along the trail to meet me around 9 in the morning. His goal was to do about 5 miles in and then turn around to hike back. Since I camped 18 miles from Harriman, this meant I needed to knock out around 13 miles by 11 in the morning. That's a tall order. So, I got moving early and left camp well before 7.

I walked extremely quickly and managed to run into Nick at the top of the ridge around 11:30 am. It was great to see him especially since he's a Rangers fan and he was rocking a Devils t-shirt. We took a short break as the terrain was becoming more demanding. Short, frequent and steep ascents and descents accompanied by large rocks that required the use of your hands in addition to your feet made the hiking more challenging (and more enjoyable, in my opinion).

It took about 2 hours for us to reach the parking lot near Arden Valley Road. We hopped in Nick's pickup truck and drove south down Route 17 to the Rhodes North Tavern in Sloatsburg, NY. We ordered some Lagunitas Little Sumpin Sumpin beers (I don't think I've ever seen this gem on tap) split some nachos and then I tried to tackle a 14 oz burger that rivaled the legendary AT Burger in Hot Springs, NC. I conquered the burger, but the battle left me weak and I was overcome by the French fries.

Nick gave me a ride to the supermarket to purchase some hamburgers and hot dogs (and black bean burgers for Great P) for a small 4th of July celebration in the woods. He had already obtained one of those flexible coolers so I could pack everything in for tomorrow night. We returned to the parking lot to find the rest of the Trail Family already there. Nick brought me an absurd amount of venison jerky he acquired from a friend so I passed some out to the other thru-hikers there.

Fingerboard shelter was only 4 miles away, but they felt very long with a full cooler hanging from my shoulders. I cooled off with a dip in Island Pond and then tackled one of my favorite sections of trail: Lemon Squeezer. This short, uphill rock formation starts with a slanted walkway that narrows as you progress forward. It's impossible to get through the without scraping your pack a bit. Next, there's a challenging rock scramble that causes you to contort your body in a way you didn't think was possible. Again, all of this happened with a 10 lb cooler on my chest, which ripped shortly after Lemon Squeezer, lasting for a whopping 2 miles.

The "reliable" water sources according to our guide were basically dry, which forced us to collect water from some undesirable, stagnant pools. When we finally reached our campsite, the hole in the cooler forced us to make some grave decisions. We chose to sacrifice the burgers tonight and save the indestructible hot dogs for tomorrow evening.

DAY 102

Starting Location: Fingerboard Shelter
Destination: Stealth Campsite near Anthony's Nose
Today's Miles: 16.7
Trip Miles: 1404.4

Jul 4, 2016 - I woke up at 3 in the morning to urinate as I do just about every night, but, tonight, I noticed that someone else had pitched their tent in our campsite after we had all fallen asleep. I didn't think anything of it, but when I finally woke up, one look at the pack hanging on the nearby tree told me it was none other than Princess Peach. It had only taken him 3 days to catch us after taking 2 zeros at home. He had hiked 94 miles in 3 days to do it - that's a lot of hiking.

We only had 16.7 miles from our campsite to Bear Mountain and the small town of Fort Montgomery, NY. However, I was completely wiped from yesterday. On top of that, the heat and the bugs sapped all of my motivation for the day's plans.

One of my hobbies out here has been natural navigation or finding my way without map and compass. While I'm definitely improving, I, for the life of me, cannot tell direction (North, South, East, West) in the middle of the woods on a foggy day. However, while walking today, I had a revelation. All of the large rocks were clearly oriented in the same northeastern direction. The striations on top of the rocks also pointed in the northeastern direction. Furthermore, the south side of the rocks were far more jumbled and broken up than the north side. All of this indicates the rocks were formed by a glacier moving slowly in the southwest direction. Now, I have a clear cut compass in the middle of the woods regardless of whether the sun is out. Fascinating.

I stopped at the top of the peak just south of Bear Mountain and took in the view of the Hudson River, the Bear Mountain Bridge and Bear Mountain before tackling the next few miles. On the other side of Bear Mountain, I descended into two zoos. The first was an annoyingly large group of tourists camped out for the holiday near Hessian Lake that clogged the trail near the bottom of the mountain. I distinctly heard three foreigners whisper that I was a professional hiker. I stopped and purchased a jumbo pickle on a stick from an Amish food stand before walking past the most disgusting pool I've ever seen (people were actually waiting in line to pay for access to this cesspool) and through the second zoo.

The second zoo was actually a zoo. However, it was so sad seeing animals like foxes, bobcats and bears trapped in tiny enclosures with no room to run while idiots gawked at them. I walked quickly through this zoo as it made me angry.

The Trail Family waited on the south side of the bridge while Jingle, Peach, and Great P walked to Fort Montgomery for a resupply and some beer (and cider for Great P). My left butt cheek had started to disagree with my right butt cheek and the resultant chafing was rapidly becoming uncomfortable. Matt and Tom's gift of the Gold Bond Friction Defense stick suddenly turned into the greatest gift I've ever received.

We crossed the bridge with hot dogs and beer and stealth camped near the top of Anthony's Nose, which provided an absurdly beautiful view of the river and the bridge. Hot dogs, beers and a nice fire put a nice end to our holiday even though we didn't have the day off. We even stayed up until almost 11 pm...whoa.

DAY 103

Starting Location: Stealth Campsite near Anthony's Nose
Destination: Clarence Fahnestock State Park Campground
Today's Miles: 19
Trip Miles: 1423.4

Jul 5, 2016 - It had rained during the night and everyone slept in pretty late. Despite the rain, it was unfathomably humid outside - it literally felt like I was swimming all day. The rocks were wet, which meant bad news for me seeing as my shoes have zero traction when the rocks are wet. I warned everyone I would fall at least once. About two miles later, my feet flew out from under me and my bag of garbage was launched into the woods as my ass hit the ground. Peach and Training Wheels witnessed this and had a good laugh.

About 5 miles into our hike, we stopped at a deli just off the trail and got some food while we laid out our tents to dry. Suffice it to say I ate a lot of chocolate frosted donuts (I believe 11 was the magic number).

Peach and I decided to just bang out the remaining 14 miles without taking breaks so we could relax and attempt to cool down at the Clarence Fahnestock State Park campground. I had the new Blink-182 cd to keep me entertained. I did fall very hard, though. We were walking along a raised dirt platform with steep drops on either side. I reached up to adjust a strap on my pack and walked right off the side. I tumbled down about 10 feet before a rock broke my fall - I wasn't hurt, just very dirty. Still, I definitely need to be more careful.

We reached the park around 4 pm and helped ourselves to a hot chicken sandwich. The last two miles in the punishing sun really took its toll on our bodies so a real sandwich was deemed necessary. I was so drained and exhausted, I just wanted to go to sleep. We walked almost a mile to the campground (the campground was free, but the three campsites reserved for AT hikers were holes compared to the other sites) and I took what must have been a 30 minute shower. I cleaned my clothes a bit while in there, too. The water at the campground wasn't potable so we had to walk another quarter mile down the busy road to get that.

Peach actually managed to secure a hitch and get beer again. While I hadn't planned on drinking anything, it did make the bugs more bearable. The heat and the bugs are out of control lately. I've always avoided hiking during the summer for both of those reasons. Now, I don't have a choice and it definitely takes away from my enjoyment of the trail. My body has too many bug bites to count. I miss the winter and I maintain that a 25 degree day is far preferable to the weather lately. It took a while to fall asleep because I was sweating so profusely.

DAY 104

Starting Location: Clarence Fahnestock State Park Campground
Destination: Morgan Stewart Shelter
Today's Miles: 14
Trip Miles: 1437.4

Jul 6, 2016 - The bugs this morning were so obnoxious, I left camp as soon as possible carrying my coffee with me. Even at 7 am, you could tell the day would be unbearably hot and humid. The forecast was 95 degrees and 90% humidity. The first 10 miles were bearable thanks to the Wimbledon radio - Roger Federer was playing Marin Cilic in the Quarterfinals. Federer, down 2 sets to love, fought off 3 match points to pull off a 5 set comeback victory that got me unbelievably pumped up.

At the 10 mile mark, with sweat literally cascading down my body, we decided to wait out the hottest part of the day at a deli 0.3 miles off trail. They had a picnic table and a shady camping area where hikers could attempt to cool off. I even managed to nap, which was far better than being awake during the midday onslaught of the sun. The deli had turkey roll-ups with stuffing and gravy and a side of Cajun rice with sausage and chicken. It was amazing. Pretty much every other hiker had the same idea as us - Great P, Croc, Napster, Easy E, Flipper, Mint, Pepper, Olive Oil and Forest.

Since today and tomorrow would be easier days, we killed about five hours at the deli before hiking the last four miles to the shelter. Even at 7 pm, with the sun down, I arrived at the shelter drenched in sweat. With no breeze and the bugs swarming greedily, I couldn't even dry off. I dumped a bottle of water over myself so I could convince myself I was somewhat clean and crawled into my tent. I'm not sure how, but I managed to fall asleep pretty quickly.

The heat, humidity and swarms of mosquitos are leaving me drained, exhausted and totally without motivation to hike more miles. It's still hard to be negative, though, seeing as every other hiker is going through the same misery. Since we're in it together, it's pretty easy to have a good time and just take the bad with the good. That doesn't stop me from daydreaming of winter all the time.

DAY 105

Starting Location: Morgan Stewart Shelter
Destination: Danbury, CT / Appalachian Trail Railroad Station
Today's Miles: 10.9
Trip Miles: 1448.3

Jul 7, 2016 - In a similar situation to yesterday, the bugs were just awful this morning so I left camp as quickly as possible. Today we would hike only about 11 miles to the Appalachian Trail Railroad Station where Peach's friends, Lyndsay and Megan, were picking us up for a nero in nearby Danbury, CT.

Shortly after leaving camp, I needed to leave the trail to take care of some smelly business. I can honestly say that squatting down in the leaves absolutely drenched in sweat and with bugs assaulting my exposed privates may have been my low point on the trail so far. I was bit multiple times in the areas under my shorts, which made walking immediately uncomfortable.

After that, I walked as fast as possible to get out of the woods knowing that an air conditioned hotel room was waiting for me. I hiked 11 miles in under 3 hours. Another deli was down the road with a camping area where I could wait for Peach, Great P, Lyndsay and Megan.

About an hour later, everyone arrived at the deli. Another thru-hiker had been showing me the video of the latest police shooting in Dallas. It's one of maybe 3 or 4 major news stories that have reached me out here and it's a solid reminder of how much I do not miss hearing the news. This world out here may not necessarily be real, but it certainly is a better place. Ignorance is definitely bliss sometimes.

Anyway, Lyndsay and Megan brought us to the supermarket for a quick resupply and some pizza. I actually only had 2 slices which brings my running total to 135. The rest of the afternoon was literally spent in a Super 8 hotel room chatting, sipping beer, eating Chinese food, resting, and playing True American from New Girl, which was a freaking blast. The air conditioning, shower and laundry (in that order) were indescribably satisfying. Great P had his first shower in 12 days.

I had a chance to talk with Survivor today – he's closing in slowly. He may have Lyme Disease, but he got antibiotics for it and should be fine.

DAY 106

Starting Location: Danbury, CT / Appalachian Trail Railroad Station
Destination: Ten Mile River Campsite
Today's Miles: 9.8
Trip Miles: 1458.1

Jul 8, 2016 – Today started with Roger Federer's semifinal match against Milos Raonic. I watched the first 2 sets in the hotel room, but had to listen to the rest as I hiked. It was a very disappointing 5 set loss and I don't really have anything more to say about that.

Jingle, Training Wheels, and Sweets took a zero yesterday at Wheels' Aunt's house (nicknamed The Grevort) so we decided to take another short day to wait up for them (sort of). Our goal was the Ten Mile River Campsite with the hope that we would have a chance to swim and cool off. It was a short 9.8 mile day.

The three of us took a short break at the Wiley Shelter where we met a man named Woody (this was his real name as it was his first day on trail. He had decided to start in NY and hike to Maine and then hike from NY south to Georgia). This guy was a hoot with a 65 lb pack, 10 pairs of socks, 7 changes of clothes, at least 9 days' worth of food, a massive butane fuel canister AND an equally large propane tank. Woody insisted that the second propane tank was his only luxury item that he used to soften the large quantity of hash oil he carried with him. We all chimed in with pointers and explained that most hikers have less than 2 full pairs of clothes. He seemed grateful for the help.

Another mile north along the trail and we found two older gentlemen, Walt and "Rambo", doing Trail Magic. Walt's son had completed the trail in 2014 and he had heard about Trail Magic often. Both guys said they tried Trail Magic once and enjoyed it so much that they continue offering burgers, dogs, fruit, beer and snacks whenever they have time. I can't wait to pay it forward in the coming years after I summit the mythical goddess named Katahdin.

We finished our short day with a pretty good hill. The first 200 yards were tough as I worked through my burger and beers, but I felt stronger with every step I took. At the top, Peach and I almost simultaneously agreed that we needed to open the throttle back up. We had needed a break on the long days for sure, but enough is enough - we needed to get back to 18-20 mile days immediately.

Our campsite tonight was on the banks of the 10 Mile River and could not have been any better. There was a breeze, the water was cool, but refreshing and we had all afternoon to enjoy it. Eventually, I made a small fire on a rock in the middle of the river (fires were not allowed in the woods, so this was my loophole) and cooked up some dinner with my feet in the water. I don't think I'll top that any time soon.

DINNER ON A ROCK IN THE MIDDLE OF THE RIVER.

DAY 107

Starting Location: Ten Mile River Campsite
Destination: Silver Hill Campsite
Today's Miles: 18.9
Trip Miles: 1477

Jul 9, 2016 - Technically, I crossed out of New York and into Connecticut yesterday. However, I crossed back and forth across the border a few times before finally leaving NY, which happened today. That's 9 states down and 5 to go!

Princess Peach, Great P and I had 18.9 miles to the Silver Hill Campsite. The terrain as we exited NY and entered CT has become noticeably more challenging and I would only expect it to continue to do so. Today, we had a few pretty tough climbs, which we honestly haven't tackled consistently for a while now.

The weather was definitely cooperating today - the sun was gone, the breeze was blowing, the humidity was gone and the temperature had dropped into the mid-seventies. All those factors definitely turned a very challenging day into an extremely enjoyable one. The climbs had me breathing hard and sweating pretty profusely, but it felt good to get away from the persistent ridge line that haunted PA and NJ and summit some real mountains again - even if they are only around 1,500 feet tall.

Our last descent brought us to the banks of the Housatonic River, which we followed for about 4 miles to the campsite. I sat on a rock right next to the river and just watched the water flow by for about 30 minutes. It was extremely relaxing, I would have fallen asleep if it wasn't for the chill brought on by the breeze and my sweaty shirt. You won't hear me complain, though - the chill was so welcome after the hot hell we've baked in for the past two weeks or so.

We ran into Chicken Feet and Salty at the campsite, but, otherwise, we had the place to ourselves. It was a pretty unique campsite complete with a pavilion, a patio, a privy, grass, a bench swing and a picnic table. Even though there are no campfires allowed in CT, the temperature drop forced our hand. We rolled away a massive section of fallen tree, built a fire ring with rocks, and got a blaze going. The next morning we would simply remove the rocks and then roll the trunk over the logs so no one would know.

Chicken Feet brought a large roll of salami to share with everyone and seemed to be his usual self again. Lately, he has seemed pretty stressed, but no one knows why. It's hysterical to watch this tiny Vietnamese man curse and say simple American words like 'awesome'.

THE IRON THRONE OF THE APPALACHIAN TRAIL

DAY 108

Jul 10, 2016 - It rained during the night, but that's good. The more humidity the sky sheds, the cooler it should be, right? It looked like rain again that morning and I was hoping the sky would open up. However, the rain never came and the first 8 miles or so were horribly humid and wet. I must have been bit by at least 5 Mosquitos and 2 deer flies.

It remained humid all morning, but early on in our hike, we saw a sign for a Trail Magic picnic in Falls Village, CT. This motivated the 3 of us to bang out 15 miles before noon. As we walked into town, the rain finally came and cooled everything down - it was glorious.

So, sopping wet, we walked up to the best Trail Magic we've received on trail so far, in my humble opinion. Burgers, dogs, omelets, bacon, fruit, a whole table of desserts, three different pasta salads, Gatorades, beer, wine and several tubs full of resupply stuff including food, Ziploc bags, toiletries and even parachute cord were completely at our disposal. Panda, who thru-hiked last year, organized the impressive event. It was incredibly well supplied and well organized.

I got to talking with Panda and the one thing she mentioned that stuck with me is that the process of rejoining society is unavoidably "horrible".

It's a year later and she is still not adjusted. So, I have that to look forward to...

After the Trail Magic was over, we walked into the center of town to check out an auto show that was taking place. I walked into the Falls Village Inn to grab a beer at the bar. When I tried to order the beer, the bartender said, "I can put it into a to-go cup and you can drink it outside". I said I would wait for my 2 friends to see what they wanted to do, but he simply repeated his previous statement. It took me a few more seconds to realize he was politely kicking me out of the bar, presumably because of the smell I was exuding. I can now say I have been kicked out of a bar for excessive body odor. Still a little shocked, I walked outside where I found a few cheap beers and listened to the cover band, which we mistook for karaoke since they were not very good.

After talking with Jingle, Sweets, and Training Wheels, we decided to just stay at the Toymakers Cafe in town, which offered free camping. It was a shorter day - only 14.8 miles - but the company at the campsite was great. We ordered pizza (Tim, I'm at 141 slices), Legs and Verge joined us, and we just sat in the yard and talked. Great P overdid it with a bottle of whiskey and passed out in his unprotected tent. When the skies opened up a little later, we slipped his rain fly on and climbed into our own tents.

DAY 109

Starting Location: Falls Village, CT / Toymaker's Cafe Campsite
Destination: Guilder Pond Picnic Area
Today's Miles: 20.4
Trip Miles: 1512.2

Jul 11, 2016 - A slow morning had me leaving camp around 8 am to start an ambitious 20.4 miles to the Guilder Pond Picnic Area. The terrain looked very challenging today with no less than 4 significant summits - Mt. Prospect, Bear Mountain, Mt. Race, and Mt. Everett.

The first section of the hike paralleled the Housatonic River until I saw a large waterfall. With no hesitation, I took off my clothes and jumped into the pool at the base of the falls for an early morning bath. Then, with wet clothes, I started on the 1st climb of the day.

As my trail name entails, I enjoy the uphill and today was no different. Peach, Great P and I plowed through the first 14 miles by 1 pm. I opted to take a long lunch break at the top of Bear Mountain on top of a large rock observation tower with beautiful panoramic views of CT below.

Mt. Race proved to be just as scenic as Bear Mountain, and had a 0.6 mile section of trail that followed the edge of a steep cliff. At 77 degrees and breezy, the hike was a lot of fun even with the sun beating down on us.

I felt great until I hit Mt. Everett - 1 mile straight up and then another mile straight down to our campsite. When I say straight up, I mean any steeper and the treads on our shoes would not have been able to grip the large, smooth rocks that comprised the side of the mountain. The use of our hands was necessary to maintain balance as we ascended the rock face.

Needless to say, it felt good to hit the picnic area and stuff some hot food into our stomachs. We had actually been aiming for the shelter 0.4 miles farther down trail, but the picnic area was so inviting, that we just set up there. Despite actually looking, it was only after we set up that we saw the 'No Camping' sign - whoops.

As far as the high school drama, Great P apologized to Legs today for sleeping with her and then, essentially, avoiding her for 500 miles.

DAY 110

Starting Location: Guilder Pond Picnic Area
Destination: Mt. Wilcox North Shelter
Today's Miles: 21.9
Trip Miles: 1534.1

Jul 12, 2016 - MOSQUITOS! I woke up this morning and lay in my tent for a while. Without moving my head, I could count 12 of these bugs from hell. I dreaded unzipping my screen and stepping out into No Man's Land where I would most certainly be assaulted. I managed to pack up camp in less than 20 minutes and practically ran from the picnic area with breakfast in my hands.

I hiked a quick 8 miles in the cool morning air to the intersection of Route 7 with hopes of catching a hitch into Great Barrington, MA to do some laundry. You can only wear the same socks for so many days before the buildup of gross matter starts to actually damage your feet. I would not be getting a shower, unfortunately, which makes 5 days without a proper one.

On top of the mountain this morning, I looked out to find the surrounding peaks protruding from a literal sea of clouds. This has consistently been one of my favorite views on trail. Next thing I know, my descent plunges me down into the clouds blocking the sun completely.

Hitchhiking was a piece of cake - as soon as I threw my thumb out there, an elderly woman in the first car we saw pulled over her minivan to give the 3 of us a ride into town. We were dropped off in a plaza containing a grocery store, a laundromat and the Great Barrington Bagel Company (they claimed to be the 'Best NY style bagel sandwich - we'll see about that).

Great P got the laundry started, Peach went to the grocery store and I walked to the deli to grab sandwiches for everybody. I ordered 2 sandwiches for myself including a sausage, egg and cheese on an everything bagel. While the bagel sandwich was excellent, there's just something about the bagels in northern NJ and NYC that can't be replicated anywhere else. Plus, sausage pales in comparison to the greasy goodness of Taylor Ham.

After a good 3 hours of hanging around the laundromat, we caught a hitch back to the trail. The driver actually got out of his car and offered us blunts rolled with his homegrown marijuana. I politely declined, but that was so nice of him.

I started up the first significant hill of the day and as I summited, I noticed that the trail started to go down the same side (west) of the ridge that I just came up. As I descended, I wondered why the trail builders couldn't just keep the trail flat until it crossed over the ridge. But then, I heard Peach coming in the opposite direction. Shit. Somehow, I had turned myself around and walked down the southbound portion of the trail I had just walked up. Both frustrated and amused at myself, I turned around and climbed the hill for a second time. I was happy to see that the trail did end up passing over to the east side of the ridge.

The next 12 miles were fairly uneventful unless you count the swarms of flies and Mosquitos constantly badgering me. I wear my headphones just so I don't have to listen to them buzzing near my ear. I reached the shelter that was our destination for the night and couldn't find Great P anywhere. I left a message with Scavenger and pressed on to find some better campsites. I didn't find one until 2 miles later at the Mt. Wilcox North Shelter.

Sweaty and tired, I started to pitch my tent with an absolutely incredible number of mosquitos and flies incessantly pestering me. I stuck my trekking pole into the ground and it snapped cleanly in half. I lost it. Incredibly frustrated, I took the rest of the pole and destroyed it on a nearby tree. Finally, out of breath, covered in numerous new welts, I set about honing a tree branch to temporarily hold up my tent while the bugs continued to bite.

After 45 minutes, I finally had my tent up and I just sat inside hiding from the bugs while I tried to calm down and dry the sweat off my body. Great P and Peach rolled into camp around then and saw my situation. Luckily, I could use Great P's spare pole to make my tent a little sturdier than it was with the stick.

I ate a quick dinner in my tent (the other two did the same – it's really not possible to sit outside anymore regardless of bug nets or bug spray) and tried to stretch out my stiff legs. I hiked 21.9 miles today, which makes nearly 43 in two days over much tougher terrain than I've seen recently. Tomorrow, I will need to tone it down a bit.

It feels ridiculous that something like bugs is a serious mental challenge on this trip, but it's tough to explain just how bad they are. Throw in the humidity, high temperatures, and sore muscles, and this just fucking sucks.

DAY 111

Starting Location: Mt. Wilcox North Shelter
Destination: Upper Goose Pond Cabin
Today's Miles: 14
Trip Miles: 1548.1

Jul 13, 2016 – The three of us wanted to continue putting in big miles, but we also heard great things about the Upper Goose Pond Cabin, which was only 14 easy miles away. It was yet another early start and a quick exit from camp to escape the unrelenting bugs. I caught up with Lucky, Lolly and Cal only to find out that at the lake between the North and South Wilcox shelters, I had missed a moose taking a drink from the pond. Unfortunately, I had already passed that pond yesterday.

Great P and I reached the first road crossing where I intended to grab some water before our first and only climb of the day. A chalkboard sign on the side of the road caught my eye and I discovered a little wooden closet filled with sodas, Gatorade, snacks, fresh eggs and a power strip so hikers could charge their phones. Two children kept the closet stocked and asked hikers to pay a small amount for each item using the honor system. It was a pretty cool set up and I gladly left a dollar for a cold Mountain Dew.

Scarfoot, Longcloud, Scavenger, Lucky, Lolly and Cal joined us just as we were about to continue hiking. It was actually a very nice day so we had no problem hanging out by the closet and chatting for a while.

With help from my Mountain Dew, I crushed the only mountain standing between me and the Upper Goose Pond Cabin. The cabin was a half mile off trail and situated next to Upper Goose Pond. This place was beautiful - it had 17 bunks with mattresses, a living room with a fireplace and kitchen table downstairs, a kitchen, a covered porch, picnic tables everywhere, two privies and campsites out back. The place was taken care of by a happy couple: Paul and Wendy.

After some introductions, I set up my tent (the bunks are still not worth the risk of snorers) and then ran down to the lake to rinse the filth off as best I could. The water was unbelievably refreshing and I treaded water as long as my diminished upper body could.

Peach and I then signed out one of their canoes and paddled out to the island in the middle of the lake. He wanted to race back - he would swim and I would row the canoe. Of course, I won and he nearly drowned during the underestimated 300-400 yard swim back to the shore.

I made an early dinner and just relaxed for the rest of the afternoon while I read some of the outdoor magazines left on the coffee table inside. Finally, we got a game of Monopoly going on the porch with Peach, Great P, Scarfoot and Scavenger. While I successfully negotiated a few blockbuster trades, Great P quietly built houses on the yellow spaces and crushed everyone in less than 90 minutes. It was probably the fastest game of Monopoly I've ever played. At least Scavenger didn't win...

DAY 112

Starting Location: Upper Goose Pond Cabin
Destination: Dalton, MA / Tom Levardi's Backyard
Today's Miles: 20.6
Trip Miles: 1568.7

Jul 14, 2016 - Paul and Wendy made blueberry pancakes and coffee for the 5 of us in the morning. Paul is a pastry chef so, needless to say, his pancakes were pretty fantastic. Breakfast was before 7 so we were still able to start hiking early after our very satisfying stay at the cabin. I've said it before, but it's places like Upper Goose Pond Cabin that make the AT so unique and enjoyable.

It was tough to get into hiking this morning. Lately, this has been happening much more frequently. While I'm definitely still enjoying the trail, my enthusiasm has been waning a bit. The heat, humidity, bugs and general wear and tear on my body make it a lot harder to get excited about hiking 20 miles every morning. I've heard that most hikers just want to finish as they get closer to Maine and I'm starting to understand why.

We only had one tough climb during our 20.6 mile hike into Dalton, MA (the trail runs right through the center of town). Otherwise, the walk was quick and easy - we arrived around 3 pm. We knocked on the door of Tom Levardi, whose house was located directly on the trail, and asked if we could camp in his backyard. He's been allowing hikers to camp there for 36 years now.

Tom went above and beyond by doing our laundry and driving us to the supermarket for a resupply and the Chinese buffet where he joined us for a large meal. We also borrowed his bikes and rode to the Dalton CRA, which offered free showers. After 7 days without one, you can imagine how wonderful it was.

Helton, one of the Warrior Hikers (he had to leave the trail due to an aneurism in his abdomen), lives in MA and drove down to meet us. It was great to see this guy again though it's a shame he had to leave the trail. We went to the local pub (Jacob's) and were joined by Rafiki, Zippy, Goat (it's always cool meeting people with similar or the same names), and Colonel Mustard. The latter two were from Montreal and were some of the first hockey fans I've met on trail. It was a relief to finally be able to speak the same language with them.

Things escalated quickly at the bar and it was very late before we called it quits and headed back to Tom's for the night. On the way to Tom's, Zippy and I were sidetracked by the lights still on at Crane Currency, the only company in the country responsible for manufacturing the paper that US currency is made from. Zippy was very attractive (or at least 'trail attractive') and we were flirting hard, but when I made my move, she insisted she had a boyfriend waiting for her at home. I failed again.

DAY 113

Jul 15, 2016 - This morning is only the third morning on trail I have been hungover, but it was a doozy. Breakfast food was a necessity and it needed to be found quickly. Helton drove us to the Misty Moon Diner in the adjacent town of Pittsfield, MA where they had a breakfast food challenge: The Godzilla - a 12 egg omelet with four meats, four cheeses, and eight different vegetables, home fries and four pieces of toast. All of that needed to be eaten in 30 minutes. I didn't have high hopes of finishing, but who am I to turn down a breakfast challenge of this magnitude? What would Ron Swanson do?

The Godzilla came, saw and conquered. I managed to eat all 12 eggs, but all the other ingredients proved too heavy on an already fragile stomach. The omelet was out-of-this-world delicious, but, honestly, even if I had just hiked 20 miles and did not feel like I had been hit by a truck, I still would have failed. That amount of breakfast food is just too heavy. The waitress gave me two Ziploc bags so I could pack out the greasy goodness I had left over.

After breakfast, Helton drove me to the outfitter so I could purchase my new pair of Kelty trekking poles. I also caved and snagged some bug spray because I was near the breaking point with the bugs.

As soon as I returned to Tom's, I laid down in the shade of a large maple tree in his backyard and slept for a few hours. All of us were in pretty bad shape and were not ready to start hiking again.

Finally, as 3 pm rolled around, we got our act together. Princess Peach, Great P, and I hiked a whopping 4.2 miles to the Crystal Mountain Campsite where we gave up and made camp. We justified our short day with the fact that we had hiked 17 days straight of at least 10 miles.

After a campfire reheated the Godzilla for dinner, I retired to my tent early to get some reading done. In the distance, I could hear a thunderstorm rolling in, but couldn't tell if it was headed our way. The forecast only had the chance of rain at 20%.

All of a sudden, an intensely loud and long clap of thunder sounded right above our heads. Then the rain started falling. With dismay, I realized I made a rookie mistake by pitching my tent in a shallow, hard, dirt basin devoid of any dead leaves or cushion. The rain drops caused the dirt to bounce up and spray the netting of my tent. Puddles quickly formed around the bathtub floor of my tent and, as the rain started to fall harder, I realized I had a pretty big problem on my hands.

The small puddles quickly grew into one large, muddy puddle that threatened to spill over the bathtub floor and into the interior of my tent. I pushed down and discovered the floor of my tent was literally floating. When my crocs and shoes literally floated away, it was time to make some moves as swimming seemed inevitable.

I grabbed my rain jacket, opened the screen and stepped out of my tent barefoot - the puddle completely submerged my foot up to the top of the ankle. Cursing, I grabbed both ends of my tent and lifted it with everything inside to transfer it to a bed of dead leaves nearby. I was careful to leave the rain fly draped over the interior, but everything was already wet. I turned around and cursed even louder - my pack was face down in the puddle and nearly submerged. I quickly grabbed everything and transferred it underneath my rain fly.

When I went to re-pitch my tent, I realized the stakes were still in the ground under the puddle (I keep using the word puddle, but let's be real, it looked and felt like a small pond and rain was still falling). For almost 20 minutes, I stomped barefoot through the pond scraping up dirt trying to feel around for my stakes. I managed to find 3 and remembered Steel had given me an extra one that I kept stored in my pack for emergency situations. If this wasn't any emergency situation, I don't know what is.

I finally managed to re-pitch my tent, but now that everything I owned was sopping wet, the plastic butts of my new trekking poles kept slipping on the plastic dimples of my tent. This issue and a large rock near my left stake caused my tent to collapse 3 times. I used small wads of Leukotape and slid them between the butts of the trekking poles and the dimples of my tent, which, thankfully, did the trick. I crawled into my tent and used a microfiber towel to wipe up as much water as possible from my bathtub floor, my quilt, and my sleeping pad. I managed to get rid of a few puddles, but everything was still wet.

Even the clothes I was wearing were dripping wet as I finally lay down and tried to relax. I told myself that the wetness kept me cool in the humid atmosphere of my tent. I also knew this would turn into a funny story eventually, which served to help lighten my mood. Despite the chaos, I managed to stay pretty calm during the whole affair with the exception of a few loud exclamations. The fact is, I set my tent up in a really stupid spot and should know better by now. As a result, I was unprepared for the unexpected rain and paid the price. It would certainly be an interesting morning. I slipped into a surprisingly deep sleep as the rain continued to pound my rain fly.

DAY 114

Starting Location: Crystal Mountain Campsite
Destination: Sherman Brook Campsite
Today's Miles: 20.9
Trip Miles: 1593.8

Jul 16, 2016 - When I woke up, I immediately remembered the disaster that was last night. I shakily stepped out of my tent to survey the extent of the damage. I noticed that the small pond that had been my tent site had receded into the ground and I saw my fourth tent stake sticking out of the ground. With a little digging, I also uncovered my knife, which I totally forgot about last night.

The only items in my pack that miraculously stayed dry were my dirty pair of socks, my electronics, my toilet paper and my book. Basically, nothing was damaged beyond repair, which I was grateful for. I packed everything up and hung what I could off the side of my pack to dry as I walked.

Today, we would be hiking over Mt. Greylock - the highest point in MA at 3,491 feet tall and part of the Berkshires. However, the first thing we did was descend four miles into the town of Cheshire, MA to grab a coffee at the Dunkin Donuts there. We relaxed for a bit, used the facilities and charged up our phones before starting the eight mile ascent to the summit of Greylock.

A strong breeze made the ascent extremely enjoyable and even drove away the constant deer flies. At the top, I sat down outside the Bascom Lodge and caught my breath. Legs and Verge met me there along with Great P and Princess Peach, who would be having lunch with his friend Albert.

Great P said the ranger directing traffic said something about Trail Magic at the end of the parking lot. Naturally, we investigated and met Susan and Mike from Boston. Their son had hiked the PCT last year and he had guilted them into doing some Trail Magic. With McDoubles, chips, clementines, soda and iced tea, they asked us if they were doing it right. Regardless of the fact that they drove two freaking hours from Boston on a Saturday simply to give food and drink to complete strangers, we assured them they were killing it.

On the way back to the lodge, Legs and Verge invited us over to yet another car where their friend from school, Nate, met them to provide more Trail Magic. This guy had a delicious homemade pasta salad, fruit salad and homemade cookies. These cookies were huge, yet he managed to cook the moist center all the way through without even slightly burning or overlooking the edges. I was impressed.

A sign at the top of Mt. Greylock explained that, during the last Ice Age, the Wisconsin glacier moved southwest over the summit of the mountain. During that time, the summit of Greylock was covered in ice over 40 feet deep. That is just incredible. You could literally see the striations left in the rocks by the slow moving glacier.

Finally, we resumed hiking and descended into North Adams, MA, which the trail passed directly through. We made camp just 2 miles north of town at the Sherman Brook Campsite to complete a 20.9 mile day. Despite wet wood, a fire was necessary to drive away the pesky deer flies. I ran down to the sizable stream to do a full body rinse and before you know it, it was time for bed. Most of my stuff managed to dry off while I prepared dinner and the temperature dropped ensuring a comfortable night in my tent.

DAY 115

Starting Location: Sherman Brook Campsite
Destination: Melville Nauheim Shelter
Today's Miles: 18.4
Trip Miles: 1612.2

Jul 17, 2016 - It rained again last night, but, needless to say, my tent was pitched in a much safer spot. Still, after my disaster two nights ago, the rain instilled a little paranoia and I kept expecting something to go wrong.

As I crossed into Vermont, the sign for the beginning of the Long Trail appeared. The Long Trail is the oldest long distance hiking trail in the United States. It starts at the border of MA and VT and makes its way north to the US - Canada border. The AT shares the Long Trail for 105 miles until both trails go their separate ways near Killington, VT.

I had a pretty standard 17 miles to the road crossing for Bennington, VT. Standard, except for the fact I took the wrong trail for about a mile before Slim Rims realized our mistake (The Count of Monte Cristo is heating up big time and the drama has distracted me recently), and Great P fell off a boardwalk to soak his entire boot in a marsh. We took a long lunch by a stream so it could dry out a bit. Oh AND I crossed 1600 miles AND I crossed into Vermont, my twelfth state on the AT! My song when I bounded past the border was, of course, Mother, We Just Can't Get Enough, which I just can't get enough of after 1600 miles. So, actually, it was an extraordinary hike rather than a standard one.

At the road crossing, Steve called me over to his car and offered me soda, Gatorade and fruit. By talking to him, it sounds like he has a lot of free time and does Trail Magic around 4-5 times per week. He knew all the hikers names ahead of us and told us of his aspirations to hike the trail himself when he retires in two years at the age of 60.

Steve offered us a ride into town to do a small resupply (I probably had enough food to last me until Wallingford, VT, 66 miles away, but I hate having to ration my food). Great P and I also got some pizza to put my count at 144 slices.

Peach hitched into town separately and did infinitely better than us - he found a brewery I missed: Madison Brewery and Pub. I was peeved that I missed a brewery so close to trail as I continue to Brew Blaze. Peach did forget to ask for a sticker though, so his visit never happened, right?.

Once back at the road crossing, a steep 1.4 miles brought us to the Melville Nauheim Shelter where we called it a day. I only got bit by two mosquitos that night making VT immediately better than MA.

DAY 116

Starting Location: Melville Nauheim Shelter
Destination: Story Spring Shelter
Today's Miles: 17.4
Trip Miles: 1629.6

Jul 18, 2016 - Standing in our way today was Glastenbury Mountain, which stands at 3,748 feet. A gradual uphill spread out over several miles brought us to the top, which was densely covered in conifers. The summit did have a tall fire tower that was unlocked at the top. I dropped my bag, ran up the stairs and watched as I crested the tree line to a panoramic view of the surrounding mountains. To the north, I could see Stratton Mountain and Bromley Mountain beyond, both distinguished by their ski slopes.

I ate a quick lunch at the top of the tower and then continued hiking. Our goal for the day was a river 20 miles away from where we started, but thunderstorms soon changed that. The rain started coming down and I quickly became pretty soaked, but that didn't stop me from stopping at every pond to check for signs of moose. I've been seeing their tracks in the mud recently, but so far, they have only served as a tease.

I met Peach at the Story Spring Shelter 17.4 miles into our hike and we decided to call it a day on account of the rain. Of course, immediately after we made our decision at two in the afternoon it stopped raining and the sun came out. However, shoes and socks had been taken off so there was no going back.

Great P and I set about making a fire with the wet wood. I constructed a layered teepee and stuffed a large pile of dry birch bark in the center. Even with the wet wood, the birch bark burned so furiously that we had a fire in practically no time at all. The smoky fire drove away all the deer flies and made the afternoon very enjoyable.

Jellydog, who we hadn't seen since Tennessee, stopped in for lunch and we had a chance to catch up with him. Shortly after he left, Legs and Verge showed up and decided to stay basically ensuring we would have a good time - it's literally impossible not to with these two. We also had an older gentleman hiking the Long Trail decide to stay - his name was Cardinal65. I speak for everyone when I say the first thing that entered everyone's mind was that 'Cardinal65' was an AOL screen name. He was nice enough, but literally took notes of everything we said for his "book". There were also three other Long Trail hikers there - Ben, Piper, and Sara - that we kept running into, though they never seemed to want to hang out around the fire.

DAY 117

Starting Location: Story Spring Shelter
Destination: Bromley Shelter
Today's Miles: 23.1
Trip Miles: 1652.7

Jul 19, 2016 - Today, I was pretty excited to hike up and over Stratton Mountain at 3,936 feet - as a skier, it just feels unexplainably satisfying to hike over a mountain I've never skied before. The weather was freaking unbelievable with temperatures in the 70s and a consistent breeze. I practically ran up the mountain as the weather had me so jacked up with adrenaline.

There was another fire tower atop Stratton where I realized that while we were on Stratton Mountain, the ski slopes were actually on North Stratton Mountain, the peak just north of where I was. There was also a plaque at the summit explaining how the view from Stratton was what gave Benton McKaye the idea for the Appalachian Trail back in the 1920s.

The view, the excellent weather and the terrain I was hiking through really impressed upon me how beautiful Vermont actually is. My favorite place in the world is easily upstate NY near Schroon Lake and Lake Placid. Well, Vermont was nearly identical and I just couldn't get enough of it. Since entering Vermont, it was like someone flipped a switch: the number of bugs had dramatically decreased, the weather had cooled down significantly, the ponds and lakes are crystal clear, clean and refreshing, the woods are filled with beautiful birches and sweet smelling pine trees, and the towns are small and welcoming. Three days in and Vermont is easily my favorite state on the trail so far.

After Stratton, I hiked past Stratton Pond and couldn't resist taking my clothes off and swimming. The air was cold and Peach insisted on staying dry, but as soon as Great P and I dove in, we were joined by Lucky, Lolly, Cal, Piper, Peach, and Slim Rims.

Eventually, I got moving again and several hours later, I arrived at Route 11 where I hoped to catch a ride into Manchester Center, VT with Great P and Peach to do some laundry. The laundromat was right next to the Mountain Goat Outfitter (I showed my battered Darn Tough socks to them and received another pair free, but unfortunately, did not receive any other discounts for sharing my name with them), a beer store, a supermarket and a pizza joint. Does it get any better than that?

I split some beers with Peach, which we packed out, and crushed 6 slices of pizza. I also packed out four more. Three hours later, we were back on trail. We hiked three more miles uphill to Bromley Shelter completing a 23.1 mile day. While we had an excellent time around the campfire with Mouse, Slim Rims, Old Toe, Legs, Verge, Little Whip, our beers and leftover pizza (154 slices, Tim) I realized too late that we screwed up. It was a beautifully clear night AND it was a full moon. If we had hiked just one more mile to the summit of Bromley Mountain, we could have sat on the ski lift while we watched the sun set and the moon rise at the SAME time. I was so upset once I realized this and it will remain one of the only things I regret on this whole trip.

It helped that Slim Rims shared her weed chocolates with Great P and I. Before long, we were both giggling uncontrollably like school girls at the dumbest things. While I don't like smoking, consuming edibles is a completely different story. The high also helped me fall asleep in the shelter tonight, as there were very few campsites available at the shelter.

DAY 118

Starting Location: Bromley Shelter
Destination: Little Rock Pond Shelter and Tenting Area
Today's Miles: 17.8
Trip Miles: 1670.5

Jul 20, 2016 – On the heels of our big day yesterday, the Tenacious Tripod resolved to hike a shorter day today – 17.8 miles to the Little Rock Pond Shelter and Tenting Area. Even though the day was shorter, it was by no means easy as we summited 4 mountains: Bromley Mountain, Styles Peak, Peru Peak, and Baker Peak.

I arrived at the top of Bromley Mountain with Legs and we took some pictures on the ski lift while we lamented the fact that we missed out on the glorious cowboy camping opportunity. I continued on to Styles Peak where I shared my last beers with Peach and Legs at a gorgeous overlook.

CHILLING IN THE SKI LIFT AT THE TOP OF BROMLEY MOUNTAIN

For most of this trip (and most of my life, I guess), Peach and I have been reliving the punk rock music that got us through middle school and high school. On the descent from Styles Peak, we both put on the Say It Like You Mean It album by the Starting Line. Between the music and the outstanding weather, we literally ran down the mountain past Old Toe, Little Whip, Ben, Sara, and Piper. These 5 Long Trail hikers were honestly in awe of the Tenacious Tripod - between our stories, the beer, pizza and our speed, it was very obvious they were impressed. Don't get me wrong, I'm not bragging, but two nights later, we distinctly overheard both Old Toe and Little Whip tell someone on the phone about the "three hikers that packed out seven beers each and ran up and down mountains". Go big or go home.

I continued hiking along the picturesque Vermont section of trail until I arrived at Little Rock Pond. I sat with Legs and Longcloud for a while staring out at this lake that reminded me so much of my favorite Paradox Lake. We watched as a lone loon splashed around and made its characteristic calls that echoed off the mountains around us.

Just then, I turned around to see someone hiking southbound and mechanically said hello. I turned back to the pond and then did a double take. A man of about 40 was hiking completely naked. Today is July 20, exactly one month after the summer solstice, so we were thinking he just got the date wrong. However, why didn't he realize no one else was naked? Furthermore, we all realized he very clearly had no tan lines, which suggested he hiked naked pretty often.

Anyway, Legs, Verge, Great P, Peach and I swam to the other side of the lake to examine a large rock that looked to be a promising cliff jumping spot. Only the smaller rock proved to be safe - while jumping was fun, swimming back and forth across the large pond after an 18 mile day was not. I was physically exhausted and nearly ate everything in my food bag later that night.

We made another huge fire to drive the few bugs away and enjoyed yet another perfect night by the campfire. Everyone there was just high on everything Vermont had to offer, especially after all the demoralizing aspects of PA through MA.

DAY 119

Starting Location: Little Rock Pond Shelter and Tenting Area
Destination: Summit of Mt. Killington
Today's Miles: 24
Trip Miles: 1694.5

Jul 21, 2016 - We had another slow, lazy morning, but had some pretty ambitious plans for the day. We were to hike 24 miles to the summit of Mt. Killington where we hoped to make camp. That meant a long four mile climb to 3,908 feet at the end of a longer day.

I booked it out of camp around 8 am and flew to the first road crossing where I hoped to catch a hitch into Wallingford, VT to pick up a resupply package from Mom. To my dismay, the road had barely any traffic. It took Slim Rims and I nearly 30 minutes to catch a ride. Conversely, as soon as I got to the post office, no less than three people offered me a ride back to the trail. Two of these offers I was forced to refuse since I needed to sort through my package first.

As usual, my Mom outdid herself with the contents of my package. However, I did request my spare ground sheet for my tent - instead, she sent me a synthetic sleeping bag liner. Close, but not really, Mom. I ended up giving the liner to the guy who gave me a ride back to the trail head.

I hiked another six miles to the Clarendon Gorge parking area where Goldberry again surprised us with Trail Magic! This time, she brought us homemade quiche and fresh rhubarb squares along with watermelon, chips, sodas and Gatorades. Honestly, it was just good to see her again.

After dunking my shirt in the nearby river to help me cool down, I resumed hiking up Beacon Hill. While not especially long, Beacon Hill was very steep. A false summit and the subsequent incline had me panting for breath and forced me to stop several times. Over 100 miles in 5 days and that damn swim across the pond yesterday had finally started to wear me down. At the top, I still had about 8 miles to go.

About 5 miles before the summit of Mt. Killington, Great P, Peach and I took one final break under a bridge on some rocks next to a river to grab a snack. We had passed probably our most significant milestone yet - less than 500 miles to go to Katahdin! We took a moment under the bridge to reflect and think about that for a bit while Peach and I drank a celebratory beer.

For the next 5 miles, as I worked my way up to the summit, I thought about this milestone. While it is extremely exciting to have the end of this endeavor in sight, did I really want this trip of a lifetime to end? Maybe it was just the renewed energy supplied by Vermont that may soon wear off, but no, I did not. I thought back to my worst moments on trail - getting norovirus in the woods, my infected toe, the pain in my knee, getting flooded in a thunderstorm - and realized that I now appreciate those obstacles more now than I do my triumphs. People always marvel at all the small sufferings thru-hikers go through and immediately dismiss them in deference to the comforts that normal life offers. But I know that going back to work at a company in a field that doesn't especially interest me, whether it's in an office or in the field, will have me absolutely craving those sufferings. There's a reason people return to the mountains again and again and seek out the mental clarity provided by nature, that special focus born of high stakes undertakings. I'm beginning to have a true understanding of this sentiment and to realize with a stark calmness that there are things in life more important than a large, steady paycheck and the approval of my peers with respect to conformity.

The last 0.2 miles to the summit of Mt. Killington was alarmingly steep, but was so incredibly worth it. The world opened up below me as I stood on the bare rock and looked around. I crossed to the other side of the mountain and stood next to the gondola as I gazed at the surreal looking ski signs without the customary white backdrop of snow. I made camp in a small copse of pine trees and watched the intense wind rock my tent. It would be an interesting night, but damnit the sunset was worth it.

DAY 120

Starting Location: Summit of Mt. Killington
Destination: Campsite at the Inn at Long Trail
Today's Miles: 6.3
Trip Miles: 1700.8

Jul 22, 2016 - After five long days in a row (about 20 miles per day), the three of us agreed we deserved a reward day. As a result, our ambitious plans were to hike 6.3 miles to Route 4 and Brew Blaze all day. And that is exactly what we did.

We descended the steep trail from the Killington peak and quickly finished our 6 miles. We caught a hitch from Matthias into the city of Rutland, VT. Since the Hop'n Moose Brewing Company didn't open until noon, Great P, Peach and I walked into Clem's for a breakfast burrito and, quite unexpectedly, a couple beers.

After breakfast, we stood outside the brewery and waited for it to open. Noon came and went, but no one came to unlock the door or flip the 'Closed' sign around. Puzzled, we waited nearly 15 minutes until a couple simply walked up, opened the door and walked inside. Needless to say, we felt pretty foolish.

The brewery was pretty good and offered at least 10 different varieties of beer including cider for Great P. However, the bartender was horrible and was the reason we ended up leaving after only an hour. We walked down the street towards Route 4 in the hopes of getting a hitch to the Inn at Long

Trail, but were sidetracked by the BK Lounge where I slaughtered their dollar menu by ordering 20 nuggets and a spicy chicken sandwich.

A woman named Carol finally gave us a ride (hitching has been a little harder up here) and we were dropped off at the Inn at Long Trail, a famous hiker destination. The Inn was actually built in the early 1900s as a lodge for the Green Mountain Trail Club where they could rest after performing trail maintenance. The Inn was literally built for hikers. The AT used to run right through the Inn, but the government eventually moved the trail a half mile west to government owned lands. It's a shame seeing as the Inn was a valuable piece of history for both the AT and the LT.

At the Inn, we met Lucky, Lolly and Cal who were nice enough to buy us our first round. They had actually gotten engaged at the top of Mt. Killington and celebrated the same night at the Inn at Long Trail.

After a beer, Peach and I (Great P didn't feel like going) started trying to hitch 11 miles east to the Long Trail Brewery (I never realized the brewery was named after the actual Long Trail). It took us nearly an hour and three separate hitches to make it there, but, thankfully, it was worth it. The brewery was nestled at the bottom of a ridge line and next to a river – this made sitting out on the deck a very pleasant experience.

Eventually, we started to make our way back to the Inn – Yogi'ing (the term for starting a conversation with someone in the hopes of catching a ride) in the parking lot was unsuccessful so we were forced to hitch on Route 4. We were picked up by a professional fisherman who drove us all the way back.

The bartender handed me a pub menu that playfully offered hiker foods such as Ramen, tortillas, instant coffee, etc. After realizing it was a joke, I ordered the nachos and a hot dog and continued sharing beers with Lucky, Lolly, Ben, Piper, Sara, and Old Toe. We all drank until about 10 pm (which is extremely late for hikers) while we listened to a live Irish band called Shakespeare in the Alley.

The day was a resounding success and I had two more brewery stickers to show for it. I retired and walked back across the street to my tent.

DAY 121

Starting Location: Campsite at the Inn at Long Trail
Destination: Stealth Campsite after Chateauguay Road
Today's Miles: 14.9
Trip Miles: 1715.7

Jul 23, 2016 – Mama Mountain Goat had another visit planned – she would meet us in South Pomfret, VT, on Sunday to spend a day and a half up here. That meant an easy 2 days since South Pomfret was only about 25 miles away. Today, our goal was the Lookout 18 miles from our starting point.

After packing up, we walked back across the street to the Inn and ordered some breakfast. Old Toe joined us at the table and we chatted about both the Long Trail and the Appalachian Trail. The breakfast was excellent just like everything else at the Inn.

The day was pretty humid so it felt like we swam the first 10 miles. I stopped in at the shelter to grab some lunch after a fairly steep incline. Princess Peach and Great P joined me shortly and we discussed the thunderstorms that were supposed to be coming in the afternoon.

Great P was beat so he decided to just stay at the shelter that night. However, I pushed on another 6 miles to the top of the next hill and pitched camp quickly in a leafy stealth spot – I wanted to get set up before the rain began. The increased winds, falling temperature and loud claps of thunder signaled the storm was just about to explode.

Sure enough, about 5 minutes later, just after Peach made us some coffee, the skies opened up and we were caught in a wildly intense storm for about 15 minutes. I quietly sipped my coffee and had some dinner in my tent while the weather raged all around me. I was thankful that the hail that was forecast did not appear. I know I've been in a lot of thunderstorms at this point, but it's always a nerve racking experience. Sitting in my tent is just about all I can do in the woods where I am at the mercy of falling trees.

I had trouble falling asleep after the storm because I felt so gross (today is 9 days without a shower). Tomorrow could not come soon enough.

DAY 122

Starting Location: Stealth Campsite after Chateauguay Road
Destination: South Pomfret, VT / Lebanon, NH / Hotel
Today's Miles: 10.3
Trip Miles: 1726

Jul 24, 2016 - When I stepped out of my tent this morning, it appeared the storm left the woods immediately around me unscathed. Knowing we only had 9 miles to get to South Pomfret, we took our time eating breakfast. Great P actually caught up before we were done eating.

At the top of the first hill, we came to the Lookout. The Lookout is simply a cabin that sits on private property with a beautiful view of the surrounding land. The owners allow hikers to sleep in the cabin and enjoy the view. The platform on top of the structure gave us a panoramic view of the north and our first glimpse of the mighty White Mountains of New Hampshire that we've heard so much about.

The rest of the walk to South Pomfret was uneventful save for a man named Bob thrusting some of his home grown zucchinis on us as we walked into town. We soon arrived at Teago's General Store and bought some sandwiches to eat while we waited for my Mom to arrive.

Mom arrived around 1:30 pm and drove us to the Fairfield Inn and Suites in Lebanon, NH where we would be staying for the next two nights. After 10 days without a proper shower (I only rinsed off in three ponds), the massaging shower head could not be adequately described in words.

Laundry was just as satisfying except all of our clothes still smell after one wash cycle. It's all relative though. Mom also graciously brought me some supplies including my fourth pair of trail shoes, my fishing pole and reel (Thanks, Nick) - I definitely want to fish in the backwoods of Maine for some dinner.

Once we got into town, we realized just how bad the thunderstorm last night was - power was out in half the city and trees were down everywhere. We also heard that Legs and Verge, who were hiking just ahead of us yesterday, did indeed get hit with hail.

Four incredibly clean people left the hotel in search of some dinner. We selected an Italian place named Lui Lui next to the EMS and LL Bean outfitters. I needed a new pair of Superfeet insoles as the ones currently in my shoes had 1,200 miles on them - I realized they were cracked and worn all the way to the plastic. I was hoping this was the reason I was developing plantar fasciitis in my right foot and new insoles would remedy it before my feet became too painful.

Dinner was delicious and plentiful - with full stomachs, we actually drove to the movie theatre where the four of us saw The Secret Life of Pets. It was just as hysterical as the previews made it out to be. Even Peach, who had been giving me crap about wanting to see it for a month now, admitted he enjoyed it.

DAY 123

Starting Location: Lebanon, NH / Hotel
Destination: South Pomfret, VT / Lebanon, NH / Hotel
Today's Miles: 0
Trip Miles: 1726

Jul 25, 2016 - On my zero day, I managed to sleep in until 7 am - I already missed the sunrise and the sounds of the birds in the dark hotel room. I stole out of the room quietly so my Mom could continue sleeping and helped myself to coffee and an enormously large breakfast in the hotel lobby. I relaxed in the room for a few hours on a full stomach until around noon. By that time, I was already growing restless just sitting around. The four of us hopped in the car and went to the supermarket to resupply. My Mom and I pigged out on a plate full of the mozzarella sticks and chicken wings from the hot food trays.

Next up was a trip to Hanover, NH, home of Dartmouth University. We will actually be passing through Hanover tomorrow as the trail runs directly through the town / campus. Mom went off to shop while Peach, Great P and myself stopped at Molly's restaurant (a whopping 50 yards from the car) to grab some beers (or margaritas if you're Great P). My Mom finally arrived and everybody ordered lunch except me - I had about 12 mozzarella sticks in me. We started talking to the bartender - in two weeks, she was moving to Oregon into a $700,000 house she's never seen before with a boyfriend who works as a movie director in Jamaica. She's a bartender and a karaoke DJ: DJ Hot Wheels. Oh and she's already been divorced at the age of 25. I mean you can't make this shit up - I could practically see my Mom's mind blowing up as this lady tells us all this.

After Molly's, we drove down to West Hartford, NH to check out the Harpoon Brewery to continue this Brew Blazing adventure. A scoop of ice cream at the nearby shop was $4 so I walked directly to the brewery to drink some beer and collect another sticker. My Mom talked to us about life and Peach pushed all of her buttons as it is ridiculously easy to do. Our final stop for the day was the Seven Barrel Brewery in Lebanon, NH - yet ANOTHER brewery checked off our list and ANOTHER sticker collected. Peach actually ate a quick dinner and then hitched the two miles back to the hotel while my Mom was shopping. Mom joined Great P and I shortly after running her errands. We ordered some dinner, sipped some beers (or ciders if you're Great P and cosmopolitans if you're my Mom - I don't think she's ever ordered one she doesn't think is too strong) and actually stayed for trivia. The trivia here was pretty standard, I suppose - six rounds of 10 questions with cards that allow a team to double down on a round and to earn the points for a specific question for free. However, the method in which the prizes were awarded was just bizarre. To make a long story short, we came in last place and walked away with three of the six candy prizes, which were awarded after each round. The winners of each round had the choice of selecting the topic of the next round or a box of candy. Last place for each round received the remaining option. So, basically, people chose questions over candy...it's bizarre I know. After trivia, we drove back to the hotel and got another good night's sleep. I needed it sorely especially since I felt a cold coming on. I think it's pretty ironic that I get a cold on my day of rest, but I guess I'll have to deal with it. It will not be fun mouth breathing up the White Mountains, which I will be hiking later this week.

DAY 124

Starting Location: South Pomfret, VT
Destination: Stealth Campsite north of Dartmouth
Today's Miles: 21.7
Trip Miles: 1747.7

Jul 26, 2016 - After another gourmet continental breakfast at the hotel, my Mom drove us back to the trailhead in South Pomfret. To make up for our zero, we were looking at 21.7 miles into Hanover, NH - that's right, today we would be entering our 13th state on the AT!

The hiking itself was pretty mild with a few unremarkable ups and downs. As always after a zero, it's just tough getting back into things. A warm, slightly humid day didn't make matters any better, but as walking is literally my job right now, sometimes I'm obliged to hike even when I don't want to. The Count of Monte Cristo and his twisted revenge plots kept me more than entertained.

Ten miles into the hike brought me to West Hartford, VT. A Sobo hiker had remarked to me, "Make sure you jump off the bridge", but I literally had no idea what he was talking about. As I crossed said bridge into town. I looked down and realized exactly what he was talking about. On the other side of the bridge, another Nobo hiker, Captain Red, hailed me and told me a lady named Linda was doing Trail Magic on her front porch. She was serving soda, coffee, muffins, chips, meat sticks and crackers. It seemed like nearly every hiker on the trail stopped in at her place. Linda even left the house and told us we could stay and hang out.

Anyway, after indulging in some refreshment, I waited for Peach so we could jump off the bridge. Great P had sent a message ahead that he was taking it slow and would meet us in Hanover. The bridge jump wasn't quite as good as the James River, but still very enjoyable and refreshing.

Another 10 miles brought me to a stream where I stopped to fill up on water. All of a sudden, I heard an ear splitting crack and a massive oak tree fell in the woods about 100 yards in front of me. I guess it was a good thing I stopped for water. Clambering over fallen trees had become a theme all day – that storm two nights ago really did some damage.

Another mile along the trail had me crossing the Connecticut River into New Hampshire! Dartmouth students sunbathing on the beach or practicing crew looked up as I let out a yell. Only two states left!

Finally, I walked into the town of Hanover and right into the middle of the Dartmouth campus. I sat on a bench on the green while I waited for Peach and thought how odd it felt to be sitting around all these college kids with my hiking gear.

When Peach arrived, we walked along the trail to a pizza place called EBA – Everything But Anchovies. No, I actually did not get pizza because they had a chicken sandwich special that I couldn't pass up. While eating, I perused a list of Hanover Trail Angels I picked up at Linda's. These Trail Angels offered to put up a certain number of hikers for the night in their own homes. That's hospitality. I called all 10 numbers on the list – three were either out of town or already full, but I never heard back from the others. Our only option was to hike to the other side of town and stealth camp right behind the baseball field.

DAY 125

Starting Location: Stealth Campsite north of Dartmouth
Destination: Lyme Center, NH / Mr. and Mrs. Cotter's Home
Today's Miles: 16.8
Trip Miles: 1764.5

Jul 27, 2016 - Legs and Verge invited the three of us to their grandparents' house tonight. They would pick us up in Lyme Center, NH, which meant we had 16.8 miles to get there. For some stupid reason, I ambitiously told Legs we would be there between 12:30 and 1 pm.

Before we left camp, Great P informed us that he would be zeroing in Hanover due to pain in his IT Band. Having suffered from the same pain for about 400 miles, I showed him some stretches and exercises that eventually resolved my issue. That sucks, though, as it was a lot of fun hiking with him. Who knows when or if we would see him again?

As I left camp, I was hailed by Colonel who I hadn't seen since Woods Hole Hostel near mile 550. Apparently, he ran out of money and actually exchanged work for food and a place to sleep for 2 months! At the end of his stay, the owners paid him some money and he traveled up to VT to continue hiking north. When he hits Katahdin, he'll go back to VT and head south back to the hostel.

Anyway, today's hike had 2 pretty significant climbs - Moose Mountain and Holt's Ledge. As I started to climb Moose Mountain, I realized just how ambitious my meeting time with Legs and Verge was. The only time I stopped all morning was to throw back a Mountain Dew from a man doing Trail Magic. Unfortunately, I quickly thanked him and explained that I could not stay and talk as I had 4 miles left to go in an hour.

I practically ran up Holt's Ledge and reached the summit literally shaking and gasping for air. My stuffed up nose made breathing much more difficult during the climb and I was nearly spent for the lengthy downhill to the road crossing. I arrived at 1:02 pm, though, so I made it. Peach arrived about 20 minutes behind me with flushed cheeks - he was understandably cursing at me for setting the ridiculous meeting time.

Legs and Verge arrived around 1:30 pm and drove us back to Mr. and Mrs. Cotter's absurdly beautiful house at the base of the mountains. The house had a porch on three sides, a garden, a barn, and a large, beautiful lawn. What more could you ask for? The Cotters had brownies, chips, salsa, and fresh raspberries laid out to keep us busy until dinner. They also let us shower and do some laundry while we waited for Training Wheels, Sweets and Jingle to arrive.

The rest of the afternoon was a blast. We played bocce ball, Pictionary, and relaxed with beers until dinner. For dinner, Mr. Cotter grilled us burgers, hot dogs and sausages while Mrs. Cotter laid out salad, chips, baked beans and potato salad.

Following dinner, I had the privilege of lighting the massive bonfire set up in the backyard. Mr. Cotter held the propane tank while I held the flamethrower and ignited the hell out of the massive pile of wood. We had to move the bench at least 30 feet back from the fire because it was so hot. We roasted some s'mores, which are actually impossible to eat cleanly with a beard, by the way.

THE TRAIL FAMILY AT THE COTTER'S HOME

Finally, those of us still awake went in the hot tub and while we soaked, stared up at the stunning night sky. It was dark enough to see the Milky Way as well as a handful of shooting stars and satellites. I was a little bummed Training Wheels did not join us in the hot tub.

DAY 126

Starting Location: Lyme Center, NH / Mr. and Mrs. Cotter's Home
Destination: Stealth Campsite near North Jacobs Creek
Today's Miles: 10.7
Trip Miles: 1775.2

Jul 28, 2016 – I had Reese's Puffs for breakfast this morning! It must have been the first time I've had cereal for breakfast in several years, but it was delicious. Mr. Cotter even offered to let me pack out the rest of the Puffs with me. All in all, my stay at the Cotter's was extremely nice. I'm grateful to have been invited and to have met people like Legs and Verge on the trail. Unfortunately, even though they're slack packing a few days while at their grandparents, they're not leaving until Sunday, which means we may not see them for a while. I really hope they catch up because it's a real pleasure hiking with them.

Peach and I were dropped back off at the road crossing at about 10:30 am. Mr. Cotter seemed genuinely impressed by the amount of beer we consumed yesterday. I did not feel well (the beer may or may not have had something to do with this) – I didn't get a lot of sleep, my cold had deteriorated, and I had to make 3 excursions off trail because I had diarrhea. Smarts Mountain (about 3,500 feet) slapped me around for nearly 2 hours before I reached the top. The view from the fire tower was worth it, but barely, as I was struggling pretty hard.

I descended to South Jacobs Creek where I tried to rehydrate. Peach walked up and saw that I did not look well so he suggested we call it a day at North Jacobs Creek just up the hill. I gratefully accepted and we set up in a stealth spot halfway up Mt. Cube. I made a small fire to cook dinner and was literally asleep by 6 pm.

DAY 127

Starting Location: Stealth Campsite near North Jacobs Creek
Destination: Beaver Brook Shelter
Today's Miles: 23
Trip Miles: 1798.2

Jul 29, 2016 - I slept for literally 12 hours last night and woke up feeling incredibly refreshed. My nose and throat were still a little stuffed, but the rest of my body was rejuvenated. It's a good thing, too, because today I entered the White Mountains that I've heard so much about.

It's pretty common knowledge that the Whites are undoubtedly the toughest hiking on trail, but, honestly, I was looking forward to them. They may be challenging, but, supposedly, their beauty is just as unsurpassed.

Peach and I trekked over the final mile of Mt. Cube. The summit provided us with our first glimpse of the Whites in Mt. Moosilauke at 4,802 feet. It definitely did look imposing against its blue and white background. Ten miles into my hike, I caught a hitch with Peach to the Green House Restaurant for the Moosilauke Monster pizza challenge - a fully loaded 30 inch pizza for two people that needed to be eaten in 90 minutes or less. Despite my failed attempt at the Godzilla, I was and will always be absolutely certain that I can complete any pizza challenge.

The Green House restaurant was closed! Thoroughly disappointed, we hitched back the other way along the same road and settled for Moose Scoops ice cream in the small town of Warren, NH. Oddly enough, we also got to see a 73 foot tall missile randomly erected in the middle of town.

We hitched back to trail and were treated to home grown shiitake mushrooms from our chauffeur. Fully satisfied in the belly area, I continued hiking and summited Mt. Mist where I again gazed on the beast that is Moosilauke. After I walked down the north side of Mt. Mist, I had a 4 mile ascent to the summit of Moosilauke. I did get some fuel in the form of Trail Magic at the road crossing just before the ascent. Three oatmeal pies and a Mountain Dew can do quite a bit for you.

The 4 mile ascent consisted of 3 miles straight up and 1 gradual mile along a saddle to the summit. I saw my first moose on that gradual mile, but honestly wish I hadn't. Apparently, this moose had a neurological disease that caused it to walk above the tree line and stay there. Well, this moose has been up there for close to 3 weeks slowly starving to death. The moose was completely emaciated and just looked confused as it stood stupidly in the same spot. Another hiker behind me reported it was laying down when he walked past. It was incredibly sad and it's a real pity someone won't shoot it and put it out of its misery. The only reason it hasn't been shot is because whoever does it is legally responsible for removing the body (an admittedly difficult task at the top of a mountain).

Anyway, the 360 degree panoramic view at the summit of Moosilauke is tough to describe unless you see it for yourself. To the north, the mighty White Mountains stood resolute while to the south, the ridge line faded until it was lost to sight. The sun was shining, the wind was blowing, and the visibility was outstanding.

My sweat soaked shirt is the reason I ultimately had to hike down to the Beaver Brook Shelter – it was quite cold with the wind blowing so strongly. A fire had already been started by some Sobos so I was able to cook some dinner, but the tenting situation was less than pleasing. I ended up pitching on a double incline so that I constantly slid to one corner of my tent, which made it very difficult to sleep. However, I could find some solace in my 23 mile day and the fact that I had finally made it to the Whites!

DAY 128

Starting Location: Beaver Brook Shelter
Destination: Stealth Campsite near Franconia Notch
Today's Miles: 17.8
Trip Miles: 1816

Jul 30, 2016 - People said the Whites were hard, but I didn't appreciate it until today. I mean, holy shit! The elevation profile for the Whites recorded in our guide book looks like AWOL (the author) left the room and a child just scribbled mischievously all over the page. People also said the Whites were the most beautiful part of the AT and today I also came to appreciate that sentiment. Even though the hiking is hard, the terrain and the views are humbling to say the least.

This morning began with a steep downhill on the north side of Moosilauke. For almost 2 miles we descended the mountain with a cascading waterfall on our left. As soon as we hit the bottom, the uphill began again. Mt. Wolf wasn't anything special, but this mountain set up the South and North Kinsman mountains at 4,358 and 4,293 feet, respectively.

The ascent up South Kinsman was yet again parallel to a waterfall. I passed 2 swimming holes, but passing a third was out of the question. I rinsed off in the cold pool at the base of the falls and restarted my ascent. The last mile to the summit was easily the hardest and most fun hiking I've done on trail so far. The trail was so vertical that I had to stow my trekking poles in my pack and use both arms and legs to get myself up the rock faces. It took forever, but, again, I was rewarded with surreal views at the top including a glimpse of the famous Franconia Ridge! The ridge would have to wait until tomorrow.

Thankfully, the Kinsman mountains were the last uphill portions for the day. Peach and I descended to the Franconia Notch and stealth camped. We hitched into nearby Lincoln, NH to resupply and to indulge at a burger place called McDonald's. Between the 2 of us, we crushed 8 McDoubles, 40 chicken nuggets and a large order of fries. We also picked up a six pack to help us unwind back at the tent site.

Laying down in my tent was the most wonderful feeling in the world. My entire body was sore from the day's exertion. My plantar fasciitis continues to get worse, but it's easy to ignore while hiking these crazy beautiful mountains.

DAY 129

Starting Location: Stealth Campsite near Franconia Notch
Destination: Galehead Hut
Today's Miles: 13
Trip Miles: 1829

Jul 31, 2016 - I thought the last 2 days were beautiful, but I was wholly unprepared for the show today. The hike began with a 3 mile uphill struggle to get up onto Franconia Ridge. Then, I crested the tree line to behold Mt. Lincoln in front of me. It literally felt like I was walking on top of the world. The ridge fell away sharply on either side of me and, without trees to obstruct my view, I could see at least 5 miles ahead of me. The picturesque trail wound its way through rock piles marked with cairns up over Mt. Lincoln (5,089 feet), Mt. Lafayette (5,263 feet) and eventually, Mt. Garfield (4,458 feet). And of course, the continuous panoramic view was nothing short of breathtaking.

Peach and I shared a beer at the top of Mt. Lafayette and tried to control our excitement and enthusiasm. We couldn't believe where we were. Eventually, we had to keep moving (again, the combination of sweaty clothing, decreased temperatures and the increased wind made for a really cold environment).

After only 13 miles in 8 hours (just for comparison, Peach and I could routinely hike around 24 miles in 8 hours - the Whites were rudely adjusting us to a much slower hiking pace) we stumbled, exhausted, into the Galehead Hut. In the Whites, there are several huts that tourists or thru-hikers can stay in for a hefty fee of $125 per person. These huts have no showers or electricity and must be hiked to, but they do offer homemade dinner and breakfast. It's common for these huts to offer 'work for stay' to between 2 and 3 thru-hikers each day. Today, Peach and I were lucky enough to be those thru-hikers at the Galehead Hut.

We sat around, relaxed, and read from 4 to 8 pm until dinner had been served to the paying guests. We got the leftover pasta shells, peas, bread and curry soup. It was pretty tasty despite the fact that it was a bit cold. Our sleeping quarters on the floor of the main dining room was clogged with guests until after 9 pm. I was freaking exhausted and didn't want to wait so I cowboy camped on the front porch and allowed the cool breeze to lull me to sleep. Mola, Diatom and Helter Skelter showed up late and were granted floor space for sleeping.

DAY 130

Aug 1, 2016 - Breakfast at the Galehead Hut was served at 7 am so the thru-hikers had to be up and out of the hut by 6 am. Peach and I stuck around while we heard breakfast being served inside and hungrily waited until the leftovers were available. At around 8 am, Erica, the hut master, offered us leftover eggs, oatmeal, gingerbread cake, canned peaches and coffee.

Following breakfast, the three of us (an older gentleman named Walkman was also doing work for stay) began doing our 'work'. The work consisted of sweeping all the floors and cleaning out the bunk beds. Erica had stated yesterday that the work would take about 2 hours, but we were finished in less than 45 minutes. The only downside to the work for stay in my opinion was that we had too much time to sit around. Otherwise, the work we had to do was most definitely worth the homemade food we were served even if it was just leftovers.

Our actual hike began with a doozie this morning. We had a 0.8 mile hike up the side of South Twin Mountain (4,902 feet) that was literally more vertical than a staircase. I was just thankful it was at the beginning of the day rather than at the end. The views at the top were worth it as the Whites continued to dazzle. However, looking out, I could clearly see some rain moving in.

The rest of the day was mostly downhill into Crawford Notch, but it rained for about half of the hike down. The footing on the steep downhill slopes was insanely treacherous especially considering my shoes had zero traction on the wet rocks (My shoes have never had good traction, but they did solve all of my other foot problems after Damascus. I just dealt with it, but the Whites are less forgiving than the rest of the trail.) As I neared Zealand Falls Hut, I fell and tore up my left forearm on a rock. Peach and I took refuge at the hut and I washed off the blood that was dripping down my arm, which was enough to alarm the other hikers there.

I beat Peach in consecutive games of cribbage (the student has overtaken the master) and we waited for the rain to stop. I treated myself to some coffee and slices of cake that were for sale. Napster bought the $2 bottomless soup and ate 11 bowlfuls.

Peach and I got moving again and descended to Crawford Notch, the gap between the Franconia Ridge and the Presidential Range. Peach needed to pick up a package at the AMC Highland Center 3 miles off trail so we hitched a ride from a crabby old man that consistently complained about the challenging features of the Whites. Still, we arrived at the center and walked in cold and wet to pick up the package.

As it turns out, the concierge told us the package was actually at the holding center 3 more miles down the road at the Mt. Washington Resort. With hopes of returning to the trail and stealth camping near the road, we hitched again to the resort. This place was fancier than a resort you'd find in Bermuda – it looked like a white and red castle surrounded by a 9 hole golf course and a field full of horses. I can't tell you how odd it felt walking into a lobby where a woman was having her portrait painted while dripping wet and smelling like a literal asshole – I hadn't showered or laundered in about 6 days. While Peach was told that the post office was closed until 9 am the next morning, I sat on a cushioned couch and allowed it to soak up the water from my shorts. I discreetly inched down the couch periodically to allow a new, dry section of couch to soak up some more water.

So, we had to walk all the way back to the road and hitch back to the Highland Center.
It took about 20 minutes to get a hitch while we stood shivering in the windy rain. At this point, we decided we would cave and get bunks at the Highland Center for $75, which included the dinner and breakfast buffet. This way we would be able to shower, dry all our equipment, and reset a bit. Plus, we hadn't paid for lodging since Duncannon, PA.

At the bunkhouse, I met Spielberg, Chili Pepper, El Alto, Spider, and Cookie, who I already knew. We all crushed the buffet and then I beat Peach again in cribbage before falling asleep.

Tomorrow, the Presidentials!

DAY 131

Starting Location: Crawford Notch / AMC Highland Center
Destination: Stealth Campsite near Sphinx Trail
Today's Miles: 14.5
Trip Miles: 1858.2

Aug 2, 2016 - Today was a day to remember on trail. While I still think the Franconia Ridge was more majestic, the Presidential Range did not disappoint by any means. The entire range stretches for almost 23 miles with the famous / infamous Mt. Washington serving as its pinnacle at 6,288 feet. Our goal for the day was to hike over Washington and stealth camp below the tree line a couple miles beyond.

On the way to breakfast (the amount of bacon I consumed was close to disgusting), Elyse at the concierge, who had given us the hitch back to the Highland Center last night, stopped me to hand me Peach's package. While it was great we didn't have to wait until 9 am, it was obvious that someone overlooked the package yesterday at the Highland Center. Peach was a little frustrated when he found out.

Anyway, we caught a hitch back to trail with another hiker named Grandma and started up Mt. Webster (3,910 feet). About halfway up, I slipped on another rock, but instead of sliding, my legs went up and I fell bodily onto the rock. My thigh and the underside of my upper arm slammed into the edges of the rock while my other forearm scraped against another rock. It's amazing how much can pass through your mind in less than a second, but, immediately, I thought I broke my arm - I unconsciously thought that I'll go to the hospital, wait for a day or two and then get back on trail wearing a cast. I immediately regretted the fact that I'd probably lose my friends as they continued hiking. But once I gave my mind some time to assess the situation, I realized I just bruised my arm, ripped up my other forearm pretty badly and had a dead leg. I was in pain and bleeding pretty profusely, but things could definitely be worse. Regardless, it was not a good way to start a hike through the Presidential Range.

I resumed limping up the trail – on the bright side, my leg was completely dead so I couldn't feel the burn as I worked my way up the mountain. It did, however, hurt quite a bit. After another hiker forced me to stop so he could clean up my arm with some antiseptic, I reached the summit of Mt. Webster where the view made everything hurt just a little less. Two songs got me pumped back up: "My Body" by Young the Giant and, of course, "Tubthumping" by Chumbawumba. Grandma tried to tell me that Tubthumping was actually a song about politics – I politely told him to fuck off.

The top of Mt. Webster afforded me my first view of Mt. Washington – it was covered in so much crap (cell towers, buildings, and weather instruments, etc.) that it reminded me of the mountain from the home planet of the Monstars from Space Jam. Still, it was cool to see it in the distance all day and continue striving for it.

I hiked over Webster and Mt. Jackson (4,052 feet) to arrive at the Mizpah Hut for a much needed water resupply and lunch break. I kept it short, though, because the weather was looking good on Washington and that doesn't happen very often. The top of the mountain is cloudy over 300 days out of the year due to its height and steep faces and literally protrudes into the jet stream. It also is known for having the worst weather in America and, arguably, the world. One hundred fifty-seven people have died hiking Washington and it boasts the fastest recorded wind speed in the world at 212 mph. Another cool fact that I read while reading about the geology of the Presidentials is that about 460 million years ago, Mt. Washington was 8 miles higher than it is today, which is considerably higher than Everest! That's a hell of a lot of erosion.

Anyway, I continued hiking and crested Mt. Pierce (4,312 feet) and Mt. Franklin (5,004 feet). Washington was next. I stopped in at the Lake of the Clouds Hut, a mere mile from the summit, to fill up on water and clean out my wounds again (one of the employees was visibly alarmed and asked if I needed medical attention). Then, I was on my way and before you know it, I was at the summit! People drive their cars up there, take a cog train up there (it's actually thru-hiker tradition to moon the people on the cog train, but since a few hikers have been arrested recently, I regretfully refrained) but I walked 12.5 miles uphill to get there. That's a damn good feeling.

PEACH AND I AT THE TOP OF MT. WASHINGTON

I had a snack at the top with Peach, Sherpa, Napster, and Grandma (not just a snack, but a fantastic Whoopie Pie containing nearly 800 calories), waited in a freaking line to take a picture at the summit and started making my way down the trail. Tourists at the top were amazed at how far we've walked to get here and a few wished me congratulations. Thanks, but I'm not finished yet.

Peach and I hiked another 2 miles to the intersection of the Sphinx Trail and started hiking down a ravine to find a stealth spot below tree line. Luckily, we found what must have been the only grassy spot in the Whites above the tree line a couple hundred feet off trail set up home for the night. It was cold and breezy with a clear blue sky above us just the way I like it.

"My body tells me no, but I won't quit because I want more... Cause I want more!"

DAY 132

Starting Location: Stealth Campsite near Sphinx Trail
Destination: Stealth Campsite near Pinkham Notch
Today's Miles: 11.5
Trip Miles: 1869.7

Aug 3, 2016 - After our memorable day yesterday, all we had to do today was finish up the Presidential Range and hike into Pinkham Notch. That was only 11.5 miles and mostly downhill except for the only significant summit of the day: Mt. Madison (5,366 feet). I woke up to a frigid morning above tree line and above 5,000 feet - there was so much condensation on my tent that it was completely saturated. Luckily, a brilliant sun was rising in the northeast to dry it off while I sipped Peach's coffee to warm myself.

I quickly hiked the 5 miles to Madison Hut in the hopes of finding some leftover breakfast. I was not disappointed as a huge bowl of oatmeal was placed on the table. I also did pay $1 for a piece of marble cake, which was definitely worth it. At the hut, I ran into Jellydog again who had finally caught his friends Panda, Mumbles, and Whiplash. We all watched Peach literally run down the mountain singing at the top of his lungs and had a good laugh.

Although I showered 2 days ago, my shirt smelled like a rotting animal carcass. Whenever I hiked uphill and tucked my nose forward, I would actually stop and look around to see if I could find the source of the horrible smell until I realized it was me. That's the difference between a synthetic shirt (what I was currently wearing) and a Merino wool shirt (what I started the trail with). Although I did not need a resupply, I insisted to Peach that we hitch into Gorham, NH to do some laundry. He smelled just as bad so he agreed.

As I descended from the summit of Madison, I took one last look around at the unique landscape that exists in the rocky world above tree line before plunging into the boreal world of the conifers. We arrived at Pinkham Notch early – around 1 pm – and secured a ride to town without even sticking out our thumb. Three young ladies from Michigan were finishing up a section hike and offered to give us a ride.

Laundry was a success if you consider that all my clothes still causing me to recoil in disgust a success (the gentleman who gave us a ride back to trail made bluntly pointed out that we had wasted our money at the laundromat). At the very least, I removed the crusty stuff from my socks so they didn't create hot spots. Peach and I walked across the street to Mr. Pizza and had ourselves some calzones and $8 pitchers of PBR.

We each grabbed a 6 pack for the evening and finally got a hitch back to the notch where we would be stealth camping, which had been our specialty for a while now. We found an awesome spot right next to a creek where I could clean off. I set up my tent on a bed of soft, decomposing pine needles and got a fire going. We were soon joined by Cookie, Jellydog, Whiplash, Panda and Mumbles to make for a pretty excellent night.

DAY 133

Starting Location: Stealth Campsite near Pinkham Notch
Destination: Stealth Campsite south of Rattle River Shelter
Today's Miles: 19
Trip Miles: 1888.7

Aug 4, 2016 – Ok, so I tackled Moosilauke, soared over the Franconia Ridge, and survived the Presidential Range. The only section left in the White Mountains along the AT was the Wildcat Range – 19 miles over 9 peaks. That was the ambitious agenda for today.

The hike began with yet another grueling climb up Wildcat Mountain (Peak E – 4,066 feet), which proved to be a lot of fun since it was at the beginning of the day and it was full of those vertical rock scrambles that involve the use of your whole body. It's pretty freaky when you pause on an up step and realize your pack is literally pulling you backwards off the rock face. You either recover or you fall for a long time. The summit of Wildcat was extremely picturesque with the gondola (it's a ski mountain) set before the Presidential Range with Washington looming in the background.

The next 4 miles consisted of brutal up and downs over Peaks D, C and A (3,990, 4,278 and 4,422 feet, respectively). Four peaks in the first 6 miles! We made an insanely steep descent into Carter Notch where we stopped in the Carter Notch Hut for some lunch. This would be the last hut I would see in the White Mountains.

Whenever I hear the word 'notch', I've come to expect an extreme of some sort. Carter Notch was no different. Following the insanely steep descent into the notch was an equally vertical ascent, but to an even higher elevation. Just when I thought I hit the summit of Carter Dome, I realized I only reached the edge of the dome. The last quarter mile of the ascent was awkwardly pitched on the rock face so that my calves were the only thing preventing me from sliding down. My calves were on fire by the time I reached the summit.

The dome provided one last look at the Presidential Range before we plunged back into the tree line. The day was still young and I had 4 more mountains to climb before I could lay down to sleep, which I couldn't wait for, by the way. Over the next 8 miles, I summited Mt. Hight (4,653 feet), Middle and North Carter Mountains (4,610 and 4,539 feet, respectively) and, finally, Mt. Moriah (3,976 feet). I then descended about 4 miles to the Rattle River Shelter.

After all that, exhaustion isn't even the right word anymore. It did feel good, though, knowing that we knocked out the entire Wildcat Range in one day. Peach and I found a stealth spot across the Rattle River next to one of the better swimming holes we've seen on trail. You could actually jump off a rock and do a can-opener without fear of hitting the bottom. We made a small fire, sat back and reflected on the day's work. Peach looked at me and said, "Well, we did it again, Goat". Go big or go home. Jellydog, Whiplash, Panda and Mumbles joined us yet again for some revelry in the swimming hole and around the fire.

We worked our asses off the past few days and when we crunched the numbers, realized we averaged 16.1 miles through the White Mountains. That's crazy.

DAY 134

Starting Location: Stealth Campsite south of Rattle River Shelter
Destination: Stealth Campsite near Page Pond
Today's Miles: 10
Trip Miles: 1898.7

Aug 5, 2016 - As a reward for our hard work yesterday, Peach and I planned on heading back into Gorham, NH for some breakfast food. I was hoping it would cure some of the aches and pains coursing through the battered body the Whites had left me with. So, at Guldie's, I ordered the following: 2 scrambled eggs with American cheese, hash browns, 1 English muffin, 1 buttered bagel, 1 kielbasa, and 1 giant pancake (this thing was about 14 inches in diameter and substituted nicely for a standard short stack of pancakes). The waitress gave her usual warning that it was a lot of food. It went in one ear and out the other - she was left flabbergasted when she collected my plates with only half an English muffin remaining.

Peach had to resupply, so I took a seat in the park and waited patiently. I ran into Lucky and Lolly, who determined that they would not finish their section hike at Katahdin before being called back to teach at school. I also saw Longcloud, who was staying at the local hostel.

On top of the 2 easy miles I walked to the road this morning, I had 8 left on our short day. However, 7 of those remaining miles were uphill on a relatively humid day and my legs were screaming with every step. I also can't rid myself of the cold I acquired on my last zero - every few hundred yards, I cough up some phlegm or blow my nose on the ground. It screws with my breathing as I ascend and that's why it bothers me.

Well, I made it to Page Pond, but I crawled the entire way, stopping every few hundred yards to catch my breath and quench the fire coursing through my limbs. Even my upper body was sore from yesterday, though that's not saying much since I can barely do 20 pushups nowadays. On the bright side, I now have less than 300 miles remaining in my trip!

Being a huge hockey fan, I like to think of this hike as my own Stanley Cup seeing as I'll never actually win the real one. When I watch playoff hockey, the game reaches a climax of fervor and excitement when the Stanley Cup is in the building. Knowing the cup is within reach just sets everyone on edge. Players and fans alike want nothing more than to reach the end of the game and see the Stanley Cup presented in all its glory. But, once the cup is revealed, then it's over and the long wait for next season begins. Well, I don't have a next season and I've always wanted the playoffs to last as long as humanly possible (with the exception of that game when the cup is in the building). So, rather than run to Katahdin, I am going to enjoy the hell out of these last three weeks. I'll get my Stanley Cup, but, honestly, it's all about the playoffs right now.

Once I set up in a stealth spot near Page Pond, I sat on a rock on the edge with Peach and cooked some dinner over the fire. I wanted to try my fishing setup tonight, but the pond was bursting with lily pads, which would have entangled the fishing line. There will be plenty more lakes – if I catch just 1 fish and eat it for dinner, carrying all the gear for 2 states will have been 100% worth it.

Unfortunately, I still haven't seen any signs of moose. Actually, there have been countless sightings of moose tracks and piles of scat, but no signs of the actual animal.

DAY 135

Starting Location: Stealth Campsite near Page Pond
Destination: Full Goose Shelter and Campsite
Today's Miles: 13.5
Trip Miles: 1912.2

Aug 6, 2016 - If I thought Maine would be any easier than the Whites, I was very wrong. Maybe I was just still exhausted and didn't have enough time to fully recover physically, but I was absolutely dead from the get-go this morning. Peach and I were trying to maintain a 15 mile per day pace, but I wasn't sure it was sustainable in this terrain.

Our first mountain of the day was Mt. Success, which is ironic because as soon as you get to the top, your success is rewarded by a view of the next peak sticking up like a giant, majestic middle finger. It's been this way for almost 2 weeks now. In this particular case, it was the three peaks of Goose Eye Mountain. It's funny, though, because as I peered at Goose Eye, I couldn't determine where the trail actually went up the mountain. I immediately dismissed the bare rock face directly in front of me because there's no way a hiker could climb it.

Before I could tackle Goose Eye, I crossed the border between New Hampshire and Maine. I also passed the 1900 mile mark. I was officially into my 14th and final state! As I contemplated this, I realized I had been just standing in the middle of the trail staring at the sign for almost 10 minutes. I have never doubted for a second that I would finish this thing, but I guess the reality of my thru-hike really hit home at this moment. I was going to summit Katahdin. A section hiker named Sasha broke my reverie and we took each other's picture.

As it turns out, the bare rock face on Goose Eye was indeed the trail. Sections of rebar had been installed in the rock face so that I literally climbed a ladder to the top. As ridiculous as this is, the views at the tops of these peaks were stunning with the wind whipping from west to east.

I continued on to Full Goose Campsite and Shelter where Peach and I decided to call it a day. Since it had rained a bit and we were still exhausted, we would save the Mahoosuc Notch for first thing tomorrow morning. This way, it would be safer, we would be less drained and it would be more enjoyable. Peach made a cribbage board out of a piece of wood and we played a few games while we ate dinner. We were eventually joined by Sherpa and Scavenger.

DAY 136

Starting Location: Full Goose Shelter and Campsite
Destination: Frye Notch Lean-to
Today's Miles: 15.5
Trip Miles: 1927.7

Aug 7, 2016 - As I left the shelter this morning, Scavenger absently addressed me by my trail name. Consequently, about 20 yards down the trail, I heard a total stranger yell, "Bye, Mountain Goat! I've been following your blog - you have beautiful writing". Momentarily stunned, the only response I put together was "Thanks!". She finally yelled "Hakuna Matata!" as a sort of proof that she actually did read my posts. I just laughed and kept walking.

The Mahoosuc Notch is widely recognized as the most difficult mile on the AT. AWOL's guide actually labels it as "most difficult OR fun mile of the AT". It is a jumbled mass of boulders between two mountains that requires thru-hikers to scramble as they have never scrambled before. The notch is also known to be very cold because, since it is situated on the north side of a mountain, it literally never sees the light of day - piles of snow and ice can often be seen in some of the crevices under the rocks even during summer.

I tucked my trekking poles into my pack and started scrambling. Almost immediately, I ran into a Sobo that said he had been in the notch for almost 90 minutes...for 1 mile! The oversized rock scramble was an absolute blast as I scaled boulders like a spider only to swing down the other sides like a monkey. The entire mile took me 42 minutes (I was curious to see how long it would take) and was satisfyingly tiring as I used my entire body for the length of the notch.

Immediately after the notch, I climbed the Mahoosuc Arm, which was just a prolonged vertical rock scramble similar to what I experienced throughout the Whites. As much fun as I had, it was a relief to descend into Grafton Notch around 10 miles later.

I walked into the parking lot and I heard a woman say, "Mountain Goat?". Again, stunned, I turned to her and asked her how she knew that because I certainly didn't recognize her. It turns out that her name is Satellite and she also reads my blog! She had set up some Trail Magic in the parking lot only 15 minutes previously and I was the first hiker she ran into. Two readers in 1 day in the backwoods of Maine. I couldn't believe it. Needless to say, I was flattered and enjoyed getting to know Satellite a bit. She's crazy about the AT and loves to meet hikers on the trail despite our smell. Thanks again for the Trail Magic!

Satellite's food and refreshment powered me up Baldpate Mountain's west and east peaks. It was a boost I definitely needed. As I sat at the summit, I looked west and realized rain was moving quickly in my direction. With only 1.8 miles to the Frye Notch Lean-to, I rushed as fast as I could down the north side of Baldpate (meaning that I crawled with earnest as it was just as steep as everything else these days) and arrived at the shelter just as the drops began to fall.

It was only a passing shower, though, so I proceeded to get a fire going as a section hiker went to bed in the shelter at 4:30 pm. He left all his garbage on the bench in front of the shelter and snapped at Peach when he tried to ensure that the guy would wake up to put his stuff away so the mice wouldn't have a field day. Then, just as this guy fell back to sleep, a Sobo Hot Toddy doppelgänger showed up at the shelter. The resemblance to the real Hot Toddy was so uncanny that I was left very disturbed. Seriously, Peach and I just looked at each other and couldn't even laugh because this woman was so similar. We were both clearly thinking the same thing.

Even though the section hiker was an unreasonable prick, Longcloud, Peach and I also slept in the shelter due to the low temperature and high winds outside.

DAY 137

Starting Location: Frye Notch Lean-to
Destination: Andover, ME / Little Red Hen Campsite
Today's Miles: 14.6
Trip Miles: 1942.3

Aug 8, 2016 - Today was our first relatively easy day since before Moosilauke. During our 14.5 mile trek to the road crossing for Andover, ME, we only had one significant climb out of Sawyer Notch - there's that damn word 'Notch' again and yes it did live up to its connotation.

This morning, before I left camp, I noticed the mouthpiece for my water bladder had been compressed on the ground causing most of the water to spill out and get soaked up by the bottom of my pack. I refilled the bladder and left camp. Immediately, I noticed droplets of water landing on my calves and the back of my shorts were soon saturated with water. I assumed it was just the water my pack had soaked up, but as I went to take a sip of water, I noticed my bladder was empty. When I refilled, I failed to screw the cap of the bladder on completely. Two liters of water had slowly seeped through my entire pack and down my shorts. Ugh.
I couldn't do anything about it except wait until I reached town to dry everything so I just continued walking while water continued to drip onto my legs.

When I reached South Arm Road where Peach and I hoped to hitch into Andover, I tried to clean myself off in the river a bit. Eight days without a shower and 6 without laundry were messing with my mind again. I constantly caught the horrible scent my body exuded and I could actually feel the slimy layer of built up sweat on all my clothes. To put this in perspective, when I woke up this morning, my socks, which had been left out by the fire to dry, were stiff like a new sponge or a washcloth that is left unused for a week. I could actually snap them and watch the salty crust break off and fall to the ground.

I needed a hitch into town because I was completely out of food, but it took nearly an hour to catch a ride - there was so little traffic in that hour that the 4th car to pass us picked us up. We were dropped off at the Andover General Store where Peach and I ordered food and watched the Olympics for once (it's actually painful having to miss the Olympics especially since we usually can't even see results due to lack of cell service). I ate 2 hot dogs and 4 slices of pizza. I also ordered another pie to pack out tomorrow (168 slices, Tim).

We set up our tents in the backyard of the Little Red Hen Diner and Bakery. They were closed, but we had heard from Sobos that it was cool to stay there. I left a note on their front porch anyway explaining our situation and guaranteeing them that we would buy breakfast in the morning. The rest of the evening was spent reading and drinking some beer while the sun set.

DAY 138

Starting Location: Andover, ME / Little Red Hen Campsite
Destination: Stealth Campsite near beach of Sabbath Day Pond
Today's Miles: 17
Trip Miles: 1959.3

Aug 9, 2016 - As promised, Peach and I walked into the Little Red Hen promptly at 6:30 am for some much needed breakfast. I love breakfast food, but I was really craving their Mountain burger consisting of a huge homemade beef patty, bacon, cheese, and sautéed steak. The waitress at the breakfast bar liked our note and obliged us both by making the burger for us. Both of them were gone before 7 am and we were both extremely satisfied.

I was about ready to go when the chef pulled a pan of fresh blueberry crumb muffins out of the oven. I caved and devoured the warm goodness saving the muffin top for last, of course. Again, I opened my mouth to ask the waitress for the check when the chef pulled out another pan of fresh orange cranberry crumb muffins out of the oven. The aroma stopped me in my tracks and I couldn't help it - I indulged yet again. Amazing.

By this time, the Olympic news had us glued to the television. Peach and I looked at each other and abruptly decided to zero right then and there (after ensuring the Little Red Hen did, in fact, serve beer). Ten minutes later, we came to our senses and were packing up our stuff. Then, we proceeded to hitch a ride back to trail. A lady named Sarah offered us a ride.

I had a pretty steep incline up Old Blue Mountain (You're my boy, Blue!) immediately after the South Arm road crossing, but the rest of the 16.7 mile day wasn't too strenuous. I also summited Bemis Mountain and started a long downhill toward Moxy Pond where I hoped to find a stealth spot and make an attempt at fishing.

Moxy Pond showed no signs of even a bad campsite so I pushed another 2 miles to Sabbath Day Pond. I found an absurd beach with stealth spots directly across the trail where I set up. I immediately ran into the shallow, warm water and bathed fully and completely. You don't fully appreciate showers until you haven't had one in 8 days.

Next up was my first attempt at fishing on trail. Despite having a complete backpacking set up, I had no idea what I was doing. I had never strung a pole before, but I thought I could figure it out. Plus, Longcloud came by a little later and was able to point out to me where I had gone wrong. I waded out about 80 yards into the lake and cast out. The water was extremely shallow so I didn't have much hope of catching anything, but man it was fun standing there in the refreshing water with the sun setting before me. I gave it a half hour and then had to get loving so I could actually make dinner before dark. We even had a small campfire on the beach – it was perfect. The lake did have leeches, though, and I'm talking like 6 inch long leeches. I've seen Stand By Me and that's all the leech experience I'll ever need.

DAY 139

Starting Location: Stealth Campsite near beach of Sabbath Day Pond
Destination: Rangeley, ME / The Hiker Hut
Today's Miles: 9.4
Trip Miles: 1968.7

Aug 10, 2016 - When Peach and I woke up this morning and pulled our sweat soaked clothes on for the 7th day in a row, neither of us could handle it. We decided then and there to hike a short day to Rangeley, ME and snag bunks at the Hiker Hut, which was just 0.3 miles off trail.

The actual hiking today was very easy and I listened to Sherlock Holmes' adventures to help pass the time. The only problem with Holmes is that every time I come across another hiker, the standard exchange of pleasantries causes me to miss several crucial details to the mystery. Then, I try to rewind the audiobook, but my fingers are so wet with sweat that my touch screen doesn't even work. It's frustrating.

I completed the 9.7 miles to the Hiker Hut before 11 am and spoke to Katherine, the owner's wife, about securing a bunk. Unfortunately, the bunk room was full, but Peach and I could split the couple's suite next to the river (it's basically just a lean-to) for the same price. Done deal. I gave Peach the bed and I took the floor. I essentially begged Katherine to do our laundry and she obliged for only $1. She put white vinegar in with the detergent and, for the first time all trip, I was unable to tell which socks were my hiking pair and which were my sleeping pair. This hostel was very unique because there was no electricity or running water. The outdoor shower was simply a pump, propane heater, and a water supply bin manually filled with water from the adjacent stream. It reminded me of one of those outdoor showers at a beach house (the only good part of the beach, if you ask me) - the hot water combined with the cool, gentle breeze creates a pleasantly unique sensation.

Peach and I were shuttled to town with Cookie and ate some lunch at the Red Onion - I crushed yet another entire pizza pie (176 slices, Tim). The next stop was the ice cream place in town followed by Sarge's, the local pub. Since we weren't being picked back up until 7 pm, we had a solid 5 hours to watch the Olympics. Cookie and Longcloud soon joined us along with a Sobo that was Councilman Jam's doppelgänger. While watching the Olympics, I noticed a bumper sticker on the bar that read "Pond Hockey Tournament 2010, Rangeley, ME". Anybody that knows me can vouch for how excited I was by this 6 year old sticker. This town was my kind of place.

On the way back to the Hut, Steve, the owner, dropped all of us at the grocery store for a resupply. Since I didn't need a resupply thanks to Mama Goat's last package, I just stocked up on Whoopie Pies, which are apparently, very popular in Maine. I can't get enough of them - each pie is 800 calories with each macronutrient nicely represented and they're freaking delicious.

Steve made popcorn and we all sat around the fire chatting about the trail until I called it quits relatively early to get some sleep. Tomorrow would be a big day as Saddleback Mountain stood in our way.

DAY 140

Starting Location: Rangeley, ME / The Hiker Hut
Destination: Stealth Campsite near Perham Stream
Today's Miles: 15.3
Trip Miles: 1984

Aug 11, 2016 - I left the Hiker Hut about 7:30 am after some coffee and a Whoopie Pie for breakfast. My hike today was a comfortable mixture of easy and difficult terrain. It started with a rejuvenating 3 mile walk to the base of Saddleback Mountain (4,120 feet), which is a popular ski resort up here.

Next, of course, was a 2 mile climb up Saddleback, but the last mile was completely above tree line. It's amazing how that can change the perspective of a hike - the first mile was a hot, sweaty ascent through the pines with no wind while the second mile was simply stunning. Slope and distance doesn't matter when you're in that other world above the trees. The wind gusts and thankfully wicks the sweat off your body while you gaze around at the stunning landscapes (and ski slopes in this instance).

After Saddleback, I had another 3 miles of up and down hiking in the alpine environment while summiting The Horn (4,021 feet) and Saddleback Junior (3,655 feet). The trail switched back to downhill for another 3 miles and once again 2 miles back uphill where I hoped to find a nice stealth spot near Perham Stream.

Peach and I kind of have a reputation for finding the best stealth spots on trail and having fires at nearly all of our campsites (for some reason, most other hikers try to stay at established campsites or shelters and, at this point on the AT, almost no one bothers to start fires anymore). Our priorities are water (preferably swimming holes), fire pits, and good, rainproof tenting in that order. As I arrived at Perham Stream a good 2 hours before Peach, I managed to bathe yet again. The stream was raging and large enough to fully submerge myself. I also watched a group of river otters play around for a while which may have been the cutest thing I've ever seen. I found a secluded tent site, too, but it didn't have a fire pit. It did, however, have a piece of scorched earth from a previous fire so I hauled rocks in from the stream and made my own. Cookie joined us and Peach and I grilled up some Taylor Ham.

It was supposed to rain 1-2 inches tonight and this would be my first rain since I was flooded a few weeks ago. I was a little stressed and paranoid to be honest with you. I was almost positive that my rent was in a safe spot, but the previous disaster gave rise to some doubts. I rolled sticks into the edges of my newly acquired ground sheet and put small rocks on top to create a barrier on the uphill side of my tent. This way, if rain started to accumulate, it should flow under the ground sheet rather than the bathtub floor. We'll see if it works.

DAY 141

Starting Location: Stealth Campsite near Perham Stream
Destination: Stratton, ME / Spillover Motel
Today's Miles: 16.9
Trip Miles: 2000.9

Aug 12, 2016 – There was no rain during the night, but the sky this morning looked like it was about to explode. I quickly packed everything up and put my rain cover on my pack just in case. Then, Peach and I shared some coffee before the 16.9 mile hike to Stratton, ME today. Coffee goes well with Whoopie Pies. Who knew?

As I left camp, I immediately started ascending Lone Mountain in some disgustingly humid air. The sweat poured down my face and, honestly, I wished it would rain. Less than 2 miles after camp, the sky obliged me with nature's free shower and laundry service. Rain can be a glorious thing.

On the down side, rain meant slippery rocks and roots as I ascended and descended Spaulding Mountain, South Crocker Mountain (4,040 feet), and North Crocker Mountain (4,288 feet). I managed to fall only once resulting in some minor abrasions on my already scabbed up forearms. That's a miracle considering how horrible the traction is on my shoes. With no exaggeration, I can say that my name brand Crocs have better grip than my Oboz.

It rained for about 7 hours and nearly the whole time it took me to reach the road crossing that led to Stratton. While rain is great in small quantities, hiking for an extended period of time in the rain usually results in some form of chafing. This experience was no different - extreme chafing occurred in both my groin areas. Gold Bond was liberally applied and, since that stuff is actually magic in stick form, the chafing gradually subsided.

About a mile from the road crossing, I came across a large, hand built sign in the dirt that read 2,000 miles! I remarked at how ridiculous a distance that is - you don't fully appreciate that until you've walked every foot. I still had 189 miles to go, but it was time to celebrate a bit in Stratton.

Peach and I caught a hitch to town and tried to find a place to stay. We started with the Stratton Motel where we ran into a couple of hikers I haven't seen since at least the Shenandoahs: New Hampshire Bob, Weebles (she had taken some time off for family events so she decided to flip flop up to Katahdin and hike south). Scavenger and Slam were also there. Since there were 2 weddings this weekend in Stratton, everything was booked except for the Spillover Motel. Peach and I split a room there with Weebles and Moonshine - Yes, Moonshine, who had gotten off trail a few weeks ago, was back in Maine and was driving out from Portland to meet us for the night!

We took showers and did a bit of gross bathtub laundry while we waited for Moonshine to arrive. My lunch consisted of a homemade peanut butter and fudge bar I spontaneously picked up at the general store. It must have weighed 2 lbs and filled me up like nothing I've ever eaten before. The Olympics were also on so our gloomy, rainy day was looking up pretty quickly. Cookie, Longcloud and Slam had split the adjacent room.

Moonshine arrived around 5 pm and brought all the resupply mail drops he never ended up using much to the delight of everyone. He was barely recognizable without his beard. We caught up a bit - he's well on his way to starting up his construction business again. Then, all 7 of us hopped in his truck and drove to a place called The Rack for some dinner. I ordered beer and another pizza pie, which, of course, I crushed (182, Tim). I can't tell you how much fun that meal was, but Cookie did a pretty good job capturing it with the picture she took. It's amazing the sort of relationships everyone builds out here. I hiked with Moonshine for only 1 month and I'll be in touch with him for many years to come.

After dinner, we headed back to town and realized that every store and gas station had closed at 9 pm despite the fact that it was a Friday night. That meant the only beer we could drink was across the street from the motel. Afterwards, Moonshine set off some fireworks he brought from home - I slipped inside just as the landlord came out to yell at him.

DAY 142

Starting Location: Stratton, ME / Spillover Motel
Destination: Stratton, ME / Stratton Motel
Today's Miles: 0
Trip Miles: 2000.9

Aug 13, 2016 – Moonshine left the motel early because he had to get to a wedding this afternoon. The rain showed no signs of slowing down this morning so Peach and I decided to take our last zero in Stratton. One of the weddings was actually at the Spillover Motel so we caught a ride back to the center of town to the Stratton Motel where I secured us couch spots for $10.

The reunion in Stratton continued with the arrival of Sherpa, Jellydog, Whiplash, Mumbles and Panda. Even 188 miles from the end of this trip, I continue to meet new people like Solo, Romani, Jester (finally, a hockey fan from Minnesota), and Bombadil (this is Legs and Verge's Dad who I was hoping to run into – unfortunately, the knee problems he had been having since mile 1200 had finally forced him off trail). I was hoping Legs and Verge themselves would catch up today, but I never heard back.

Today was a true zero – I had a frozen pizza at 10 in the morning (188, Tim), resupplied on Whoopie Pies, and just sat around drinking, playing board games and watching the Olympics all day. Peach and I played some cribbage at the White Wolf Inn and I played Weebles in some ping pong and pool at the Stratton Plaza later that night. I know this all sounds very well and good, but zeros are really hard. Sitting around all day is actually a very tough thing to do, certainly tougher than hiking 17 miles in the rain. Still, the all-star cast at the Stratton Motel practically demanded a zero.

MOONSHINE VISITING IN STRATTON, MAINE.

DAY 143

Starting Location: Stratton, ME / Stratton Motel
Destination: East Flagstaff Lake Campsite
Today's Miles: 17.9
Trip Miles: 2018.8

Aug 14, 2016 – So, I definitely drank a bit too much last night – it was those damn Not Your Father's Root Beers that are just so easy to drink. It didn't help that Peach put on a pop punk playlist from the early 2000s halfway through the six pack...

While most hikers are some of the friendlier people I've met, there are a few assholes. I got up from the couch to pee in the middle of the night as usual, but when I came back a Sobo had thrown all of my stuff on the floor and said to me, "I paid for this couch". Thankfully, I was pretty out of it and just went to sleep on the floor, because the only other options were to make a scene or physically roll him onto the floor and take the couch back. Peach woke up and feebly told him to get lost, but whatever. I definitely couldn't believe it, though.

Hiking up the famous Bigelows is as good a hangover cure as any, I suppose, though I definitely struggled up Bigelow Mountain (4,145 feet). I refueled with some food and water at the top, which definitely made me feel a bit better. I moved on to Avery Peak (4,090 feet) and then Little Bigelow Mountain. Apparently, you can see Katahdin and Mt. Washington from the summit of Bigelow Mountain on a clear day, but today was too cloudy. I fell a few times today and managed to bend both of my trekking poles. I thought they were beyond repair, but managed to fix them at camp. Hopefully, they can last through the 100 mile wilderness because I need them to hold up my tent.

After tackling the Bigelow peaks like a zombie, I made the long descent down to Flagstaff Lake where I set up camp in yet another dreamy spot right next to the lake. A short walk brought me down to a pebble beach where I took a short swim to clean myself off. An equally short walk brought me to a large rock overlooking the lake where I cast out with my fishing pole for about an hour and a half. Unfortunately, I still haven't gotten even a nibble. I had to settle for another Taylor Ham and cheese wrap for dinner around the fire.

I was still exhausted from the night before and a 17.9 mile day isn't exactly rest. I went to bed pretty early and read the Chronicles of Narnia. I'm definitely too old for these books, but I've never read them and always wanted to. I fell asleep to a few loons singing a naturally distorted lullaby. They might be the most unique birds - they just play around in the water and make hysterical noises all the time.

DAY 144

Starting Location: East Flagstaff Lake Campsite
Destination: Caratunk, ME / Stealth Campsite
Today's Miles: 19.1
Trip Miles: 2037.9

Aug 15, 2016 - Waking up this morning reminded me that while my mind may not want this hike to end, my body is begging for rest. I don't have any serious injuries, but the little things add up. My hands, forearms and even upper arms look like someone attacked me with several sharp forks. My knees and feet constantly and relentlessly ache like they've just received a beating. I have pack rash (blisters and open sores) on my hips and my back just above the tailbone that won't go away. My plantar fasciitis has been status quo lately, but at least a few times a day the muscle in the bottom of my foot has the disturbing feeling like it's a frayed rope that is slowly having its threads snapped - it's not especially painful, but that can't be good. Lastly, I most definitely have nerve damage in both my feet because many (not all) of my toes constantly tingle and have delayed, tingly responses to contact. Despite all of this, I managed 19.1 miles today to Caratunk, ME.

My situation is far from unique because every thru-hiker at this point is suffering from similar maladies. Slam's pack rash makes mine look like a joke. New Hampshire Bob definitely has a broken toe judging by the size and color of it. At the age of 66, his response to the reasonable suggestion of going to the doctor was, "Ah, I don't give a shit" (this guy is great by the way). Peach's knees are far worse than my own. Cookie's feet look like she's walked on broken glass for 2,000 miles. Everybody still gets blisters. Whatever the problem is, you deal with it and keep walking - that's thru-hiking.

Anyway, this morning was the easiest terrain I've had since PA (minus the rocks, of course). All I had was 2 small hills to warm me up and then it was about 16 flat miles into Caratunk, ME. There was a catch, however: just before Caratunk was the Kennebec River. Now, the Kennebec is about 400 feet wide and is extremely dangerous to ford because there are 3 hydro plants positioned upstream. When the hydro plants release water into water, which they do at least once a day, the water level and current increase very rapidly. For this reason, an outfitter in Caratunk provides ferry transportation across the river and hikers are warned not to ford the river. The ferry runs between 9 am and 2 pm so I had to hike 19.1 miles by the early afternoon if I didn't want to be stuck on the south side of the river.

I left camp 6:15 am and stopped for only 10 minutes to grab a snack and refill on water. This will sound crazy, but walking on flat ground all day made my legs ache more than walking up and down. In fact, any small hills I encountered throughout the day made my legs feel a bit better. I guess the changes in elevation force you to use different muscles while walking along flat ground forces you to use the same muscles the whole time. I made the ferry by 12:45 pm - it turns out, the ferry was just a small canoe with an operator. The canoe had a white blaze in the bottom of it signaling that it was officially part of the AT. I actually helped row across the river so I definitely earned those 400 feet.

Once in Caratunk, I yog'ied a ride to Northern Outdoors 2 miles down the road to attempt the Exterminator burger challenge: 2eight ounce beef patties, 1 fried chicken breast, 1 fried egg, a ball of fried mac and cheese, onion rings, fried pickles, bacon, tomato and lettuce served with 1 pound of steak fries in 30 minutes. I failed yet again, but I did get through the entire burger and half the fries. Regardless, the burger was genuinely delicious and may be the best I've had on trail so far.

Northern Outdoors was also home to the Kennebec River Brewing Company (no, they didn't have a sticker). I still managed to take down a beer after the Exterminator destroyed my belly. This place was amazing though – hikers could take free showers, there was a pool with volleyball (it's disgusting how useless we all are at anything other than walking), and a hot tub. I'm pretty sure they had laundry, too, but I figured I would just take care of that in Monson.

After all these shenanigans, I got a shuttle back to the trailhead and stealth camped right next to the parking lot. I tried to read a bit, but fell asleep almost immediately.

DAY 145

Starting Location: Caratunk, ME / Stealth Campsite
Destination: Moxie Bald Mountain Lean-to
Today's Miles: 18.8
Trip Miles: 2056.7

Aug 16, 2016 – After our leisure activities at Northern Outdoors yesterday afternoon, it was back to work this morning with an 18.8 mile hike to Moxie Bald Mountain Lean-to. Again, it was fairly easy terrain today with only 2 small mountains to clamber over: Pleasant Pond Mountain and Moxie Bald Mountain. Both of these were almost relaxing climbs considering what we've been subjected to the last 200 miles or so.

I took a really nice lunch break at Moxie Pond – halfway through my ford, I set up on a large rock and had the breeze cool me down while I listened to water trickle past me. I was still hoping to see a moose, but still no luck on that front.

Once I reached the lean-to, I was very careful to set up my tent in a safe place as it was supposed to rain pretty heavily that evening. My paranoia was still strong since my disaster just north of Dalton, MA. I checked and rechecked my setup to ensure that flowing water would not build up around me. A beautiful lake was situated right next to my camping spot – I had intended to fish, but the water was very shallow. I settled for a fire and a nice warm dinner instead.

I was forced into my tent pretty early because the No-See-Ums were relentless.

These tiny bugs are worse than mosquitos because you don't see them until you've been bitten and sometimes not even then. I caught up on some journaling and read my children's book. When the rain started, I sat in my tent with my headlamp on just staring at the ground for almost 20 minutes until I was confident my setup would withstand the deluge. That was a nerve racking 20 minutes, though, so sleep came easily.

DAY 146

Starting Location: Moxie Bald Mountain Lean-to
Destination: Monson, ME / Shaw's Lodging
Today's Miles: 17.9
Trip Miles: 2074.6

Aug 17, 2016 - It rained quite a bit during the night and the rain continued into the morning. I was rudely awoken by a drop of condensation that caused me to bolt upright in panic thinking that the rain had bested me yet again. The No-See-Ums were dreadful again this morning so Peach and I skipped our morning coffee and got moving early.

I had 17.9 flat miles to Monson, ME, the southern terminus of the 100 mile wilderness. It rained for most of the morning, which was rather annoying - usually, the rain is very refreshing, but I just wasn't feeling it today. In fact, today was one of those days I just didn't feel like hiking at all. The deceptively flat terrain made my legs ache like they do after walking through an amusement park all day.

I had 2 rivers to ford today - and, unlike most of the rivers we've had to "ford" lately, these were wide and deep enough that walking through the water was actually necessary. I stood staring at the water for a few minutes debating whether or not I wanted to take my shoes and socks off. Finally, I just said screw it and walked through the knee-deep water with everything on. It was already raining anyway.

Another bizarre thing I noticed in the woods today is that autumn was already underway this far north. Leaves had started to change color and had already begun to accumulate on the forest floor. It's only mid-August!

When I don't feel like hiking, I just keep moving for fear that I'll stop and get stuck somewhere. So, I finished my nearly 18 mile day by 12:30 pm. While waiting for Peach, I ate an entire jar of cinnamon raisin peanut butter. Breakneck, who was forced off trail with less than 300 miles left because of 2 broken bones in his foot, randomly arrived at the trailhead and gave me a ride to Shaw's Lodging in Monson, ME.

I've only stayed at about 5 hostels the whole trip, but I sure do pick the right ones. This place was incredible - I was immediately treated to a beer upon arrival and, since I was tenting in the backyard, offered a shower. I did laundry and then explored this small mansion equipped with a full resupply and gear shop, 3 bunkhouses, 3 bathrooms, a cabin, and a restaurant quality kitchen that supposedly produced a legendary breakfast every morning. The staff - Poet and AJ - were very down to earth and accommodating.

Peach, Cookie and I headed to the community center in town where we pre-registered for our permits for Katahdin. Our summit date will be August 25. Next up was lunch / dinner at the Lakeshore House followed by relaxing the rest of the evening.
I needed a large resupply to get me through the next 100 miles. The 100 mile wilderness meant no towns or resupply points for the next 100 miles. I would be completely off the grid.

Later that night, I somehow got into a conversation with Poet about life and how the AT changes you whether you realize it immediately or not. This guy was a high school teacher for nearly 15 years during which he hiked the AT with his wife. After falling in love with the hiker community, Poet took a risk and purchased Shaw's 2 years ago. He loves every second of it. Even if purchasing the hostel hadn't worked out, he insists he wouldn't have regretted it because if he hadn't taken the risk, he wouldn't have been able to bear always wondering what would have happened if he did.

When I explained to Poet my situation, he actually urged me to try to marry engineering to something related to the great outdoors. Worse comes to worse, if I hate it, then I could just pull myself out of the field like I already had to hike the AT. Poet even went so far as to offer me a potential work for stay position in the hostel in the future that would keep me busy while I figure out what I want to do. While I don't plan on taking him up on this offer, it just goes to show what this hiker community can be like. The last piece of advice Poet provided was to never make a decision based on money - it's just not worth it if there's no enjoyment associated with the large paycheck. These words really echoed the thoughts and conclusions that had already been bouncing around in my head during my long, quiet walks in the woods.

DAY 147

Aug 18, 2016 - Peach and I actually volunteered to help out with some trail maintenance this afternoon so the 100 mile wilderness would have to wait a few hours. All logistics aside, I only had 1 thing on my mind when my eyes opened this morning: breakfast.

When I saw the size and quality of the kitchen at Shaw's yesterday, my expectations for breakfast unintentionally skyrocketed. Breakfast also turned out to be free since we had signed up to help out with the trail maintenance. I walked into the kitchen for a cup of coffee and caught Poet cooking up a storm. At least 50 strips of bacon graced the grill and his famous hash browns were sizzling in 3 giant cast iron pans. Three eggs were cooked to order for each hiker and bottomless blueberry pancakes were piled in the center of the table. I was salivating. As a bonus, Cookie is a vegan so when she was served bacon, she slid her pieces discreetly onto my plate. Even though everything was delicious, the hash browns stole the show. Golden and crunchy potato cubes fully buttered up and seasoned are hard to do correctly, but Poet crushed it.

Anyway, the rest of the morning was spent catching up on my writing while I waited for the shuttle to bring us to the trail maintenance event. AJ shuttled about 7 of us to the Jo Mary road about 30 miles into the 100 mile wilderness where we would be unloading logs from a truck. The logs would eventually replace the bog bridges that we walk on for very wet sections of trail. The whole event was supposed to take about 4-5 hours, but since several people volunteered, we were completely done in less than 2. The trail has provided so much these past 5 months so it felt good to give back a bit. I definitely want to get involved with this type of volunteer work when I get home.

Peach and I had planned to get back on trail and hike a shorter day into the wilderness, but when we arrived back at the hostel, our wildest dreams had come true: Sweets, Jingle, Training Wheels, Verge and Legs had arrived! It turns out we would all be summiting on August 25. Therefore, we decided to zero one last time so we could all hike out together tomorrow. Despite all the good things that I've experienced on trail, the chance to hike the last 115 miles with my closest trail family eclipsed everything. Our paths had crisscrossed several times over 2,000 miles of backcountry and a twist of fate had once again brought my favorite people together for the finale. If only Moonshine, Steel, Great P, and Survivor had been with us as well...

It was an excellent afternoon as we investigated the Spring Creek barbecue joint next door (it had been closed yesterday with a sign out front that actually read "Closed - Out of Food") and caught up with each other. Spring Creek (remember the creek in Hot Springs, NC?) must be a lucky name because the pulled pork sandwich was so juicy it was difficult to eat.

I picked up another pizza for dinner and we played corn hole and Scattegories into the evening. I downed 4 of the pizza slices bringing me to 200 pizza slices since I started hiking on March 25. I still had 4 slices I would pack out with me tomorrow. As I lay down to sleep, I realized everything was working out wonderfully and couldn't wait to start the 100 mile wilderness tomorrow.

DAY 148

Starting Location: Monson, ME / Shaw's Lodging
Destination: Cloud Pond Lean-to
Today's Miles: 19.1
Trip Miles: 2093.7

Aug 19, 2016 - After another serving of Poet's immensely satisfying breakfast food, it was time to get back to trail. The seven of us (Peach, Wheels, Jingle, Sweets, Legs, Verge and myself) had a plan to summit on Thursday, August 25 very early in the morning (not necessarily to catch the sunrise, but just to beat out the day hikers and have the summit to ourselves for a bit). We would push to get through the 100 mile wilderness in 5 days and arrive at Abol Bridge on August 23, which is positioned immediately outside the boundary for Baxter State Park (BSP). Then, extremely early on the 24th, we would each cross the boundary into BSP to register for one of the 12 coveted camping spots at the Birches Lean-to. It would only be a 10 mile hike from Abol Bridge to the Birches and would set up our summit day very nicely. On the morning of the 25th, we would only have the 5 mile hike up to the summit and, of course, the hike back down (which was not to be underestimated). Appropriate celebrations would follow in nearby Millinocket, ME on the evening of the 25th where we all had bunks reserved at the AT Lodge.

Over recent years, there has been a lot of negative back and forth between BSP and thru-hikers. BSP has a very strict policy of wilderness first and recreation second. While there are certainly thru-hikers who abuse BSP's rules (Scott Jurek, for instance, who sprayed champagne all over the summit when he completed his record breaking thru-hike), most thru-hikers want to be as respectable as possible to a landmark as revered as Katahdin. So, even though there are some thru-hikers who give the rest of us a bad name, BSP does a very poor job of making their regulations and logistical options known to thru-hikers. For example, if I don't get a spot at the Birches (it's first come, first served on the day of - basically, the first twelve to sign the register just outside Baxter are guaranteed spots later that evening), I can either hike several miles into the park and try to yogi a spot at the full Katahdin Stream Campground or hike a grueling 20 mile round trip summit from Abol Bridge to Katahdin and back down. Neither of those are desirable options, which is why getting a spot at the Birches is so important. My point is that most thru-hikers have no idea these options exist. The only reason we know is because we asked everyone and their grandmother. The only employee present to help us at the ATC visitor center in Monson had never done the hike and really had no idea what our options were. That's frustrating. Peach had a great idea to publish an article to the Appalachian Trials website detailing complete guidelines for a thru-hiker's last 15 miles.

Anyway, AJ gave us a ride back to the trailhead and I set out to start the 100 mile wilderness. The reason it's called the 100 mile wilderness is that for a stretch of 100 miles, there are no resupply options, no towns and very little cell service. We were on our own and had to carry all our supplies for at least 5 days, though it takes some people as long as 13 days to complete this section of the trail.

During the first 3 miles of this beautiful day, I passed by 5 ponds and walked through a dense forest of maple, beech, and the dominant white birch, fir, cedar and pine trees. The trail, as it's been through most of Maine, is a layer of decomposing pine needles interspersed with tree roots and rocks on top of a thin layer of topsoil. On either side of the trail, ferns and thick, soft layers of moss are abundant. It's very unique, extremely tranquil and smells very pleasant.

About 7 miles in, I came across a large waterfall called Little Wilson Falls with a deep pool at the bottom. I climbed down the rocks and made my 3rd attempt at fishing. An hour later, I still had nothing to show for my efforts. It was most frustrating.

Several miles later, I stopped at a brook with another deep pool to read for a while. I couldn't resist the water, though, so I stripped to my boxers and sat in the pool as I let the small waterfall cascade over my shoulders. It was like a cold version of those fancy pools you find at resorts in those tropical places. This was way better.

Though most of the day was spent going up and down small hills, I ended my day with our only significant climb in Barren Mountain. I met Goat, Jellydog, Whiplash, Panda and Mumbles at the top where we scaled the old fire tower for some stellar views. I proceeded to the Cloud Pond Lean-to to finish my 19.1 mile day. Chores included the usual: taking a bath in the lake, building a fire and cooking some dinner. Two section hikers arrived and I was immediately impressed by their setup. Though their fishing attempts failed, while I was building a fire, I noticed them gutting and skinning a red squirrel they had shot earlier in the day. Apparently, it's open season all year long on red squirrels. They had a saw for cutting actual firewood and a large pot to cook some gourmet pasta. That's how it's done.

To my immense disappointment, Training Wheels was the only member of our Trail Family that didn't convene at the Cloud Pond Lean-to. She had stopped about 3 miles short of the lean-to to set up camp in a stealth spot. Ever since I met her at mile 273 in Hot Springs, NC, I had to admit I had quite a crush on her. Under normal circumstances, I would have definitely asked her out. However, in less than a week, we would be going our separate ways. Missouri and New Jersey aren't exactly close to each other. After the exciting prospect of spending the entire 100 mile wilderness around her quirky personality, I was understandably disappointed to find that I probably wouldn't see her at all given our aggressive schedule.

DAY 149

Starting Location: Cloud Pond Lean-to
Destination: Sidney Tappan Campsite
Today's Miles: 18.6
Trip Miles: 2112.3

Aug 20, 2016 - I woke to one of those mornings that are just cold enough to make your sleeping bag the most comfortable thing in the world. The prospect of Peach's coffee did the trick of getting me out, though. I had another big day today - 18.6 miles to the Sidney Tappan Campsite.

Today's hike had significantly more ups and downs today as I approached Whitecap Mountain where I would catch my first glimpse of Katahdin as long as the weather cooperated. A few hours into my hike, I took a break on a cliff overlooking the gorge south of Whitecap and had some lunch. I found myself thinking of all the things I'm going to miss about this hike. Eating lunch on a cliff, on a summit or on the banks of a river literally everyday is right there at the top of the list. I've even had lunch while literally sitting in a river - I mean, how can you beat that? Sleeping outside is far and away what I will miss most of all. Don't get me wrong, I miss sleeping in a bed sometimes, but now that I'm comfortable outside, I find that I sleep much better than I ever used to. I don't set alarms out here or worry about time - the sun and the moon govern my days. I'll miss the freedom and the simplicity of life in the backcountry - water, food and shelter are my only concerns. I'll miss hitchhiking and yogi'ing and all the crazy stories associated with them. I'll miss being hiker trash. I'll miss having people look at me like I'm a zoo animal because deep down I know that it's the other way around. I'm honestly dreading reintegration back into society, but I know I'll figure it out.

With 7 miles left in my hike, I stopped at a river crossing that required fording for another snack. I put my feet in the water and had a conversation with a ridge runner that policed the ford. The Gulf Hagis trail 2 miles north was apparently a tourist destination and the lady was making sure people forded the river safely. It was then that I realized the 100 mile wilderness isn't actually that wild considering there was a parking area less than a mile away.

A gradual 7 mile climb brought me to the Sidney Tappan Campsite a few miles short of Whitecap. I built a fire and waited for everyone else to arrive. The usual crew was on their way, but we were also joined by Goat, Jetson, Curly, and Footage. Peach took out his guidebook and began reminiscing. For a while now, he's been looking back to where we were on the trail with the mileage we have left to hike. It's funny because all the "big" climbs we did - Blood Mountain, Trey Mountain, Albert Mountain, etc. - are just a joke compared to what we've been hiking since Vermont. I mean just today, we hiked the equivalent of about 4 Trey Mountains in elevation and considered it a relatively easy day. And I remember Trey Mountain as one of my most difficult climbs on trail. Everything is relative.

DAY 150

Starting Location: Sidney Tappan Campsite
Destination: Antlers Campsite
Today's Miles: 25
Trip Miles: 2137.3

Aug 21, 2016 - Even though I hung a bear bag last night, mice, squirrels and / or chipmunks managed to chew yet another hole in my food bag. Luckily, they must have gotten tired after actually creating the hole and didn't get to any of the food. Footage and Curly were not as fortunate. They're ruthless out here.

Whitecap was the first and only mountain on the agenda today. I was supposed to get my first view of Katahdin from the north side of the mountain. However, my hopes were not high as I watched clouds billowing across the summit of Whitecap. The wind was strong enough to blow me off course and make rock hopping much more difficult. As expected, Katahdin was shrouded in cloud - the only piece I could see was the top left corner. I would get another shot at the 'Greatest Mountain' ('Katahdin' actually means 'Greatest Mountain' in the local Native American tongue) in another 30 miles or so.

The rest of the day was a 21 mile stretch of flat terrain devoid of excessive rocks and roots. It was very pleasurable hiking and I made great time throughout the day. I stopped at the Cooper Brook Falls Lean-to to do some fishing. The brook right in front of the shelter had a small waterfall that created a deep swimming hole. I could actually see the brook trout swimming around at the bottom. I was at it for almost 2 hours, but the fish wouldn't catch on the hook! Every time I cast out, I watched the fish attack my lure, but I still didn't catch anything. I changed lures and even tried a piece of pepperoni, but still no luck. It was extremely frustrating – apparently, I am not a very good angler.

Since I still had 8 miles to go to reach the Antlers Campsite, I gave up the fishing and got moving again. The Antlers Campsite was freaking beautiful – a sprawling bed of pine needles with 2 fire pits on a peninsula in the Jo Mary Lake. There was a huge rock beach so of course I rinsed off as best I could.

Jellydog, Whiplash, Mumbles and Panda were already there. They had pushed big miles the past 2.5 days so Jellydog's friend could be picked up from Joe Mary lake via C-plane. The pilot had promised to bring them a case of cold beer. So, for almost 3 days, this case of beer was the only thing driving them to do 25+ mile days...and the pilot forgot it! Even worse, as the pilot revealed the bad news, he cracked open a cold soda and started drinking it right in front of Jellydog and co. Needless to say, none of them were in a good mood.

I got a fire going and made a ground shattering food bag trade with Peach – I gave him 2 tuna packets and he gave me a jar of peanut butter. That's bartering at its finest. Goat, Curly, and Jetson caught up and joined us by the fire. Talk of our summit dates and the logistics surrounding Baxter State Park consumed our conversation. We were close.

DAY 151

Starting Location: Antlers Campsite
Destination: Rainbow Stream Lean-to
Today's Miles: 21.7
Trip Miles: 2159

Aug 22, 2016 - It poured all night and continued into the morning. Rain in the morning is kind of nice because everyone sleeps in a bit hoping the rain will stop and allow us to safely pack up camp. Unfortunately, I had to shit and that drove me from my tent into the rain very quickly. Of course, by the time I was done with that, I was already wet so I just went ahead and packed up my things. Everyone else followed suit with the exception of Peach, who refused to get out of his tent until the rain stopped. He made coffee in his vestibule and slid out my steaming cup, which I drank leaning against a tree in the pouring rain.

The rain cleared up around mid-morning and I was cruising. Rather than stop and take a break, I just pushed 21.7 miles to the Rainbow Stream Lean-to and set up early. I had another chance to see Katahdin this afternoon, but even though it was clear near me, the top half of the mountain was enveloped in clouds. My goal may continue to hide, but I'm still closing in with only 30 miles left on my thru-hike.

Luckily, Bigfoot, Toasty and Fire had already gotten an impressive fire going with wet wood. That saved me a ton of work for a hot dinner and allowed me to relax and bathe briefly in the stream. I was joined by the usual crew (except Training Wheels who still hadn't caught up) and Panda and Whiplash. It was a beautiful night and everyone was starting to get palpably excited.

Scavenger passed through and returned Sweets' jacket, which she had dropped. Scavenger kept moving because he was aiming to summit on August 24. I still remember that fourth night on trail when Peach and I met Scavenger. Though he's certainly worked his way into our good graces, he was a pain in the ass know-it-all at the outset of our journey. I remember looking at Peach during the first few days on trail and saying, "You know he's going to summit with us, right?" Well, it turns out he wouldn't be, though summiting one day apart 2,000 miles later is pretty damn close.

I walked back up to my tent and threw a rock to hang a bear bag. The rock got caught on the branch and when I pulled it loose, the rock flew right past my head and went completely through the tarp in my tent. My tent made it literally 2,159 miles in damn near perfect condition and I destroy it hanging a bear bag. As I've said before, hanging bear bags is always an interesting affair, to say the least.

DAY 152

Starting Location: Rainbow Stream Lean-to
Destination: Stealth Campsite near North End of 100 Mile
Wilderness
Today's Miles: 14.7
Trip Miles: 2173.7

Aug 23, 2016 - Today, I would pass out of the 100 mile wilderness near Abol Bridge on the border of Baxter State Park. I had an easy 14.7 miles to hike to put me in a position to hike to the Birches Lean-to near Katahdin Stream Campground in BSP tomorrow.

As I hiked up to the Rainbow Ledges, I was really hoping for a look at Katahdin, which I still hadn't seen. At last, I looked to my left through a picturesque opening in the trees and there stood this impressive monolith. I felt like I was back in Florence, Italy, looking at Michelangelo's "David" again - I just sat there stunned and staring at the stark, jagged peak. I must have been there for 20 minutes just trying to appreciate what this mountain meant to me. It hadn't been real until that moment.

When I finally managed to tear my eyes away from Katahdin, I actually looked at my phone. Apparently, Uncle Paul had been trying to contact me regarding Paradox Brewery for some time. For some odd reason, I chose this moment to call him back. I've always looked up to Uncle Paul and his opinion has always mattered to me because he doesn't deal in bullshit or sugarcoat the truth. He tells it like it is. After briefly discussing Paradox Brewery, he asked me how the trip was going. I told him I was standing 20 miles from my goal and looking, for the first time, at the "Greatest Mountain". Even through the phone, I could hear his usual business-like tone break and I could tell he was genuinely impressed as he congratulated me. That simple break in the tone of his voice meant more to me than perhaps any other accolade I would receive from people.

I flew through the last 6 miles to the Abol Bridge at the north end of the 100 mile wilderness. I set up camp quickly in a stealth spot just south of the road while I waited for Peach to catch up. Peach, Goat and I walked up the road into the campground to get some food and beer at the restaurant there. We found Jellydog and Mumbles there – both had beers in their hand after having been teased for the last 5 days.

Sweets, Legs, Verge, Whiplash, Panda and Jingle arrived a little later. Training Wheels finally caught up and we finally caught New Hampshire Bob. The gang was all here for the grand finale, though Jellydog's crew would be hoofing the 15 remaining miles early tomorrow morning to summit on the 24th. We all bought some snacks and beer from the camp store and crammed into a picnic table next to the Penobscot River with the shadow of Katahdin looming over us. I saw my first bald eagle as it swooped down over the river and settled on a branch with the sunset as a backdrop. After hours of shenanigans by the river, the sun set and everyone headed back to our stealth camp to make a fire and continue the good times. Jellydog, Whiplash, Mumbles and Panda had plans to get up at 2 am and start hiking for the summit 15 miles away. They found a random air horn in the woods and promised they would blow it when they were leaving camping in the middle of the night.

A FAMILY MEAL IN KATAHDIN'S SHADOW NEAR ABOL BRIDGE

While everyone roasted hot dogs and sausages over the fire, Peach, Verge, Legs and I walked the mile north to the sign-up sheet for the Birches Lean-to to ensure we snagged one of the 12 coveted spots. The sign-up sheet had only 2 rules: 1. Only put your name down at the time you are entering BSP (Do not put your name down and then head back south to Abol Bridge) 2. Do not sign up for other people.

Well, we broke both of the rules but only because Verge pressured us into it. Not really, but they're more like guidelines anyway. Honestly, though, we wrote that all 8 of us arrived at 6 am and we fully intended to be there that early. Call us horrible people if you will, but it's a cutthroat business getting those spots at the Birches and there was no way we were missing out. We weren't sure what Goat's real name was so we dubbed him Albert O'Neil. Even this little excursion was a blast. We were singing along to The Final Countdown by Europe and some Lion King songs.

Days like today will make it extremely hard to leave the trail. It's already starting to feel bittersweet as I get closer and closer. Hiking something like the AT condenses friendships – an inconsequential amount of time in the real world might as well be an eternity out here. Sitting at that picnic table, I realized I've made some pretty good friends out here and it'll be tough to say goodbye.

DAY 153

Starting Location: Stealth Campsite near North End of 100 Mile Wilderness
Destination: The Birches Lean-to and Campsite
Today's Miles: 10.2
Trip Miles: 2183.9

Aug 24, 2016 - I was jolted awake by the sound of the air horn at 2:43 am. It was followed by the whoops and yells coming from the guys leaving camp. Everyone still in their tents raised a cheer in response - that's easily the most pumped up I've ever been at 2:43 am in the morning. Though I didn't hear it, Legs insisted they were playing The Final Countdown as they were packing up.

Everyone else was up early to get to the sign in sheet for the Birches by 6 am. When we got there, we, of course, knew that the list was full, so we all sat at a nearby picnic table and had some breakfast. Another thru-hiker, Thundersnarf, joined us - I don't like to talk negatively about another hiker, but this guy was a straight up pain in the ass. He persistently complains about literally everything and just never stops talking. During a lull in our conversation, he randomly comes out and says, "Confession time...I stole a trail maintainer's lunch and water and then ran away laughing". Yea...unfortunately, it appeared he would be summiting with us.

Since it was only 10.2 miles to the Birches Lean-tos and Campsite, today was an extremely lazy day - a victory lap of sorts. The entire hike was flat and ran parallel to a river that provided numerous swimming holes and waterfalls. Our whole group (nicknamed 'Super 8' on the trail registers) hiked together - we walked casually through the woods and stopped for anything and everything remotely interesting. Our first swimming hole had a small waterfall - Verge got everything started by wading very slowly and creepily into the water. Peach splashed her and then Legs and I jumped in. Before you know it, I was in my boxers literally holding onto slippery rocks for dear life fearing I would slide down the waterfall. When I got out, I realized I had a few small leeches on my legs. Gross!

Next, we took a break by a waterfall that looked like a small Niagara Falls and had yet another snack. We forded 2 rivers (the look of consternation on Verge's face as she looked for a way across the river is something I'll never forget) and finally arrived at the Katahdin Stream Campground at the base of the mountain. The ranger, Ed (this guy was incredibly nice, accommodating and stocked full of good, helpful information) checked us into the Birches, where we got settled and ran into New Hampshire Bob. Super 8 played some card games, built a fire and had some more food. Peach, Goat and I planned on waking up at 1:43 am to hike up Katahdin in time for sunrise so we attempted to go to bed around 6 pm. But sleep was impossible - it felt like the night before Christmas. I don't know when I managed to actually fall asleep, but it didn't matter. Adrenaline and excitement alone were the only fuel sources I needed for one final climb in the morning.

DAY 154

Starting Location: The Birches Lean-to and Campsite
Destination: Katahdin / Millinocket, ME
Today's Miles: 5.2
Trip Miles: 2189.1

Aug 25, 2016 - As I mentioned, I just couldn't sleep last night. I tossed and turned until 1:30 am when I got up to relieve myself in the privy. When I returned to the lean-to, I expected to find a groggy Peach and Goat slowly packing up. Instead, they were both completely animated and ready to go. I played Mother, We Just Can't Get Enough and was so jacked up, I felt like I would explode. The three of us filled up on water, dropped our trekking poles off at the ranger station (the poles would just hinder us while rock scrambling) and commenced our night hike at 2:19 am.

The hike up Katahdin consisted of almost 4,300 feet of elevation gain spread over 5.2 miles - that's intense. The beginning of the trail consisted of mostly stone steps, but it evolved into what was described to me as a vertical Mahoosuc Notch - I found that to be extremely accurate. The only real flat section was the last mile above tree line, but there, the nearly vertical ascent was replaced with high winds and cold temperatures, which always feel exaggerated at 3 in the morning. The rock scrambling was incredibly enjoyable, with the darkness adding a whole new, challenging twist. Even though I furnished my headlamp with 3 brand new batteries as recently as yesterday, the light failed me about halfway up and I had to rely on my friends' headlamps and the third quarter moon that was trying to peek through the layer of cloud cover.

The three of us filled up at the Henry David Thoreau spring conveniently located a mile from the summit. The excitement coursing through my body at this point is tough to describe. Standing there, body aching and shivering as the wind howled past me, I should have been pretty miserable, but this nervous energy made me want to run towards the summit. My mind kept trying to grasp the enormity of what I'd nearly accomplished. While my mind no doubt failed, my body responded accordingly.

We crested the final hill and there was the famous sign silhouetted against a cloud covered night sky just a few hundred yards away. All of us saw it, but each of us was lost in our own thoughts. I silently raised my arms to the sky and kept moving. At 4:55 am, I stood in front of the sign at the summit of Katahdin, having completed my 2,189.1 mile thru-hike, with my arms raised up as I let out a loud roar of triumph. I kissed the sign and, honestly, despite the adrenaline pumping through my body, threw down my pack and put some layers on - it was freaking cold.

Once we were layered up, we took our summit photos in the dark. In addition to the classic photo, I also took a few of me hoisting my pack above my head like the Stanley Cup - "It weighs almost 35 lbs except when you're lifting it". I couldn't resist.

MY SUMMIT PHOTO ON KATAHDIN BEFORE SUNRISE.

Our plan was to wait up there for about 4 hours so that the rest of Super 8 could join us for a picture with the sign. In the meantime, we took cover from the wind under a large rock and made one of the better cups of coffee I've ever had. It would be the last coffee I'd be sharing with Mr. Princess Peach (on the AT, at least) after hiking about 2,145 miles with him from Low Gap Shelter just after Neel Gap. Again, it was a triumphantly bittersweet moment.

As we sat there bundled up and taking cover from the wind, the sun started to rise and shed some light on our surroundings. At least 20 lakes stretched away to the south, the Knife's Edge stood out starkly to the east and a startlingly steep ravine plummeted from the summit to the north. I could see the last mile of the trail and continually watched expectantly for the approach of my friends.

Once the sun was up (the sunrise was blocked by cloud cover, but an hour later, the sun shone through and it turned into a gorgeous morning), the three of us slackpacked the mile out on the Knife's Edge trail to Pamola Peak. Pamola Peak actually used to be taller than Katahdin, but a large section of rock had broken off and tumbled down the side of the mountain. Pamola is the Penobscot Native American tribe's God of Thunder and Protector of the Mountain. This God causes cold weather and has the head of a moose, the body of a man and the wings and feet of an eagle. They call it Knife's Edge because the trail is 3 feet wide in some sections with literally nothing but sheer cliffs falling away on either side. One misstep and you'd fall for 4,000 feet. From a distance, the trail actually looks like a serrated knife balanced so that the edge is pointing up. Peach literally jogged the trail so he was watching me on the last descent from Pamola. The only way I could get down was to jump down about 8 feet to the next landing. I knew something was wrong and Peach confirmed my suspicions by saying I was at least 30 yards off trail literally trying to descend a cliff face. This trail was easily the most fun, most tiring and most dangerous thing I've ever done. If the rocks had been wet, the trail would have been completely impassable.

Anyway, we returned to Katahdin by around 8 am and still had to wait about an hour for Sweets, Jingle, Legs, Verge, and Training Wheels to arrive. The three of us sat on a rock and watched as everyone approached the summit with smiling faces and loud cheers, each touching the sign to signal their accomplishment. There were a lot of hugs, congratulations, pictures and ridiculous poses with the sign (which is brand new this year, by the way). My favorite picture is a tie between the one I took with Peach and the group picture with all the friends that made this experience the best and most rewarding of my short life.

Training Wheels was the last one to make it to the summit. As we all watched her approaching the sign, it looked like she was going to cry. Only a couple feet from the sign, we were shocked as she deviated and, instead, sat down hard on a rock saying, "Ugh I'm so pissy right now!". Sweets encouraged her to touch the sign and she hotly responded with a resounding, "No!". So, we gave her a couple minutes and she eventually started smiling and celebrating with the rest of us.

Except for the initial excitement at reaching the summit, it honestly didn't feel like my thru-hike was over. It just felt like we conquered yet another mountain and were casually enjoying the view like we always do. It's a little cliché, but it just goes to show you that nearly everything worth remembering about this trip happened during the walk to Katahdin rather than when I actually reached my goal. Katahdin definitely lived up to its potential and all the hype surrounding it. I couldn't help feeling the journey was over - the journey, despite all the good and bad experiences, was perfect while the ending will always be bittersweet. That's true for all of my life's important moments especially my graduations from high school and college, which stick out most prominently in my mind. I'll no doubt have too much time for reflection in the coming days to process all this, but I've been more emotional writing this than I've been since that dog died in I Am Legend.

OVER 2,100 MILES TOGETHER.

Our thru-hike might have been over, but we still had a 5 mile descent back to the campground. Since we were no longer obliged to follow the white blazes, Peach, Goat and I took the Abol Trail down. Well, about three quarters of the way down, we realized we had somehow lost the trail as we stumbled down a steep trench filled with loose dirt and large rocks. It was unnecessarily dangerous – we were about 90% sure this old, disused trail would come out near the trailhead for the Abol Trail. However, I was out of water, we were all short on food and a thunderstorm was forecast for later that afternoon. Furthermore, this is the Maine wilderness in the middle of nowhere with no cell reception. So, after a brief deliberation, we made the difficult decision to turn around and hike back up about half a mile as the sun beat down on us. We had to stagger our positions to avoid sending large rocks tumbling into each other as they cascaded down the mountainside. This course correction sapped all of my remaining energy especially now that the adrenaline from early this morning had worn off.

When we rejoined the Abol Trail, we realized all 3 of us had walked right past a sign that pointed directly to the trail. It turns out that the wrong trail would indeed have popped out where we had thought it would, but we still made the right decision by turning around. I've read enough true stories to realize that it's those simple types of decisions which often make the difference between life and death. That may sound extreme, but in the wilderness, it's really not.

Some day-hikers were kind enough to give us a ride back to the ranger station so we could gather our things. Then, we hitched a ride to nearby Millinocket, ME where we would stay the night at the AT Lodge. I was tired, but it was finally time to celebrate with the people I'd soon have to say goodbye to. We had some lunch at the AT Cafe and signed the ceiling as part of the thru-hiker class of 2016.

Later that night, everyone gathered at the saloon down the street and had a final rambunctious night together. Beers and shots were poured and, oddly enough, baby powder was sprayed nearly everywhere (rest in peace, chalkboob). I introduced everyone to grenades - there is no better shot to celebrate with.

Around midnight, as each of us slipped further into oblivion, Peach started a ridiculous conversation with Wheels and Verge about the proper way to flirt. He jokingly attempted to demonstrate on Wheels by lifting his leg onto her shoulder, but she pushed him off and said, "If I'm going to hook up with anyone, it's gonna be Mountain Goat". Everyone within earshot just stopped, my heart beating fast. Peach gladly moved out of the way and Wheels and I got to talking. Upon leaving the bar a little while later, I grabbed her hand and kissed her. Three hours later, we were still making out on a bench situated on the side of a restaurant that had gone out of business. Finally, thirst forced us back to the hostel - I got her a glass of water (this extremely small act of kindness seemed to surprise her way too much) and kissed her good night.

By the time I went to bed, it was past 3 in the morning. I had been up for almost 26 hours. It literally felt like I summited 3 days ago. Another cool factoid was that I summited on the 100th anniversary of the national park system. The land just east of BSP was actually designated a new national park today.

The next morning, Super 8 met at the AT Cafe for one last breakfast together. Peach was taking a bus back to Jersey, Training Wheels and Sweets were taking a private plane to Bangor (talk about badass), Legs, Verge, Goat and I were getting picked up by our parents and Jingle was actually hiking Katahdin again with his friends from home. I don't know when I'll see any of them again, but I'm sure we'll get together and surprise some thru-hiker hopefuls with Trail Magic in the future. I don't know if they're reading, but I want to thank them for making my adventure what it was - nature and the AT alone would've provided for an incredible trip, but it's the people that throw it into overdrive. I really cherish their friendships and, as I write this, it's already killing me knowing I won't see them for a while.

Thanks to everyone who followed me and supported me - I'll post all of the statistics and information I kept track of. Now, it's time to figure out the rest of my life, or at the very least, my next adventure. I have a feeling I've opened a can of worms - I'll always be drawn to the mountains for new adventures and because, frankly, there's nothing more satisfying or rewarding. I'll be back once I have an opportunity to process exactly what my AT thru-hike means to me, but for now, I'm out.

SUPER 8!

SUPER 8 CELEBRATING AT THE BAR IN MILLINOCKET, MAINE.

POST TRAIL

2 Weeks

Well, it's been 2 weeks since I was standing atop legendary Katahdin watching the sun rise in the northeast. Right now, I am sitting at the kitchen table of my parent's house trying to find some type of job to provide an income. The two situations could not be more different. Being home does have its perks, but I am rapidly becoming bored.

The day after my summit of Katahdin, my parents picked me up in Millinocket, and, after one last meal at the AT Cafe with most of my trail family, we drove to Bangor, ME. We were on our way to Acadia National Park, specifically Bar Harbour, for 3 days. In Bangor, a festival was being held on the waterfront and it turns out that Moonshine was there. Mama Moonshine owns a delicious food stand serving sautéed chicken and grilled vegetables and he was helping out. Needless to say, it was great to see him.

On Saturday, my family and I arrived in Bar Harbour - the first event on the agenda was a nature cruise included with our stay at the Grand Hotel. The cruise tour guide had a few interesting things to say about the history of the island and pointed out several bald eagles in the area. The rest of the day was spent walking around town exploring the touristy shops and various bars on Main Street. Dinner was the highlight of the day, as it usually is - lobster and filet mignon with a side of veggies. The day after my summit, I immediately reverted to a paleo diet and, I must say, it feels amazing to eat healthy again.

On Sunday, the three of us hiked the 7.1 mile round trip trail on Cadillac Mountain, which is the first place the sun hits in the United States when it rises every morning. I don't think I've ever seen my Dad go hiking before so I was curious to see how the hike would play out. Well, if we're keeping score, my Dad definitely fared better than my Mom. At one point, while I was inevitably waiting for my parents to catch up, I picked a handful of blueberries. When my Mom walked past me, I chucked a blueberry at my Mom's back. She thought it was a bug and proceeded to freak out. I egged her on by insisting that I saw a bug crawl down her shirt. She quickly lost all composure, took off her shirt, and, with nothing but a bra on, started smacking her shirt against the nearby blueberry bushes. People were approaching on the trail so I admitted that I was kidding and there was no bug. Totally worth it.

Other than food and drink, Bar Harbour really didn't have that much more to offer and, due to my fear of the ocean, I refused to go whale watching. With hardly anything to do, we decided to cut our losses and head home a day early. On Moonshine's recommendation, we stopped at Red's Eats, which apparently serve the best lobster roll in Maine. We waited in line for nearly an hour and confirmed that it was, indeed, one damn good lobster roll. I actually ordered the fried clams, though, as they are one of my all-time favorites.

So, late Monday night, I finally arrived home. I opted to sleep in the twin size guest bed downstairs simply because the east facing windows had no shades and the sun would wake me every morning. It's a pitiful attempt at recreating the intense calm achieved by sleeping outdoors, but it'll have to do.

Breakfast was my favorite - 3 scrambled eggs with 2 slices of American cheese in a pool of butter. After breakfast, I forced myself to shower (I do have to remind myself sometimes. In Acadia, I actually realized I wore the same boxers 3 days in a row before I remembered to change them) and got to work on compiling the statistics from my trip, creating Thank You postcards and attempting to clean my gear.

I also visited my Grandma and godson, Chase. My friends from home surprised me with a get together at our house where we caught up over some good food and drinks. I also took a drive (I forgot how much driving sucked and how much attention it actually requires) up to Connecticut to see Training Wheels before she flew back to Kansas City. I wasn't kidding when I said I wanted to take her on a date. I took her to a Greek restaurant and we walked around the bay for a while. Then, we made out in the car for a half hour before I very reluctantly dropped her back off at her Aunt's house. Frankly, it really sucks that she has to go back.

After only a day, my long checklist had been reduced to basically one item: "figure out life". If only it was that easy. I started the menial task of sitting at a computer again and looking through potential avenues of work. The only thing I know for certain is that I cannot return to the confines of a windowless cubicle.

The way I see it, I essentially have 3 options for work:
1. Take a Wilderness First Responder certification course and apply to be an outdoor leader / educator. I think this job would be a lot of fun, but my salary would take a pretty big hit and this would involve moving away from my friends and family at home. I'm not that concerned about the salary, but leaving my friends and family would definitely bother me. It was easy to drop everything and leave for the AT because I knew I would be coming back. A job is definitely more permanent than a thru-hike. I guess, if I'm being honest, I'm a little afraid of leaving home and abandoning engineering, which I've devoted nearly 8 years to.
2. Find an engineering job in an outdoor company related to product design and development. The only problem is I think a lot of these types of jobs would be sedentary and, again, would involve traveling simply because there are very few outdoor gear companies stationed near New Jersey. The salary would certainly be more comfortable, but I want to do something I would really enjoy and I don't know if engineering is that something.
3. Find a temporary, outdoor job around town in the service industry (carpentry, painting, electrician, plumbing, etc.) to simply pay the

bills and make the process of finding a more permanent job less stressful. This would be ideal because it would also provide me the opportunity to learn skills that I consider useful. Again, the salary isn't important here – I want to learn these handy skills and if I could earn a small salary to keep my head above water while I do it, that would be wonderful. I could even see if any local breweries need help.

As you can see, my mind is all over the place and I am quickly becoming a little overwhelmed with these life decisions.

The first weekend back, I drove to Broadkill Beach in Delaware to see my friends from school. Seeing my friend Tom crouched at the top of the stairs waiting to give me a hug because he heard me open the door is the best sort of welcome I could have asked for. Even though I had just gotten home, it was relaxing to forget about my difficult decisions and enjoy the beautiful weather courtesy of Tropical Storm Hermine with some of my favorite people.

During the second week home, I was back on the job hunt. I also caught up with my old boss, Nick, who had left our company to take a chance on a riskier venture in California. The opportunity fell through, and, unfortunately, he has been unemployed for more than 6 months now. At least he took a chance and went after something he believed would benefit him and his family. That's living with no regrets.

I'll continue to be hopeful as I search for jobs and look for the courage I need to take the next step in my life.

A Year and a Half Later

I look back now and the Appalachian Trail feels like it was in another life. Yet, I can still remember every detail like it was yesterday. Sometimes, the nostalgia lashes out so strongly, it's difficult to bear. I still get chills every time I drive underneath the AT overpass on 87 North. As far as life goes, I've figured out at least some of it or at least enough to leave me content in the present.

About a month after I finished my hike, I interviewed for an entry level position in southern New Jersey at a flooring company called Stonhard. I was attracted to the position because it sounded like an engineering job that was actually hands-on. Rather than sitting in an office every day, I would be working in the field training crews and developing new products. The salary was considerably less than my previous job and I would go from a managerial position back to the bottom of the totem pole. But, if I learned anything on trail, it's that money isn't everything.

Now, I've been working here for a year and a half and I honestly do enjoy it. The job consists of a healthy mixture of travel, office work, lab experiments and field trials. Perhaps best of all, I love the people I work with and am currently living with one of my coworkers. That's how I ended up in Philadelphia of all places.

I've stayed in touch with my trail family, especially Legs, Verge, Princess Peach and Training Wheels. Peach and I have agreed to get together at least once a year for an epic adventure to keep the dream alive. He ended up moving to Colorado, which makes the adventure easier and more difficult at the same time. Legs and Verge are relatively close in Massachusetts so we manage to meet up occasionally.

So, has the AT changed me? I think so. Most significantly, I appreciate the present just a little more instead of just looking ahead all the time.

What are you waiting for?

STATISTICS

During my trek, I kept track of some simple statistics:

Total On-Trail Cost: $4,935.52

I should mention that most hikers spent less than half this much and, of course, other hikers spend far more. During my trip, I frequently chose food and beer over a stay at a hostel or a hotel. As my food bag can attest, I bought and carried an insane amount of food. Most hikers also do not routinely carry six packs into the woods so they can slowly drink warm beer over several days with their friends. My parents did help me occasionally with new gear purchases and with supply packages. I am extremely grateful for this. Finally, this final cost does not include all the time and money I put into obtaining my gear prior to starting the hike. Below is a breakdown of my costs by category:

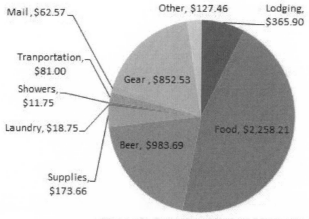

Breakdown of Trail Costs

Some other random statistics include:

- Days on Trail: 154
- Zeros: 14
- Average Miles per Day: 14.21
- Pairs of Trekking Poles: 2
- Pairs of Shoes: 4
- Number of Packs: 2
- Number of Brewery Stickers Collected: 21
- Slices of Pizza: 204

GLOSSARY

Aqua Blazing - There are actually a few opportunities for hikers to rent a canoe and paddle upriver rather than hiking.

AT – Appalachian Trail

Bald – Barren areas at the peak of a mountain or hill

Base Weight = Total pack weight – Consumables (Food, water, etc.)

Blaze – Signals painted on trees and used to mark the trail

Blue Blazing - This refers to hiking any of the side trails, easier trails, or shortcuts along the trail

Brew Blazing - This is a term I just made up to describe tailoring our hiking schedule to cater to towns that contain breweries and it's awesome. Peach and I have made it a priority to check out breweries near the trail and try new beer when we see it for sale in town. I guess it could also refer to hiking while consuming beer.

Cairn – Pile of rocks used to mark the trail and used in place of blazes when there are no trees.

Camo Blazing - A term we made up to describe hiking according to the Warrior Hikers schedule, which is predefined and part of their program (we have been doing this for a while whether it's intentional or not)

Cathole – Hole in the ground used to bury shit

Cowboy Camping – Sleeping underneath the stars without a tent

Day Hiker – One who is simply out hiking for the day or camping for one night

Flip-flopper – Hikers who hike the trail in two separate halves rather than in one continuous hike. For example, a flip – flopper might hike from Harpers Ferry south to Springer Mountain and then travel back up to Harpers Ferry to start hiking north to Katahdin.

Grey Blazing - This refers to chasing / hooking up with older women along the trail

Hiker Box – Box of free hiker food, equipment and supplies left by previous hikers

Hut – One of the cabins in the White Mountains

Lean-to – Three-sided wooden structures at shelters where hikers can sleep

Nero – "Nearly zero day". Peach and I referred to a nero as anything 10 miles or less

Nobo – Someone hiking north from Springer Mountain to Katahdin

Peach Blazing - This refers specifically to Hot Toddy putting in big miles to chase after Princess Peach

Pink Blazing - This refers to tailoring your hiking schedule according to a woman's hiking schedule with hopes of some action.

Purple Blazing - This refers to hiking while consuming wine (honestly not sure about this one, but it sounds appropriate).

Section Hiker – One who hikes the AT in sections usually over many years

Shelter – Wooden structures spaced, on average, every 8 miles throughout the length of the trail

Slack Packing – Not carrying gear for the day. Many hostels offered this option to hikers for a fee

Sobo – Someone hiking south from Katahdin to Springer Mountain

Stealth Camping – Camping in an undesignated campsite

Thru-hiker – One who hikes the AT in one continuous run within a 12 month period

Trail Angels – Providers of Trail Magic

Trail Magic – Gifts of goodwill from Trail Angels

Triple Crown – If someone thru-hikes all 3 major US hiking trails – Continental Divide Trail, Pacific Crest Trail, and the Appalachian Trail – they are said to have completed the Triple Crown.

White Blazing - This refers to actually hiking the AT by following the white blazes posted on trees rocks

Work for Stay – One who works or volunteers for a few hours at a hostel or hut instead of paying for a room

Yellow Blazing - This refers to using a car or other form of modern transportation to skip sections of the trail

Zero – A day when 0 miles are hiked

Made in the USA
Middletown, DE
19 March 2019